ANDORRA

INDUSTRIAL AND BUSINESS DIRECTORY

STRATEGIC INFORMATION, REGULATIONS, CONTACTS

International Business Publications, USA
Washington DC, USA-Andorra

ANDORRA

INDUSTRIAL AND BUSINESS DIRECTORY

STRATEGIC INFORMATION, REGULATIONS, CONTACTS

UPDATED ANNUALLY

We express our sincere appreciation to all government agencies and international organizations which provided information and other materials for this handbook

Cover Design: International Business Publications, USA

2018 Edition Updated Reprint International Business Publications, USA
ISBN 1-4330-0109-8

For additional analytical, business and investment opportunities information,
please contact Global Investment & Business Center, USA
at (703) 370-8082. Fax: (703) 370-8083. E-mail: ibpusa3@gmail.com
Global Business and Investment Info Databank - www.ibpus.com

Printed in the USA

For additional analytical, business and investment opportunities information,
please contact Global Investment & Business Center, USA
at (703) 370-8082. Fax: (703) 370-8083. E-mail: ibpusa3@gmail.com
Global Business and Investment Info Databank - www.ibpus.com

ANDORRA

INDUSTRIAL AND BUSINESS DIRECTORY

TRATEGIC INFORMATION, REGULATIONS, CONTACTS

TABLE OF CONTENTS

STRATEGIC AND DEVELOPMENT PROFILES

ANDORRA: BASIC PROFILES

Capital and largest city	Andorra la Vella 42°30′N 1°31′ECoordinates: 42°30′N 1°31′E
Official languages	Catalan[b]
Ethnic groups (2012[1])	49% Andorran 24.6% Spanish 14.3% Portuguese 3.9% French 8.2% others
Demonym	Andorran
Government	Unitary parliamentary semi-elective diarchy
• Co-Monarchs	Joan Enric Vives Sicília Emmanuel Macron (who is also the President of France)
• Representatives	Josep Maria Mauri Patrick Strzoda
• Prime Minister	Antoni Martí
Legislature	General Council
Independence	
• from Aragon	1278
• from the French Empire	1814
• Constitution	1993
Area	
• Total	467.63 km² (180.55 sq mi) (179th)
• Water (%)	0.26 (121.4 ha)[c]
Population	
• 2016 estimate	77,281[2]
• Density	179.8/km² (465.7/sq mi) (71st)
GDP (nominal)	2016 estimate
• Total	$3.249 billion[3][better source needed] (162th)
• Per capita	$36,987[4][better source needed] (26th)
Gini (2003)	27.21[d] low
HDI (2016)	▲ 0.858[5] very high · 32nd
Currency	Euro[e] (EUR)
Time zone	CET (UTC+1)
• Summer (DST)	CEST (UTC+2)
Drives on the	right
Calling code	+376
ISO 3166 code	AD
Internet TLD	.ad[f]

Andorra officially the **Principality of Andorra** (Catalan: *Principat d'Andorra*), also called the **Principality of the Valleys of Andorra** (Catalan: *Principat de les Valls d'Andorra*), is a sovereign landlocked microstate in Southwestern Europe, located in the eastern Pyrenees mountains and bordered by Spain and France. Created under a charter in A.D. 988, the present Principality was formed in A.D. 1278. It is known as a principality as it is a monarchy headed by two Co-Princes – the Spanish/Roman Catholic Bishop of Urgell and the President of France.

Andorra is the sixth-smallest nation in Europe, having an area of 468 km^2 (181 sq mi) and a population of approximately 85,000. Its capital Andorra la Vella is the highest capital city in Europe, at an elevation of 1,023 metres (3,356 ft) above sea level. The official language is Catalan, although Spanish, Portuguese, and French are also commonly spoken.

Andorra's tourism services an estimated 10.2 million visitors annually. It is not a member of the European Union, but the euro is the *de facto* currency. It has been a member of the United Nations since 1993. The people of Andorra have one of the highest life expectancies in the world and as of December 2014, according to *The Lancet*, have the highest in the world - 81 years in 2013

GEOGRAPHY

Location: Southwestern Europe, between France and Spain

Geographic coordinates: 42 30 N, 1 30 E

Map references: Europe

Area:
total: 450 sq km
land: 450 sq km
water: 0 sq km

Area—comparative: 2.5 times the size of Washington, DC

Land boundaries:
total: 125 km
border countries: France 60 km, Spain 65 km

Coastline: 0 km (landlocked)
Maritime claims: none (landlocked)
Climate: temperate; snowy, cold winters and warm, dry summers
Terrain: rugged mountains dissected by narrow valleys

Elevation extremes:
lowest point: Riu Valira 840 m
highest point: Coma Pedrosa 2,946 m

Natural resources: hydropower, mineral water, timber, iron ore, lead

Land use:
arable land: 2%
permanent crops: 0%

permanent pastures: 56%
forests and woodland: 22%
other: 20%

Irrigated land: NA sq km
Natural hazards: snowslides, avalanches
Environment—current issues: deforestation; overgrazing of mountain meadows contributes to soil erosion

Environment—international agreements:
party to: none of the selected agreements
signed, but not ratified: none of the selected agreements

Geography—note: landlocked

PEOPLE

Population: 65,939

Age structure:
0-14 years: 14% (male 4,880; female 4,527)

15-64 years: 73% (male 25,811; female 22,444)
65 years and over: 13% (male 4,196; female 4,081)

Population growth rate: 2.24%
Birth rate: 10.27 births/1,000 population
Death rate: 5.46 deaths/1,000 population
Net migration rate: 17.61 migrant(s)/1,000 population

Sex ratio:
at birth: 1.06 male(s)/female
under 15 years: 1.08 male(s)/female
15-64 years: 1.15 male(s)/female
65 years and over: 1.03 male(s)/female
total population: 1.12 male(s)/female

Infant mortality rate: 4.08 deaths/1,000 live births

Life expectancy at birth:
total population: 83.46 years
male: 80.55 years
female: 86.55 years

Total fertility rate: 1.25 children born/woman

Nationality:
noun: Andorran(s)
adjective: Andorran

Ethnic groups: Spanish 61%, Andorran 30%, French 6%, other 3%

Religions: Roman Catholic (predominant)
Languages: Catalan (official), French, Castilian
Literacy: NA

GOVERNMENT

Country name:
conventional long form: Principality of Andorra
conventional short form: Andorra
local long form: Principat d'Andorra
local short form: Andorra

Government type:
parliamentary democracy (since March 1993) that retains as its chiefs of state a co-principality; the two princes are the President of France and Bishop of Urgell, whose diocese is located in neighboring Spain; both co-princes maintain offices and representatives in Andorra

Capital:
name: Andorra la Vella

geographic coordinates: 42 30 N, 1 31 E
time difference: UTC+1 (6 hours ahead of Washington, DC during Standard Time)
daylight saving time: +1hr, begins last Sunday in March; ends last Sunday in October

Administrative divisions:
7 parishes (parroquies, singular - parroquia); Andorra la Vella, Canillo, Encamp, Escaldes-Engordany, La Massana, Ordino, Sant Julia de Loria

Independence:
1278 (formed under the joint sovereignty of the French Count of Foix and the Spanish Bishop of Urgell)

National holiday:
Our Lady of Meritxell Day, 8 September (1278)

Constitution:
drafted 1991, approved by referendum 14 March 1993, effective 28 April 1993 (2013)

Legal system:
mixed legal system of civil and customary law with the influence of canon law

International law organization participation:
has not submitted an ICJ jurisdiction declaration; accepts ICCt jurisdiction

Suffrage:
18 years of age; universal

Executive branch:
chief of state: Co-prince Emmanuel MACRON (since 14 May 2017); represented by Patrick STROZDA (since 14 May 2017); and Co-prince Archbishop Joan-Enric VIVES i Sicilia (since 12 May 2003); represented by Josep Maria MAURI (since 20 July 2012)

head of government: Head of Government (or Cap de Govern) Antoni MARTI PETIT (since 1 April 2015)
cabinet: Executive Council of ten ministers designated by the head of government

elections/appointments: head of government indirectly elected by the General Council (Andorran parliament), formally appointed by the coprinces for a 4-year term; election last held on 31 March 2015 (next to be held in March 2019); the leader of the majority party in the General Council is usually elected head of government

election results: Antoni MARTI Petit (DA) elected head of government; percent of General Council vote - 79%

Legislative branch:
description: unicameral General Council of the Valleys or Consell General de les Valls (a minimum of 28 seats; 14 members directly elected in multi-seat constituencies (parishes) by simple majority vote and 14 directly elected in a single national constituency by proportional representation vote; members serve 4-year terms); note - each voter casts two separate ballots - one for a national list and one for a parish list

elections: last held on 1 March 2015 (next to be held in March 2019)
election results: percent of vote by party - DA 37.03%, PLA 27.68%, PS-VA-IC-independent coalition 23.53%, SDP 11.74%; seats by party - DA 15, PLA 8, PS-VA-IC-independent coalition 3, SDP 2

Judicial branch:
highest court(s): Supreme Court of Justice of Andorra or Tribunal Superior de la Justicia d'Andorra (consists of the court president and 8 judges organized into civil, criminal, and administrative chambers); Constitutional Court or Tribunal Constitucional (consists of 4 magistrates)

judge selection and term of office: Supreme Court president and judges appointed by the Supreme Council of Justice, a 5-member judicial policy and administrative body appointed 1 each by the coprinces, 1 by the General Council, 1 by the executive council president, and 1 by the courts; judges serve 6-year renewable terms; Constitutional magistrates appointed 2 by the coprinces and 2 by the General Council; magistrates' appointments limited to 2 consecutive 8-year terms
subordinate courts: Tribunal of Judges or Tribunal de Batlles; Tribunal of the Courts or Tribunal de Corts

Political parties and leaders:
Citizens' Initiative or IC [Sergi RICART] (including PS, VA, IC, and independents)
Democrats for Andorra or DA [Antoni MARTI PETIT]
Greens of Andorra or VA [Isabel LOZANO MUNOZ, Juli FERNANDEZ BLASI]
Liberal Party or PLA [Jordi GALLARDO]
Social Democratic Party or PS [Vincenc ALAY FERRER]
Social Democratic Progress Party or SDP [Victor NAUDI ZAMORA]
note: Andorra has several smaller parties at the parish level (one is Lauredian Union)

International organization participation:
CE, FAO, ICAO, ICC (NGOs), ICCt, ICRM, IFRCS, Interpol, IOC, IPU, ITU, OIF, OPCW, OSCE, UN, UNCTAD, UNESCO, Union Latina, UNWTO, WCO, WHO, WIPO, WTO (observer)

Diplomatic representation in the US:
chief of mission: Ambassador Elisenda VIVES BALMANA (since 2 March 2016)
chancery: 2 United Nations Plaza, 27th Floor, New York, NY 10017
telephone: [1] (212) 750-8064
FAX: [1] (212) 750-6630

Diplomatic representation from the US:
the US does not have an embassy in Andorra; the US ambassador to Spain is accredited to Andorra; US interests in Andorra are represented by the US Consulate General's office in Barcelona (Spain); mailing address: Paseo Reina Elisenda de Montcada, 23, 08034 Barcelona, Spain; telephone: [34] (93) 280-2227; FAX: [34] (93) 280-6175

Flag description:

three vertical bands of blue (hoist side), yellow, and red, with the national coat of arms centered in the yellow band; the latter band is slightly wider than the other two so that the ratio of band widths is 8:9:8; the coat of arms features a quartered shield with the emblems of (starting in the upper left and proceeding clockwise): Urgell, Foix, Bearn, and Catalonia; the motto reads VIRTUS UNITA FORTIOR (Strength United is Stronger); the flag combines the blue and red French colors with the red and yellow of Spain to show Franco-Spanish protection
note: similar to the flags of Chad and Romania, which do not have a national coat of arms in the center, and the flag of Moldova, which does bear a national emblem

National anthem:

name: "El Gran Carlemany" (The Great Charlemagne)
lyrics/music: Joan BENLLOCH i VIVO/Enric MARFANY BONS
note: adopted 1921; the anthem provides a brief history of Andorra in a first person narrative

ECONOMY

Tourism, retail sales, and finance are the mainstays of Andorra's tiny, well-to-do economy, accounting for more than three-quarters of GDP. Andorra's duty-free status for some products and its summer and winter resorts attract millions of visitors annually, although the economic downturn in neighboring countries has curtailed the number of tourists. Andorra's comparative advantage as a tax haven eroded when the borders of neighboring France and Spain opened; its bank secrecy laws have been relaxed under pressure from the EU and OECD. Agricultural production is limited - only 5% of the land is arable - and most food has to be imported, making the economy vulnerable to changes in fuel and food prices. The principal livestock is sheep. Manufacturing output and exports consist mainly of perfumes and cosmetic products, products of the printing industry, electrical machinery and equipment, clothing, tobacco products, and furniture. Andorra is a member of the EU Customs Union and is treated as an EU member for trade in manufactured goods (no tariffs) and as a non-EU member for agricultural products.

Andorra uses the euro and is effectively subject to the monetary policy of the European Central Bank. Slower growth in Spain and France has dimmed Andorra's economic prospects. Since 2010, a drop in tourism contributed to a contraction in GDP and a sharp deterioration of public finances, prompting the government to begin implementing several austerity measures to reduce the budget deficit, including levying a special corporate tax. To bring in new revenue and diversify future sources of economic growth, the government approved in July 2012 a new foreign investment law opening investment to foreign capital.

GDP (purchasing power parity):

$3.163 billion
country comparison to the world: 180
$3.214 billion (2011 est.)
$3.227 billion (2010 est.)
note: data are in 2012 US dollars

GDP (official exchange rate):

$4.8 billion

GDP - real growth rate:

-1.6%
country comparison to the world: 210
-0.4% (2011 est.)
-1.9% (2010 est.)

GDP - per capita (PPP):

$37,200 (2011 est.)
country comparison to the world: 35
$37,700 (2010 est.)
$37,900 (2014 est.)

GDP - composition, by sector of origin:

agriculture: 14%
industry: 79%
services: 6% (2011 est.)

Agriculture - products:

small quantities of rye, wheat, barley, oats, vegetables, tobacco; sheep, cattle

Industries:

tourism (particularly skiing), banking, timber, furniture

Industrial production growth rate:

NA%

Labor force:

36,060 (2012)
country comparison to the world: 201

Labor force - by occupation:

agriculture: 0.4%
industry: 4.7%
services: 94.9% (2010)

Unemployment rate:

4%
country comparison to the world: 30
1.9% (2011 est.)

Population below poverty line:

NA% (2008)

Household income or consumption by percentage share:

lowest 10%: NA%
highest 10%: NA%

Budget:

revenues: $1.029 billion
expenditures: $1.041 billion (2012)

Taxes and other revenues:

21.4% of GDP (2012)
country comparison to the world: 151

Budget surplus (+) or deficit (-):

-0.3% of GDP (2012)
country comparison to the world: 49

Public debt:

41.1% of GDP (2012)
country comparison to the world: 86
37.7% of GDP (2011)

Fiscal year:

calendar year

Inflation rate (consumer prices):

1.1%
country comparison to the world: 29
-2.5% (2011 est.)

Exports:

$70 million
country comparison to the world: 193
$72 million (2011 est.)

Exports - commodities:

tobacco products, furniture

Imports:

$1.43 billion
country comparison to the world: 172
$1.501 billion (2011 est.)

Imports - commodities:

consumer goods, food, fuel, electricity

Debt - external:

$NA

Exchange rates:

euros (EUR) per US dollar -
0.7778 (2013 est.)
0.7185
0.755 (2010 est.)
0.7198 (2014 est.)

0.6827 (2008 est.)

ENERGY

Electricity - production:

91.24 million kWh
country comparison to the world: 201

Electricity - consumption:

562.4 million kWh
country comparison to the world: 168

Electricity - exports:

0 kWh
country comparison to the world: 96

Electricity - imports:

0 kWh
country comparison to the world: 113

Electricity - installed generating capacity:

520,000 kW
country comparison to the world: 137

Electricity - from fossil fuels:

61.3% of total installed capacity
country comparison to the world: 131

Electricity - from nuclear fuels:

0% of total installed capacity
country comparison to the world: 38

Electricity - from hydroelectric plants:

23.3% of total installed capacity
country comparison to the world: 84

COMMUNICATIONS

Telephones - main lines in use:

39,000
country comparison to the world: 170

Telephones - mobile cellular:

65,000
country comparison to the world: 198

Telephone system:

general assessment: modern automatic telephone system
domestic: modern system with microwave radio relay connections between exchanges
international: country code - 376; landline circuits to France and Spain (2012)

Broadcast media:

1 public TV station and 2 public radio stations; about 10 commercial radio stations; good reception of radio and TV broadcasts from stations in France and Spain; upgraded to terrestrial digital TV broadcasting in 2007; roughly 25 international TV channels available

Internet country code:

.ad

Internet hosts:

28,383
country comparison to the world: 109

Internet users:

67,100
country comparison to the world: 171

TRANSPORTATION

Roadways:

total: 320 km
country comparison to the world: 203

MILITARY

Military branches:

no regular military forces, Police Service of Andorra

Manpower available for military service:

males age 16-49: 22,390

Manpower fit for military service:

males age 16-49: 17,977
females age 16-49: 17,069

Manpower reaching militarily significant age annually:

male: 397
female: 347

Military - note:

defense is the responsibility of France and Spain

TRANSNATIONAL ISSUES

Disputes - international:

none

IMPORTANT INFORMATION FORE UNDERSTANDING ANDORRA

PROFILE

Geography
Area: 468 sq. km. (180 sq. mi.); about half the size of New York City.
Cities: *Capital*--Andorra la Vella.
Terrain: Mountainous.
Climate: Temperate, cool, dry.

People
Nationality: *Noun and adjective*--Andorran(s).
Population (end of 2010): 85,015.
Annual population growth rate (2010): 1.1%.
Ethnic groups: Catalan, Spanish, French, Portuguese.
Religion: Roman Catholic.
Languages: Catalan (official), Spanish, French.
Education: *Years compulsory*--to age 16. *Attendance*--100%. *Literacy*--100%.
Health: *Infant mortality rate* (2014)--3/1,000. *Life expectancy* (2008)--84 years, male and female.

Government

Type: Parliamentary democracy that retains as its heads of state two co-princes.
Constitution: Ratified in March 1993.
Independence: 1278.
Branches: *Heads of State*--Two co-princes (President of France, Bishop of Seu d'Urgell in Spain). *Executive*--Head of Government (Cap de Govern) and eight ministers (Executive Council). *Legislative*--Parliament (General Council), founded 1419, consisting of 28 members. *Judicial*--Civil cases heard in first instance by four judges (batlles) and in appeals by the one-judge Court of Appeals. The highest body is the five-member Superior Council of Justice. Criminal cases are heard by the Tribunal of Courts in Andorra la Vella.
Subdivisions: Seven parishes (parroquies)--Andorra la Vella, Canillo, Encamp, La Massana, Ordino, Sant Julia de Loria, and Escaldes make up the districts represented in the General Council.
Political parties/groups: Andorran Liberal Party, Social Democratic Party, and Andorra for Change Party.
Suffrage: Universal at 18.

Economy
GDP (2014): $3.6 billion.
Natural resources: Hydroelectric power, mineral water, timber, iron ore, lead.
Agriculture: *Products*--tobacco, sheep.
Industry: *Types*--tourism (mainstay of the economy), tobacco products, furniture.
Trade: Major activities are commerce and banking; no official figures are available. Duty-free status.
Official currency: Euro.

PEOPLE

Andorrans live in seven valleys that form Andorra's political districts. Andorrans are a minority in their own country; they make up only approximately 38% of the population or about 32,000 native Andorrans. Spanish, French, and Portuguese residents make up the other 62% of the population.

The national language is Catalan, a romance language related to the Provencal group. French and Spanish are also spoken.

Education law requires school attendance for children up to age 16. A system of French, Spanish, and Andorran public schools provides education up to the secondary level. Schools are built and maintained by Andorran authorities, who pay also for Andorran teachers. French and Spanish schools pay for their own teachers. About 32% of Andorran children attend the French primary schools, 31% attend Spanish, and 37% attend Andorran schools. Andorran schools follow the Spanish curriculum, and their diplomas are recognized by the Spanish education system. In 1997, the University of Andorra was established. The University of Andorra has two graduate schools; the Nursing School and the School of Computer Science. Students can obtain a degree in business administration, nursing, or education sciences as well as computer science. Students can also follow virtual studies with Spanish and French universities. Out of the 1,183 students enrolled in university in the 2008-2014 academic year, 460 studied at the

University of Andorra, 640 in Spanish universities, 74 in French universities, and 9 in other countries.

HISTORY

Andorra is the last independent survivor of the March states, a number of buffer states created by Charlemagne to keep the Muslim Moors from advancing into Christian France. Tradition holds that Charlemagne granted a charter to the Andorran people in return for their fighting the Moors. In the 800s, Charlemagne's grandson, Charles the Bald, made Count of Urgell overlord of Andorra. A descendant of the count later gave the lands to the diocese of Urgell, headed by Bishop of Seu d'Urgell.

In the 11th century, fearing military action by neighboring lords, the bishop placed himself under the protection of the Lord of Caboet, a Spanish nobleman. Later, the Count of Foix, a French noble, became heir to Lord Caboet through marriage, and a dispute arose between the French Count and the Spanish bishop over Andorra.

In 1278, the conflict was resolved by the signing of a pareage, which provided that Andorra's sovereignty be shared between the Count of Foix and the Bishop of Seu d'Urgell of Spain. The pareage, a feudal institution recognizing the principle of equality of rights shared by two rulers, gave the small state its territory and political form.

Over the years, the title was passed between French and Spanish rule until, in the reign of the French King Henry IV, an edict in 1607 established the head of the French state and the Bishop of Urgell as co-princes of Andorra.

Given its relative isolation, Andorra has existed outside the mainstream of European history, with few ties to countries other than France and Spain. In recent times, however, its thriving tourist industry and developments in transportation and communications have removed the country from its isolation.

GOVERNMENT

The Andorran constitution was ratified and approved in 1993. The constitution establishes Andorra as a sovereign parliamentary democracy that retains as its heads of state two co-princes.

The fundamental impetus for this political transformation was a recommendation by the Council of Europe in 1990 that, if Andorra wished to attain full integration into the European Union (EU), it should adopt a modern constitution that guaranteed the rights of those living and working there. A Tripartite Commission--made up of representatives of the co-princes, the General Council, and the Executive Council--was formed in 1990 and finalized the draft constitution in April 1991.

Under the 1993 constitution, the co-princes continue as heads of state, but the head of government retains executive power. The two co-princes serve co-equally with limited powers that do not include veto over government acts. They are represented in Andorra by a delegate. As co-princes of Andorra, the President of France and the Bishop of Seu d'Urgell maintain supreme authority in approval of all international treaties with France and Spain, as well as all those that deal with internal security, defense, Andorran territory, diplomatic representation, and judicial or penal cooperation. Although the institution of the co-princes is viewed by some as an anachronism, the majority sees them as both a link with Andorra's traditions and a way to balance the power of Andorra's two much larger neighbors.

Andorra's main legislative body is the 28-member General Council (Parliament). The Sindic General (president of the General Council), the Subsindic, and the members of the Council are elected in the general elections held every 4 years. A Sindic General and a Subsindic are chosen by the General Council to implement its decisions. They serve 4-year terms and may be reappointed once. They receive an annual salary. Sindics have virtually no discretionary powers, and all policy decisions must be approved by the Council as a whole.

The General Council meets throughout the year on certain dates set by tradition or as required. At least one representative from each parish must be present for the Council to meet. Historically, within the General Council, four deputies from each of the seven individual parishes provided representation. This system allowed the smaller parishes, which have as few as 600 voters, the same number of representatives as larger parishes, which have up to 4,300 voters. To correct this imbalance, a provision in the 1993 constitution introduced a modification of the structure and format for electing the members of the Council; under this format, half of the representatives are chosen by the traditional system, while the other half are selected from nationwide lists.

Every 4 years, after the general elections, the General Council also elects the head of government, who, in turn, chooses the other members of the Executive Council. The current Executive Council has eight ministers.

The judicial system is independent. Courts apply the customary laws of Andorra, supplemented with Roman law and customary Catalan law. Civil cases are first heard by the batlles court--a group of four judges, two chosen by each co-prince. Appeals are heard in the Court of Appeals. The highest body is the five-member Superior Council of Justice.

Andorra has no defense forces and only a small internal police force. All able-bodied men who own firearms must serve, without remuneration, in the small army, which is unique in that all of its men are treated as officers. The army has not fought for more than 700 years, and its main responsibility is to present the Andorran flag at official ceremonies.

POLITICAL CONDITIONS

Andorra held early national elections on April 3, 2011. The Democrats for Andorra (DA), a center-right coalition led by Antoni Marti Petit that included the Liberal Party, obtained 22 seats in the 28-seat General Council. The Social Democratic Party (PS), led by former Head of Government Jaume Bartumeu, obtained 6 seats. Head of Government Marti took office in May 2011. This is the sixth government formed in Andorra since the ratification of the constitution in 1993. Andorra's economy and its relations with the European Union are among the new government's top priorities.

There has been a redefinition of the qualifications for Andorran citizenship, a major issue in a country where approximately 37% are legal citizens. In 1995, a law to broaden citizenship was passed but citizenship remains hard to acquire, with only Andorran nationals being able to transmit citizenship automatically to their children. Lawful residents in Andorra may obtain citizenship after 20 years of residence. Children of residents may opt for Andorran citizenship after 18 if they have resided virtually all of their lives in Andorra. Mere birth on Andorran soil does not confer citizenship. Dual nationality is not permitted. Until 2008 non-citizens were allowed to own just a 33% share of a company, and only after they had resided in the country for 20 years would they be entitled to own 100% of a company. The country has now opened itself to foreign investors, allowing up to 100% ownership in activities and sectors considered strategic.

By creating a modern legal framework for the country, the 1993 constitution allowed Andorra to base its economy on tourism and international banking and finance. Over the short term, Andorra will continue to confront a number of difficult issues and the need to develop the institutions necessary to address them, including tax reform. In addition to questions of Andorran nationality and immigration policy, other priority issues will include a housing shortage, real estate speculation, tourism, and refining its relationship with the European Union.

Principal Government Officials
Co-Prince--Nicolas Sarkozy, President of France
Co-Prince--Joan Enric Vives i Sicilia, Bishop of Seu d'Urgell, Spain
Head of Government--Antoni Marti
Sindic General--Vicenc Mateu

Foreign Minister--Gilbert Saboya
Permanent Representative to the United Nations--Narcis Casal de Fonsdeviela
Ambassador to the United States, resident in New York--Narcis Casal de Fonsdeviela

Andorra maintains an **embassy** in the United States at Two United Nations Plaza, 27th floor, New York, NY 10017; telephone 212 750 8064 / 8065; fax 212 750 6630.

ECONOMY

Currency	Euro (EUR)
Fiscal year	Calendar year
Trade organisations	EU customs union
	Statistics
GDP	▼$3.163 billion (PPP est.)
GDP rank	180th (PPP est.)
GDP growth	▼-1.6% (Real est.)
GDP per capita	▼$37,200 (PPP est.)

GDP by sector	agriculture 14%, industry 79%, services 6% (2011 est.)
Inflation (CPI)	▲1.1% (CPI, 2012 est.)
Population below poverty line	no data
Labour force	36,060 (
Labour force by occupation	agriculture 0.4%, industry 4.7%, services 94.9%
Unemployment	▲2.9%
Main industries	tourism (particularly skiing), cattle raising, timber, banking, tobacco, furniture
	External
Exports	▼$70 million
Export goods	tobacco products, furniture
Main export partners	France 34%, Spain 58%
Imports	▼$1.43 billion
Import goods	consumer goods, food, electricity
Main import partners	Spain 51.5%, France 22.3%, US 0.3% (2003)
	Public finances
Public debt	no data
Revenues	$403 million
Expenses	$470 million
Economic aid	no data
Credit rating	A (Domestic) A (Foreign) AAA (T&C Assessment) (Standard & Poor's)

Andorra's national income was approximately $3.6 billion, with tourism as its principal component. The country has been attractive for shoppers from France and Spain because of low taxes and duty-free allowances, and it has developed active summer and winter tourist resorts. With some 270 hotels and 400 restaurants, as well as many shops, the tourist trade employs a significant portion of the domestic labor force. There is a fairly active trade in consumer goods, including imported manufactured items, which, because they are taxed at lower rates, are less expensive in Andorra than in neighboring countries.

Many Andorrans have supported the country's reform initiatives over the years, believing that Andorra's continued prosperity required fuller integration with the European Union. Andorra's tax status has had a significant effect on its relationship with the EU, with which Andorra began negotiations in 1987. An agreement that went into effect in July 1991 set duty-free quotas and placed limits on certain items--mainly milk products, tobacco, and alcoholic beverages. Andorra is permitted to maintain price differences from other EU countries, and visitors enjoy limited duty-free allowances. In June 2004 Andorra signed a series of accords with the EU in the fields of economic, social, and cultural cooperation. Tax legislation was also approved that taxed interest from monetary products and fixed-interest investments belonging to non-residents, while maintaining bank secrecy.

Although less than 2% of the land is arable, agriculture was the mainstay of the Andorran economy until the upsurge in tourism. Sheep-raising had been the principal agricultural activity, but tobacco-growing is lucrative. Most of Andorra's food is imported.

In addition to handicrafts, manufacturing includes cigars, cigarettes, and furniture for domestic and export markets. A hydroelectric plant at Les Escaldes, with a capacity of 26.5 megawatts, provides 40% of Andorra's electricity; Spain provides the rest.

Andorra's GDP - $3.66 billion (CIA), with tourism as its principal component. Attractive for shoppers from France and Spain as a free port, the country also has developed active summer and winter tourist resorts. With some 270 hotels and 400 restaurants, as well as many shops, the tourist trade employs a growing portion of the domestic labour force. An estimated 9 million tourists visit annually.

There is a fairly active trade in consumer goods, including imported manufactured items, which, because they are duty-free, are less expensive in Andorra than in neighboring countries. Andorra's duty-free status also has had a significant effect on the controversy concerning its relationship with the European Union. Its negotiations on duty-free status and relationship with the Union began in 1987, soon after Spain joined. An agreement that went into effect in July 1991 sets duty-free quotas and places limits on certain items--mainly milk products, tobacco, and alcoholic beverages. Andorra is permitted to maintain price differences from other EU countries, and visitors enjoy limited duty-free allowances.

The results of Andorra's elections thus far indicate that many support the government's reform initiatives and believe Andorra must, to some degree, integrate into the European Union in order to continue to enjoy its prosperity. Although less than 2% of the land is arable, agriculture was the mainstay of the Andorran economy until the upsurge in tourism. Sheep raising has been the principal agricultural activity, but tobacco growing is lucrative. Most of Andorra's food is imported.

In addition to handicrafts, manufacturing includes cigars, cigarettes, and furniture for domestic and export markets. A hydroelectric plant at Les Escaldes, with a capacity of 26.5 megawatts, provides 40% of Andorra's electricity; Spain provides the rest.

FOREIGN RELATIONS

Since the establishment of sovereignty with the ratification of the constitution in 1993, Andorra has moved to become an active member of the international community. In July 1993, Andorra established its first diplomatic mission in the world, to the United Nations. In early 1995, the United States and Andorra established formal diplomatic relations. Andorra also expanded relations with other nations.

Andorra is a full member of the United Nations (UN) United Nations Educational,

Scientific and Cultural Organization (UNESCO), World Health Organization (WHO), Telecommunications International Union (ITU), United Nations World Intellectual Property Organization (WIPO), World Tourism Organization, Food and Agriculture Organization (FAO), International Civil Aviation Organization (ICAO), World Customs Organization (WCO), United Nations Conference on Trade and Development (UNCTAD), International Criminal Court (ICC), International Committee of the Red Cross (ICRC), Council of Europe, Organization for Security and Cooperation in Europe (OSCE), Organization for the Prohibition of Chemical Weapons, International Center of Studies for Preservation and Restoration of Cultural Heritage (ICCROM), and Interpol, among others.

Since 1991, Andorra has had a special agreement with the European Union. In 2008, Andorra announced its endorsement of the Proliferation Security Initiative, designed to combat illegal trafficking in weapons of mass destruction.

U.S.-ANDORRAN RELATIONS

The United States established diplomatic relations with Andorra in February 21, 1995. The two countries are on excellent terms. The U.S. Ambassador to Spain is also accredited as Ambassador to Andorra. United States Consulate General officials based in **Barcelona** are responsible for the day-to-day conduct of relations with Andorra. The Andorran Permanent Representative to the United Nations, Narcis Casal, was accredited as Andorra's Ambassador to the United States in July 2014.

TRAVEL AND BUSINESS INFORMATION

Travel Alerts, Travel Warnings, Trip Registration

The U.S. Department of State's Consular Information Program advises Americans traveling and residing abroad through Country Specific Information, Travel Alerts, and Travel Warnings. **Country Specific Information** exists for all countries and includes information on entry and exit requirements, currency regulations, health conditions, safety and security, crime, political disturbances, and the addresses of the U.S. embassies and consulates abroad. **Travel Alerts** are issued to disseminate information quickly about terrorist threats and other relatively short-term conditions overseas that pose significant risks to the security of American travelers. **Travel Warnings** are issued when the State Department recommends that Americans avoid travel to a certain country because the situation is dangerous or unstable.

For the latest security information, Americans living and traveling abroad should regularly monitor the Department's Bureau of Consular Affairs Internet web site at http://travel.state.gov, where current Worldwide Caution, Travel Alerts, and Travel Warnings can be found. The travel.state.gov website also includes information about passports, tips for planning a safe trip abroad and more. More travel-related information also is available at http://www.usa.gov/Citizen/Topics/Travel/International.shtml.

The Department's Smart Traveler app for U.S. travelers going abroad provides easy access to the frequently updated official country information, travel alerts, travel warnings, maps, U.S. embassy locations, and more that appear on the travel.state.gov site. Travelers can also set up e-tineraries to keep track of arrival and departure dates and make notes about upcoming trips. The app is compatible with iPhone, iPod touch, and iPad (requires iOS 4.0 or later).

The Department of State encourages all U.S. citizens traveling or residing abroad to register via the State Department's travel registration website or at the nearest U.S. embassy or consulate abroad (a link to the registration page is also available through the Smart Traveler app). Registration will make your presence and whereabouts known in case it is necessary to contact you in an emergency and will enable you to receive up-to-date information on security conditions.

Emergency information concerning Americans traveling abroad may be obtained by calling 1-888-407-4747 toll free in the U.S. and Canada or the regular toll line 1-202-501-4444 for callers outside the U.S. and Canada.

Passports

The National Passport Information Center (NPIC) is the U.S. Department of State's single, centralized public contact center for U.S. passport information. Telephone: 1-877-4-USA-PPT (1-877-487-2778); TDD/TTY: 1-888-874-7793. Passport information is available 24 hours, 7 days a week. You may speak with a representative Monday-Friday, 8 a.m. to 10 p.m., Eastern Time, excluding federal holidays.

ANDORRA ECONOMY: STRATEGY AND DEVELOPMENTS

Currency	Euro (EUR)
Fiscal year	Calendar year
Trade organisations	EU customs union
	Statistics
GDP	$3.163 billion (PPP, est.)
GDP rank	180th (PPP, est.)
GDP growth	-1.6% (Real, est.)
GDP per capita	$37,200 (PPP, est.)
GDP by sector	agriculture 14%, industry 79%, services 6% (est.)
Inflation (CPI)	1.1% (CPI, est.)
Population below poverty line	no data
Labour force	36,060 (2012)
Labour force by occupation	agriculture 0.4%, industry 4.7%, services 94.9%
Unemployment	2.9% (est.)
Main industries	tourism (particularly skiing), cattle raising, timber, banking, tobacco, furniture
	External
Exports	$70 million (
Export goods	tobacco products, furniture
Main export partners	France 34%, Spain 58% (
Imports	$1.43 billion
Import goods	consumer goods, food, electricity
Main import partners	Spain 51.5%, France 22.3%, US 0.3%
	Public finances
Public debt	no data
Revenues	$403 million
Expenses	$470 million
Economic aid	no data
Credit rating	A (Domestic) A (Foreign) AAA (T&C Assessment) (Standard & Poor's)

Andorra's GDP in 2007 was $3.66 billion (CIA), with tourism as its principal component. Attractive for shoppers from France and Spain as a free port, the country also has developed active summer and winter tourist resorts. With some 270 hotels and 400 restaurants, as well as many shops, the tourist trade employs a growing portion of the domestic labour force. An estimated 9 million tourists visit annually.

There is a fairly active trade in consumer goods, including imported manufactured items, which, because they are duty-free, are less expensive in Andorra than in neighboring countries. Andorra's duty-free status also has had a significant effect on the controversy concerning its relationship with the European Union. Its negotiations on duty-free status and relationship with the Union began in 1987, soon after Spain joined. An agreement that went into effect in July 1991 sets duty-free quotas and places limits on certain items--mainly milk products, tobacco, and alcoholic beverages. Andorra is permitted to maintain price differences from other EU countries, and visitors enjoy limited duty-free allowances.

The results of Andorra's elections thus far indicate that many support the government's reform initiatives and believe Andorra must, to some degree, integrate into the European Union in order to continue to enjoy its prosperity. Although less than 2% of the land is arable, agriculture was the mainstay of the Andorran economy until the upsurge in tourism. Sheep raising has been the principal agricultural activity, but tobacco growing is lucrative. Most of Andorra's food is imported.

In addition to handicrafts, manufacturing includes cigars, cigarettes, and furniture for domestic and export markets. A hydroelectric plant at Les Escaldes, with a capacity of 26.5 megawatts, provides 40% of Andorra's electricity; Spain provides the rest

Andorra is principally an agricultural country with some mineral resources. Potatoes and tobacco are the main products, although there is some livestock farming. The principal raw materials are lead, iron and aluminum. The country's hydroelectric power plant supplies about a quarter of its domestic needs; Andorra is dependent on imports of electricity and other fuels from France and Spain. As a duty-free zone, the economy has expanded rapidly in recent years, trading in both European and foreign goods. The main sources of government revenue are taxes on petrol, tourism and consumer goods. Legislation introduced in 1993 aimed to promote Andorra as a financial center, supplemented two years later by another law allowing foreign residents to use Andorra as a tax shelter. There is some concern about the long-term implications of Spanish membership in the EU and the likely resulting fall in tax revenues. Andorra's main trading partners are neighboring France and Spain.

GENERAL DEVELOPMENT

POPULATION, LABOR MARKET AND TRAINING

POPULATION AND MIGRATORY FLOWS

The total population of Andorra registered a 1,3% increase in 2003, according to the demographic statistics supplied by the Interior Ministry. Thus, following the decline in the two years 1994 and 1995, the population is now continuing to grow as it did in 1996. There are now 65.306 persons residing in Andorra, the highest figure ever recorded. In terms of nationality, those with Andorran nationality have increased by 4,9% and those born in Andorra by 1,8%. In overall terms, the foreign population has grown only very slowly: the number of Spanish resi-dents has fallen slightly and the number of those with other nationalities has increased slightly.

Thus the rise in the population is therefore explained by the natural growth in the Andorran element and by a slight recovery in immigration. The rate of growth of the whole population in the period 1992-2003 was an annual 1,2%, which is a much lower rate than the 4,7% between 1987 and 1992.

The foreign population currently represents 67,7% of the total and the number of Andorrans and those "Born in Andorra" is 32,3%. The largest foreign national group is that of the Spanish, who represent 43,7% of the total, followed by the Portuguese (10,7%) and, much further behind, the French (6,8%). All other nationalities put together make up 6,6% of the total.

By area, Ordino has been the parish that has seen the biggest growth in population compared with the previous year – 8,6%, ahead of Canillo (5%) and Encamp (3,7%). Population growth in other parishes has been moderate except in the capital, Andorra la Vella which has experienced a drop (-0,4%) for the second year running.

Tourism, retail sales, and finance are the mainstays of Andorra's tiny, well-to-do economy, accounting for more than three-quarters of GDP. Andorra's duty-free status for some products and its summer and winter resorts attract millions of visitors annually, although the economic downturn in neighboring countries has curtailed the number of tourists. Andorra's comparative advantage as a tax haven eroded when the borders of neighboring France and Spain opened; its bank secrecy laws have been relaxed under pressure from the EU and OECD. Agricultural production is limited - only 5% of the land is arable - and most food has to be imported, making the economy vulnerable to changes in fuel and food prices.

The principal livestock is sheep. Manufacturing output and exports consist mainly of perfumes and cosmetic products, products of the printing industry, electrical machinery and equipment, clothing, tobacco products, and furniture. Andorra is a member of the EU Customs Union and is treated as an EU member for trade in manufactured goods (no tariffs) and as a non-EU member for agricultural products. Andorra uses the euro and is effectively subject to the monetary policy of the European Central Bank. Slower growth in Spain and France has dimmed Andorra's economic prospects. Since 2010, a drop in tourism contributed to a contraction in GDP and a sharp deterioration of public finances, prompting the government to begin implementing several austerity measures to reduce the budget deficit, including levying a special corporate tax. To bring in new revenue and diversify future sources of economic growth, the government approved in July 2012 a new foreign investment law opening investment to foreign capital.

In Andorra the evolution of its GDP presented a mixed picture based on the last data available which corresponds to the year 2012. In fact, the decrease in the economic activity of the Principality of Andorra was the most pronounced of the economies of the area. **Andorran GDP fell 1.6%** in real terms —compared to -4.3% in 2011— which represents the **gentlest fall** since GDP began to contract in 2008.

The drop in Andorran GDP was mitigated thanks to the **recovery** of certain areas of the economy and in particular certain **services**, such as **the financial sector, professional, scientific and technical services and the arts and entertainment.**

However the services most linked to tourist demand, which are one of the bases of the economy of the Principality of Andorra, continued to have a very negative impact on economic performance. **Retail trading, transportation, hotels and restaurants together took 1.1 points from the nominal gain of GVA in 2012.**

It should be stressed that despite the intensity of the economic crisis in recent years **Andorra still has one of the highest standards of living in Europe** as is shown by Andorra's relative position in terms of GDP per capita. In fact once adjusted by purchasing power GDP per capita puts Andorra in **fourth place in Europe in terms of living standards.**

In recent years **population trends** in Andorra —very much linked to the economy and the labour market— underwent a radical change in the course of the crisis as a result of the **reversal of the immigration factor**. The population estimate published by the Statistics Department of Andorra gives a more precise view of recent demographic developments in Andorra. According to these figures in **2013 the Andorran population showed a slight increase of 0.3%**, an important piece of data because it represents the first increase recorded in recent years, after the falls of 2010 (-4.5%), 2011 (-0.7%) and the virtual stagnation of 2012 (-0.02%).

DEVELOPMENT OF REGISTERED POPULATION

Spanish 43,7%
Andorrans and "born in Andorra" 32,3%
Others 6,6%Portuguese 10,7%French 6,8%

DISTRIBUTION OF POPULATION BY NATIONALITIES ANY 1996

The number of live births for 2003 has been 730,30 more than in the previous year, and the highest figure for whole of the decade. The birth rate has been around 11,2 per 1000, as against 10,9 per 1000 in 1996. The number of deaths registered has not changed since 1996 (197) and the death rate has stayed at around 3 per 1000.

As a result of the unaltered death rate, the natural growth in population has been 533 persons and advanced to 8,2 per 1000. The net gain from immigration has been 294 persons.

The structural development of the population for 2003 by age consolidates the slight tendency for it to age. Those above 65 years of age have been increasing and now represent 11,5% of the population as against 9,7% in 1990. Those between 15 and 64 represent 73,2% whilst those under 15 represent 15,3% of the total, 2,1% less than at the start of the decade.
In Andorra in 2013 there was a slowing of the rate of decline of employment and some service sectors, led by professional activities and the financial sector, created jobs. However the loss of employment was still heavy in sectors such as construction and the retail trade.

In a more long-term perspective **changes to the structure of employment** since 2007 show which groups are most affected by the changes, mainly **men earning wages below the age of 40**. The change in the structure of the workforce according to age both in Andorra and in neighbouring economies since 2007 makes it possible to identify general trends and in particular **the declining relative importance of wage-earners below the age of 40**. Andorra also shares another trait with neighbouring economies in the **comparatively poor showing of employment of men**. This phenomenon, particularly marked in Andorra, Spain and Catalonia, is explained to a large extent by **the effects of falling employment in the building industry**.

Hidden behind the recent crisis there are also fundamental trends which show the process of transformation taking place in the Andorran economy, such as the **growing importance to employment in Andorra of knowledge-intensive services** thanks to the greater power of resilience they have shown recently. The rise in the contribution of knowledge-intensive services to employment has grown faster in recent years and the **sector has gone from accounting for 23% of employees in 2007 to 28.1% in 2013**.

Prices and salaries have continued to decline in recent years in a context of excess global capacity and rising unemployment. Andorran inflation has followed a course similar to that of neighbouring economies but with the special feature that the slowing of the rise of consumer prices in Andorra has been particularly sharp. **In 2013 inflation in Andorra was the lowest of the economies in the area,** as a result of the effects of the fall in energy prices and the weakness of internal demand.
Wage increases have also slowed in recent years in a trend which has been similar to that of the Spanish and Catalan economies which have made **important gains in competitiveness** thanks to this development. **In 2013 the average wage in Andorra fell 0.7%** which reflected the fall in average remuneration in a high number of jobs, although there have also been significant exceptions such as energy, financial services and education.
Wage disparities between men and women in Andorra are still high although the gap has narrowed in recent years. In **2013 women's average salary in Andorra was 73.3% that of men**, with strong variations between sectors and activities. In 2013 the public authorities and the financial sector were respectively the sectors with the greatest and the least wage difference between men and women.

TRADE FLOWS

The boost represented by the growing spending of the emerging economies produced a **new record number of tourists in 2013**, with growth of arrivals of international tourists in the year 2013 of 5%, an increase which made it possible to reach the **historic figure of 1,087 million tourists in the world.**

In Andorra trade flows are highly sensitive to tourist spending and have shown signs of recovery throughout 2013. **Non-energy imports grew in 2013 by 4.6%, the first advance since 2005,** thanks to the growth of areas linked to the tourist trade which shows a recovery in visitors' spending.

From a geographical point of view **Spain is consolidating its position as the main external supplier of Andorra,** with a market share of Andorran imports which reached a new record of 62.7% in 2013. On the export side, **the recovery of the Spanish and French markets has been accompanied by the emergence of the Russian market.**

The increase of **arrivals of international tourists in 2013** of 4.1% reflects both **the recovery of the two traditional markets, Spain and France, and the growth of Russian tourism**. But despite this recovery of international tourism in Andorra the growth of 4.1% was less than that in Europe and the world, which has meant **a loss of market share by Andorra in the international tourist market in 2013**. Andorra was the destination of 0.21% of tourist arrivals in the world and 0.41% of tourists in the European market.

SECTORS IN THE ANDORRAN ECONOMY

After some very difficult years for the Andorran economy the **signs of recovery are there to be seen**. However, indicators for the different sectors show a **very uneven situation** and still visible difficulties in important parts of the economy.

A closer analysis reveals a **variety of different degrees of recovery from the crisis**. Thus there are sectors in which the **recovery is consolidated**, for example the financial sector, sectors which show fragile but significant signs of recovery, such as the tourist industry, and sectors still in a **process of adjustment**, such as construction.

Andorran business made quite good progress in 2013 with the **net creation of 207 establishments** which was caused primarily by the real estate sector and business services and secondly by other sectors such as hotels, retailing and industry.

Consumption of energy in Andorra dropped at a **faster rate in 2013 by -2.0%**, while electricity consumption fell by 1.6%, dragged down by lower demand from skiing resorts, distribution, hotels and restaurants. In recent years the fall in energy consumption in Andorra has been less than the fall in GDP, which has meant that **energy intensity in Andorra has risen.**

Recent figures from the **primary sector** show a relatively favourable trend linked to the **diversification strategy** the sector has followed in recent years, and which in 2013 made it possible to register a **new record of 19.9 Km. of useful agricultural land** in Andorra.

The adjustment in the **construction** industry continues without any clear signs of its bottoming out. The **shrinkage of the sector** within the economic structure of the Principality has been very severe with a loss of importance which has meant a **fall in its contribution to GVA** from 13.4% in 2006 to 7.6% in 2012 and a **fall in its contribution to total employment** from 14.4% in 2006 to 7.2% in 2013.

In the **tourist sector**, despite the 3.2% decline in visitors in 2013, an improvement is to be seen in the shape of the **recovery of tourist arrivals (4.1%) and overnight stays (4.7%)**. Growth of supply in the hotel business is being driven by more up-market establishments in line with the objective of seeking more high-quality demand.

The **registration of vehicles** increased 10.1% in 2013 and points to **an improvement of private consumption** in Andorra. This increase in registrations in 2013 contrasts with the falls seen in the two previous years, which were very much linked to the loss of population, as is shown by the fact that the rate of motorisation remained relatively stable in the period 2011-2012.

The **financial sector** is acting as the **great driving force of the Andorran economy**, as is shown by the trends of the main economic indicators —the GVA of the sector grew 4.9% in 2012 and employment in the sector increased 2.2% in 2013. This reactivation of the financial sector is basically the result of the **progress being made by the banking sector** which in 2013 produced an exceptionally positive performance. The various indicators confirm the good health of the Andorran banking industry which in 2013 increased **managed customer resources by 16% to reach 41,043 million euros**, a figure which represents a new record.

EMPLOYMENT

The number of jobs in 2003 – 33.203 average for the year – indicates a gain of 1.428 during the last year which represents quite a high year-on-year gain of 4,5%, slightly up on the 4,1% in 1996.

The average number of wage earners has been 29.088 in 2003, which represents a gain of 3,6%, much greater than for the last few years. Thus, wage earners represent 44,5% of the total population and 60,9% of the population between 15 and 64. This proportion has increased continually since 1994 and reflects a higher employment rate than that registered in most European countries.

The distribution per sector of wage earners affiliated to the Andorran Health and Social Security Fund signals a generalized positive situation in the employment market for 2003. The primary sector, which currently offers employment to 0,7% of the wage-earning population, a figure that has not varied with respect to 1996, has registered a gain in numbers Of 3,6%, a much lower increase than the 10,3% seen in 1996.

As to the industrial sector, the downward trend of the last few years has been breached and growth has been positive at 1,6%. Despite this significant recuperation, the relative weight of this sector in overall employment has continued to decrease and is now at around 4,3%.

NATURAL MOVEMENT OF POPULATION

	1996	**2003**
Biths	700	730
Deaths	197	197
Natural growth	503	533
Birth rate (per 1000)	10,856	11,178
Death rate (per 1000)	3,055	3,017
Rate of natural growth (per 1000)	7,801	8,162
Gain in immigration from updating records	117	294
Total increase in population	620	827

Source: Secretary of State for the Interior.

25 Figures from the construction industry have consolidated the positive tendency of the previous year by growing 2,2%, but it weight in the overall figure has dropped to 16,2%.

Job creation has been most apparent in the building sector and has decreased slightly in allied industries.

The biggest growth area has been in services – which represents more than three-quarters of the working population – at 4%. Hotels, catering and tourism – which has more wage-earners than any other sector except commerce – has registered a notable gain of 3%, although less than in recent years, and the participation by the sector in the overall situation has reduced slightly (17,63%), The financial sector, with 4,39% of wage-earners, which had shed workers during 1995 and 1996 (-0,2% and 0,7% respectively) has seen an increase in numbers this last year 1,8%.

The only two sectors that have shown growth of more than 5% have been Administration (5,3%) – which has increased its weight in the overall figures to 12,5% - and other services (5,6%) with a total of 20,9% of the working population as against 20,5%

EMPLOYMENT IN THE PRINCIPAL SECTORS

Primary	199		3,6		0,68	
Primary industries	497		0,4		1,71	
Construction	2.572		5,1		8,84	
Allied building trades	2.127		-1,1		7,31	
Manufacturing industry		756		2,4		2,60
Garages	409		1,5		1,41	
Food industry	1.260	-	0,8		4,33	
Tourism	5.570		4,2		,15	
Services	3.338		5,2		11,48	
Hotels and catering	4.210	2,8	14,47			
Tourist services	917		4,0		3,15	
Finance and insurance		1.276		1,8		4,39
Liberal professions	620		13,3		2,13	
Administration		3.636	5,3			12,50
Others		1.701	4,9			5,85
Total	**29.088**		**3,6**			**100,00**

Source: Andorran Health and Social Security Fund

WAGE-EARNERS 2003 VAR 97/96 % 2003

Within this last main sector there has been a notable increase in the number of wage earners in the liberal professions. Commerce – the service sector with the biggest number of wage-earners – has reinforced the timid growth of 1996 by increasing jobs by 3,2%, which has meant that the sector its overall weighting of 23,5%, around the same as last year.

TRAINING

During the academic year 1996-2003, the total number of students has been 10.593, up by 3,3% from the previous academic year and maintaining the expansive trend seen since 1995-1996. The increases are directly related to the notable expansion in the total of university-level students where numbers have increased by 17,7%. The number of schoolchildren – 88,2% of the total – has increased by 2,7%, after having fallen off slightly during the last three school years. In contrast, the number of students attending non-university courses outside Andorra has seen a significant drop. Overall, students represent 16,2% of the population, slightly higher than the 15,9% seen in the previous academic year.

The number of pupils actually studying in Andorra – as opposed to those who study outside Andorra – has increased by 2,8% - which corresponds almost exactly with the increase in the total number of students – and represents 89,4% of the total, slightly less in proportion than in the previous year. The marked rise in the number of students being educated in Spain (10,2%) and France (4,1%) during the 1996/7 academic year is due to the strong increase in the university population and who most usually must attend courses outside Andorra.

EDUCATION SYSTEM

PRIMARY AND SECONDARY LEVEL

The school population in Andorra comprised 9.344 pupils during the 1996/7 year - 88,2% of the student population – which shows an increase of 2,7% compared with the previous year, breaking the downward trend of the last three years. The increases in numbers have been quite uneven depending on the academic level. There has been a large increase at the basic secondary (20,2%) and special education levels (23,3%), although this latter represents a very small community. On the other hand, at the advanced secondary and professional 29 an increase of 18% and accentuate the growth tendency of the last two years, corroborate the expansion in investment.

As to developments in the principal sectors, the most dynamic has once again been services, although both industry and construction has also seen growth. Thus, the data from CASS reflects a notable pick-up in the number of wage earners in services (4%) in a sector that had already been growing well over the previous two years. But, job increases have also been seen in construction (2,2%) – having seen very modest growth last year – and a small increase in the number of wage-earners in industry (1,6%), which breaks the downward trend seen so far in this decade. In the case of the construction industry, a strong increase in imports of building materials reinforces the impression of a significant upturn in activity.

Within the service sector, administration and other services have been the most dynamic, certainly in the area of job creation. Tourism services have maintained the expansive trend of the last few years and commerce has also improved after years of standstill.

Lastly, the results of the regular reports by the Chamber of Commerce, highlight the better business conditions, the increase in investment and particularly the much more positive tone of business forecasts for 1998.

Turnover has been up on 2003 in all the sectors analyzed. In industry, turnover has bottomed out after the drop in 1996. In retail commerce and construction turnover has increased breaking the contraction of the previous year. And in the hotel sector, which had already registered an increase in 1996, growth has accelerated. Investment has grown in all sectors but especially strongly in the hotel sector.

Lastly, business opinion reflects a radical change in expectations, when compared with 1996. Confidence in industry and retail commerce has shown a significant improvement, with confidence well up in the hotel sector. In contrast, the construction industry is still ambivalent about business prospects.

Thus the most relevant indicators of activity tend to show a significant improvement in GDP for Andorra in 2003. Whilst waiting for the official estimates from the Ministry of Finance – which should start at the end of 1998 – which will result from the introduction of a national accounting programme and which will be the only reliable method of macroeconomic performance, we have attempted to bring up to date the figure produced by the IMF in 1994. These estimates, obtained via some fairly unsophisticated methodology and some arguable statistics, do however show some light on the tendency in economic activity. Provisional estimates for 2003 signal a growth in the GDP of about 10%.

If one excludes tobacco imports that have been very erratic during 2003, the estimates for the growth in GDP would result in a figure of about 8%. Whilst we have used the Consumer price index from Spain as a calculation factor, which could have negatively affected the estimates, there is one thing that is certain and that is that economic growth has clearly broken the downward trend of the last few years.

PRACTICAL INFORMATION AND CONTACTS FOR CONDUCTING BUSINESS[1]

The following is a list of the exports of Andorra.

Data re in millions of United States dollars, as reported by The Observatory of Economic Complexity. Currently the top ten exports are listed.

#	Product	Value
1	Malt Extract	29,654
2	Refined Petroleum	23,956
3	Stone Processing Machines	23,585
4	Concentrated Milk	21,924
5	Integrated Circuits	13,821
6	Industrial Food Processing Machinery	13,694
7	Cars	9,451
8	Rubber Working Machinery	7,909
9	Orthopedic Appliances	7,590
10	Palm Oil	6,864

Andorra is a medieval principality secluded from the rest of the world, yet only a short drive from the sparking beaches of the French Riviera, and that bustling European economic powerhouse, Barcelona. It lies in a hidden valley in the picturesque Pyrenees - and is one of the few alpine paradises in the world that is also a tax haven.What makes Andorra the ultimate personal tax haven in all of Europe is a splendid combination of features.

Take political stability. Andorra has zero leftist political parties. In fact, it hardly has any government at all. Of the 60,000 people that inhabit this alpine tax refuge, fewer than one hundred 0.4% of the total population - work for the government. There is not even a currency; both French and Spanish are recognized as legal tender.

Then there's the robust economy. Andorra is a wealthy, duty free area with no taxes of any kind whatsoever! Its postal system is free, supported by sale of Andorran stamps to collectors around the world. Labour unions are strictly forbidden. There is no hint of a "socialist mentality" among the natives.

The unregulated banking system is among the safest in the world. It is sound, prosperous, computerized, streamlined, discreet and very customer oriented. Some of the wealthiest people in the world prefer Andorra's low-profile banks to those of secretive Switzerland. You can obtain an account in Andorra and access world markets in total

[1] Materials of the Andorra Chamber of Commerce and Industry

privacy - and you can receive interest rates several percent higher than you would receive in the United Kingdom and the United States.

In Andorra there is no crime. There is free health care for everyone, including old age pensions. All internal mail is free, too! Schools are free for everyone. Most entertainment is free. Dining out in a first class restaurant before a free classical music concert is cheap. Andorra has 250 restaurants, some of Europe's best skiing and the largest number of Mercedes limousines per capita in the world. Its people are affluent. They do not pay any taxes at all.

Andorra is cosmopolitan. More than two thirds of all residents are wealthy, self-made foreigners, most of who moved to Andorra because they were fed up with government red tape and destructive bureaucracy. The adult literacy rate is 100%.

THE EXTERNAL ENVIRONMENT OF THE ANDORRAN ECONOMY

THE INTERNATIONAL ECONOMY

In 2014 the world economy suffered the worst recession for 60 years, accentuating the negative trend which had begun at the end of 2008. The world GDP recorded a fall of 0.6% in 2014, and thus ended the longest period of expansion since the Second World War. The recession has been global but more intense and longer in the developed countries, which recorded a fall in GDP of 3.2%, while the developing countries continued growing (2.5%) due to the dynamism of China and India, which only suffered a slight moderation in their rhythm of growth. The developed countries which recorded the largest falls in GDP, at -5% or more, were Japan, Italy, Germany, Ireland and the United Kingdom.

At the same time, world trade suffered a very sharp fall (-11.3% against growth of 2.8% in 2008), which was particularly intense in the case of consumer durables and capital goods, the worst affected by the contraction in demand caused by the financial crisis. The fall in world trade mostly affected the advanced economies, while imports from manufacturers in the developing and emerging countries experienced a lesser reduction, and in the case of China even increased.

The most acute phase of the recession came in the first quarter of 2014, when the GDP fell heavily in the advanced countries and the indices of confidence reached record lows. The year had started with substantial financial instability but, due to the interventions in support of the financial system which had begun to be implemented at the end of 2008, the risk in the lending markets began slowly to reduce. However, the transfer of the financial crisis to the real economy was strongly influenced by the restriction of access to credit and the increased rate of slow payments and doubtful debts. To this must be added the weakness in real estate markets throughout 2014.

Apart from the measures of support to the financial system, the serious economic situation required rapid and coordinated action from the economic and monetary authorities and, in consequence, the governments and central banks adopted measures for monetary and tax stimulation. The measures for monetary stimulus consisted in reducing interest rates and in quantitative actions to increase liquidity. Thus the European Central Bank (ECB) reduced the official rates for money on four occasions between January and May, from the initial 2.5% down to 1%, and since then has kept it stable. For its part, the Federal Reserve (FED) had already reduced its official interest rate to 0.25% in December 2008 and it was kept at that level throughout 2014. As a result of a more expansive monetary policy in the United States than in the euro zone, the interest rate differential increased, which caused the consequent rise in the value of the euro against the dollar during the greater part of the year. Finally, the Bank of England reduced interest rates three times to end at 0.5%, and the Bank of Japan maintained a rate of 0.1% throughout the year.

The quantitative measures for expansion of liquidity were based on the purchase of assets, at the same time as the national governments were extending guarantees on deposits and injecting public capital into the banking entities. But, for the moment, these measures were more effective in stabilising the banks' balance sheets than in helping to promote lending and, therefore, demand as a whole, which remained very weak until the last months of 2014. The lack of liquidity and the restrictions on credit had very prejudicial effects on consumption and investment, a fact which led to the fall in domestic demand in the advanced countries and the transfer of the crisis to the rest of the world through the fall in imports. This is why the countries more orientated to exports, such as Germany and Japan, have been those which recorded the greatest falls in GDP.

As a result of these actions, there was a progressive reduction in tension in the monetary and financial markets throughout 2014; which emerges both from the reduction of risk premiums and from the lower volatility and more intense activity in the issues markets. However, their functioning is still very far from normality due to the appearance of new financial tensions at the beginning of 2010, the consequence of the increase in the spread of the Greek sovereign debt and its contagious effect on other heavily indebted European countries.

The tax measures consisted in the functioning of the automatic stabilisers (increase in unemployment benefit and other subsidies and a reduction of tax income as a consequence of the fall in activity) and in the economic stimulus programmes approved by the various governments, such as aids for the purchase of a motorcar. At the G-20 meeting which was held in London in March it was agreed to extend the tax stimulus to a target level of 4% of the GDP for 2014. This decision caused a rapid increase in public debt in most of the countries – especially in the euro zone, the United States, the United Kingdom and Japan – and meant that the increase in the rate of indebtedness also accelerated. The high indebtedness of these economies began to generate doubts as to their solvency, first in the countries in Central and Eastern Europe and later in Greece and other countries of Southern Europe. In anticipation of this risk, the G-20 meeting referred to agreed to quadruple the financial resources of the International Monetary Fund.

In spite of the economic and financial crisis, 2014 was a good year on the stock markets. After starting the year with a downward trend, the main world stock exchanges experienced continual growth from March onwards, anticipating the future economic recovery in a context typified by the abundance of liquidity. In terms of indices, the Dow Jones and the Nikkei gained 19% in 2014, the Euro-STOXX 21% and the IBEX-35 rose by 30%.

The financial turbulence and the deterioration in economic expectations also affected the prices of the main reference currencies. The dollar continued a falling trend for most of 2014 due to the measures of support to the financial system and the economic stimulus being implemented in the rest of the economic areas as the year advanced, and also for the interest rate differential which favoured the euro zone. >

The fall in world demand and the reduction of prices of raw materials and energy reduced the possibility of a rise in inflation caused by monetary expansion. On the contrary, during the middle part of the year there was a danger of deflation in some economies, a risk which was finally removed by the rise in the price of oil during the second half of the year, after having stayed at historically low levels during the fourth quarter of 2008 and the first quarter of 2014. In fact, the price of a Brent barrel of oil closed the year at 73 dollars, as against 40 dollars in December 2008, meaning a rise in price of 85%. In 2014 as a whole, the advanced economies recorded almost no increase in consumer prices (0.1%), while in the developing and emerging economies prices rose by 5.2% on average, but still well below the 9.2% of the previous year.

EVOLUTION OF THE PRINCIPAL ADVANCED COUNTRIES

The advanced countries were those which suffered the consequences of the recession most intensely, since the financial crisis originated in the United States and extended rapidly among its main economic partners, although in the end with a greater impact on the euro zone than on the United States economy. By the end of 2008 all the developed countries had gone into recession except Japan and Italy, which had done so shortly before, and this situation continued until the last quarter of 2014, when the majority of the large economies were already recording the second positive quarterly variation in GDP. In interannual terms, the recession touched bottom in the first and second quarters and, from that point, the fall in GDP moderated; although in the last quarter of the year only the United States economy was able to record positive interannual growth, at 0.1%.

UNITED STATES

The United States economy reduced by 2.4% in 2014, the most negative figure since the Second World War, although signs of recovery began to appear during the second half of the year, due to the intervention of the United States government and the Federal Reserve to combat the crisis. The falls in private consumption and, above all, investment, were the principal features of the recession in the United States. The taxation stimulus programme and the reduction in interest rates were determining factors in restoring confidence, but did not stimulate the granting of credit, and this, added to the rise in unemployment, contributed to the stagnation in consumption and the sharp fall in investment.

In quarterly terms, during the first half of the year the United States economy still recorded negative rates and it moved out of recession in the fourth quarter after two consecutive quarters of growth. The components in the aggregate demand which contributed to the United States emerging from the recession were private consumption, representing 71% of the U.S. GDP – which had started the year with a fall of 1.5% and ended by growing by 1% – and public spending.

(a) Advance

On the other hand, the behaviour of investment

GDP AND PRIVATE CONSUMPTION IN THE was very negative in 2014, with a fall of 23%, which UNITED STATES -Rate of interannual variation had not happened since 1949. Both investment in GDP Private consumption construction and investment in equipment pulled private investment down, with the difference that investment in construction fell for the third consecutive year by around 20%, while investment in equipment suffered a strong adjustment in the [1] year. For its part, public investment showed growth [0] moderated to 1.9%, the lowest recorded for the -1 last four years, which meant that it could not act in -2 compensating for the fall in private investment. At -3 2001 2002 2003 2004 the same time, the fiscal policy applied by the United States administration was expansive, which was translated into an increase in public deficit from 6.5% of the GDP in 2008 to 11% in 2014.

With regard to external demand, its contribution to growth was positive for the second consecutive year, the consequence of a fall in imports (-14%) greater than that of exports (-9.6%). Behind the behaviour of imports was the weakness in domestic demand, while the fall in world trade explains the fall in exports. The depreciation of the dollar after the second quarter of the year encouraged a recovery in exports in the last months of the year, as the $/€ exchange rate moved from 1.307 in April to 1.393 in December. This depreciation of the United States currency contributed to improving the competitiveness of the United States and reducing its deficit on current account for the second consecutive year, situated at 2.9% of the GDP in 2014.

The crisis had a strong impact on the labour market. The rate of unemployment increased by almost four percentage points, to 9.3% on annual average, which meant the loss of more than seven million jobs during 2014. It must be remembered that at the beginning of 2008 the rate was at 4.9%, a level which could be considered as full employment.

The fall in the prices of energy and raw materials and the weakness in demand explain the historic fall recorded for consumer prices in the United States (-0.3% on annual average). During the second and third quarters the prices fell, and the subsequent recovery came in the fourth quarter as a consequence of the rise in the price of oil. The absence of inflationary pressures enabled the Federal Reserve to keep the nominal interest rate at 0.25% throughout the year, a historic minimum. In the real estate market the fall in prices also halted, mostly due to aid offered to home buyers, but the low activity in demand continued.

JAPAN

In Japan the recession was more prolonged and severe than in the United States, since it began in the third quarter of 2008 and during 2014 the Japanese economy experienced a fall in GDP of 5.2%. Japan and Italy are the only two countries to have recorded an economic decline during these two consecutive years, 2008 and 2014.

During the second half of 2014 a slow recovery began, based on the fiscal stimulus programmes and the improvement in exports associated with the recovery in world trade, in spite of the rise of the yen against the dollar. However, the economic recovery is fragile and is threatened by the danger of deflation. To avoid this danger and also to > combat financial instability and economic weakness in the country, the Japanese Central

Bank kept the official interest rate at an historic minimum of 0.1% throughout 2014. But inevitably consumer prices fell by 1.4% on average in 2014, and this deflationary prospect was a determinant for the stagnation of private consumption and investment. The high level of indebtedness in all sectors of the economy meant that deflation would increase the load of debt, and make the recovery of domestic demand impossible. On the other hand, the rate of unemployment rose by little more than one point to reach an average of 5.1% during 2014, a level which can still be considered low. In the fiscal ambit, the public deficit has gone up by six points to reach 7.2% of the GDP, as a result of the economic stimulus plans.

EURO ZONE

In 2014 the GDP of the euro zone economies also experienced a sharp fall, -4.1%, which was the first recession to be suffered in this zone since its creation. The evolution of economic activity during 2014 showed two clearly differentiated phases. During the first two quarters of the year the recession was at its most intense and reached the lowest point of the economic cycle – the fall in GDP reached 5% interannual – while in the second half of the year quarterly growth was resumed and, therefore, the recession was left behind, although not managing to achieve a positive rate of variation in interannual terms.

This fallback in GDP was attributed to a negative contribution by domestic demand, which in turn was due to a contraction in private consumption (-1.1%) and a fall in investment, more intense in the case of capital goods than in construction (-17.3% and -6.5%, respectively). This fall in investment was explained by the fall in business profits, difficulties in getting access to credit, the sharp contraction in world trade and, finally, economic instability and uncertainty. Only consumption and public investment recorded positive rates of growth (2.3% and 2.8%, respectively), due to the fiscal stimulus policies which the various governments have set in train.

The fall in domestic demand was translated into a fall in imports, of 11%, while the contraction in world trade and the rise of the euro against the dollar caused a considerable fall in exports (-13%). The current account balance for the whole of the euro zone showed a deficit, for the second consecutive year, of 0.3% of the GDP.

The labour market suffered the consequences of the fall in activity, but not so much as in the United States. In the euro zone employment fell by 2.1% and the rate of unemployment was at 9.4% on annual average, two points higher than in 2008, a year in which the rate of unemployment was at the lowest point in the historical series (available from 1993).

The weakness in demand and the fall in energy and raw materials prices meant that the rate of inflation began the year with a downward trend, to the point of entering into negative territory in June. The fall was maintained until October and the minimum in the historical series was reached in July (-0.6% annual). In the last two months of the year inflation returned to positive rates through the recovery of energy prices, and the year ended with an increase of 0.9%. In spite of this, the average variation in consumer prices in 2014 was placed at 0.3%, against 3.3% in the previous year. The underlying inflation – which excludes the more volatile components such as energy and un-prepared foods – was positive but very contained; being 1% in December, well below the price stability target of the European Central Bank (ECB) of 2%. In spite of the moderation in prices, unit labour costs went up in 2014 by 4%, as a result of a rise in salaries of 1.9% and a drop in productivity of 2%.

During 2014 fiscal policies were more expansive, the result both of a reduction of tax income through the fall in activity and of an increase in public spending in order to combat the crisis. Specifically, the public deficit for the whole of the euro zone was placed at 6.3% of the GDP, more than four points above the level of 2008, which meant an increase in the level of indebtedness of ten points on the GDP, up to 78.7%. In 2014 there was no country in the euro zone which recorded a surplus and only Finland and Luxembourg complied with the Stability and Growth Pact, which sets a cap on public deficit at 3% of the GDP. The countries with the highest deficits were Ireland (-14.3%), Greece (-13.6%) and Spain (-11.2%), and those which had the highest public debt/GDP ratios were Greece and Italy (115%), followed by Belgium, Germany, France and Portugal.

All the member countries, without exception, were in recession in 2014, but some were more deeply so than others, with regard basically to three factors: the weight in the economy of the sectors most affected by the crisis, such as the automobile industry and real estate; their orientation to exports, and their level of public deficit and indebtedness. The economies which were most affected by the fall in the automobile sector were Germany, Belgium, France, Spain and Italy, while the fall in exports mostly affected Germany, Finland and Ireland. Finally, the collapse in the real estate sector had substantially recessive effects especially in Spain and Ireland. In short, the countries which recorded the deepest falls in GDP were Ireland, Finland and Slovenia (-7% or more) and Germany and Italy (around -5%). In contrast, of the larger European economies, France was the country which had fallen back least in economic terms (-2.5%).

With regard to inflation on annual average, all the member countries recorded very moderate rates in 2014, between the maximum of Malta (1.8%) and the minimum of Belgium (0%) and, further, three countries recorded falls in prices, specifically Ireland, Spain and Portugal.

Finally, in the ambit of the process of integration into the European Economic and Monetary Union, it must be remembered that Slovenia joined in 2007; Cyprus and Malta in 2008 and Slovakia in 2014, so that there are now 16 member states in the EMU.

EVOLUTION OF THE PRINCIPAL EMERGING AND DEVELOPING COUNTRIES

The behaviour of the emerging economies was more positive than that of the developed economies, to the point that some of these countries took on the role of motor of the recovery in the world economy. In this sense mention must be made of the economies of China and India, for which the recession only meant a slowdown of between two and three points in their GDP growth rates. Also in Brazil the impact of the crisis was milder and shorter, as its economy grew in the fourth quarter of 2014 by 4% and the fall in the year as a whole was only two tenths. In that country the entry of capital, which allowed an expansion of credit, and the fiscal stimulation, encouraged domestic demand in such a way that private consumption became the great leader of the recovery during the second half of the year. In contrast, Russia, the fourth member of the BRIC group, suffered a considerable recession on account of its higher degree of integration with the advanced economies.

In the specific case of China, the strong growth of credit – more than 30% in 2014 – was the key to promoting investment, which also grew by 30%, and private consumption, which went up by 15%. The fiscal stimulus, which meant moving from a surplus of 1% of the GDP in 2008 to a deficit of 1.8% in 2014, also contributed to the expansion in domestic demand. The rapid recovery of the Chinese economy showed in maintenance of its rhythm as an importer of raw materials and was responsible to a great degree for many developing countries, particularly in the Middle East and North Africa, maintaining positive growth rates. India followed a similarly expansive road, led by domestic demand, although with more imbalance between public deficit and the balance on current account.

In general, the factors which made Asia less vulnerable to the financial crisis were the high levels of reserves, the low exposure of their financial systems to toxic assets and the high savings rate, which gave their governments more room for manoeuvre. Further, the recovery in the Asian economies came in a more balanced way, with both external and domestic demand taking part in it.

With regard to Latin American economies, on the whole there was a fall of GDP of 1.8% in 2014. The > case of Mexico stands out with the GDP down by 6.5%, leading the deepest recession in the continent. The gradual recovery of the United States economy after the summer was a determinant for the increase in exports from the area, above all from Mexico, and in short for the recovery of the Latin American economy as a whole in the last quarter of the year.

1.4. PROSPECTS

In 2010 the world economy has begun a slow recovery but at rhythms which vary widely between areas. According to the latest IMF report in July on economic prospects, the world GDP will resume growth in 2010 with a rate of 4.6%, four tenths more than was estimated in April. This growth will be stimulated by the dynamism of the emerging countries (6.8%), while recovery will be weaker in the developed economies, with an increase of 2.6%. In these latter, the high rates of unemployment and public debt, the only partial recovery of the financial system and, in some countries, the financial difficulties of families, are complicating the reactivation of domestic demand.

To this must be added the new tensions that have appeared in financial markets, although on this occasion the origin is not in the United States, as was the case with the failure of Lehman Brothers in September 2008, but in the euro zone and concerned with the crisis regarding the Greek debt and the growing lack of confidence of investors in the solvency of the more indebted European countries. These strong tensions are making the economic recovery in Europe more fragile.

To meet this situation, in May 2010 the Ministers of Economy of the European Union (ECOFIN) agreed on the creation of a financial mechanism to rescue countries in the euro zone which have difficulties in paying their public debt, in order to stabilise the financial system and shield the European currency against possible speculative attacks. The agreement consists in providing a fund of 750,000 million euro, 500,000 contributed by the EMU countries and the rest by the IMF, which will enable financial support to be given to countries in the euro zone which are finding difficulties in refinancing the debt. This agreement was arrived at after it was concluded specifically for Greece, for which 110,000 million euro was granted (30,000 to the charge of the IMF). At the same time, the ECB has started to purchase public debt to give liquidity to the markets.

In consideration for these exceptional measures, the governments of the euro zone countries have undertaken to accelerate the reduction of the public deficit, which has taken the form of multiple plans for adjustments in public spending. The first countries to approve these plans were Greece, Portugal, Ireland, Spain and Italy, but later they were joined by less indebted countries such as Germany. The German adjustment, of 80,000 million up to the year 2014, combines a reduction in social spending with new taxes on air travel, financial transactions and nuclear energy.

The spread of the Greek crisis to the public debt markets of other EMU countries and fears of the effects that the austerity measures could have on growth in 2010 and 2011, have dragged the quotation of the euro down, so that it lost 14% of its value in the first five months of the year, arriving at a point below

1.2 dollars, the lowest value of the last four years. The stock markets also recorded generalised corrections downwards for the same reasons. The central banks, for their part, have kept their interest rates at the minimum levels reached in the previous year and, following the latest financial tensions in the euro zone, the ECB has put a brake on the initiative of gradual withdrawal of some of the exceptional measures for liquidity introduced during the most critical phase of the financial crisis.

In this context, the economy of the euro zone has grown by only 0.2% during the first three months of the year, which confirms the slow recovery in the European economy, still clearly at a lower rhythm than that of the United States and Japan, economies which grew in the first quarter by 0.8% and 1.2%, respectively. In Europe, the two leading economies, France and Germany, have made timid advances, of one and two tenths respectively. The forecast of growth for the euro zone for 2010 is placed at around 1%, and will come mostly from exports, since consumption and public investment will fall back as a result of the austerity measures, and private consumption is not forecast to grow.

In the United States the recovery is being much more rapid than in Europe and is sustained on the variation of stocks and, to a lesser degree, on the recovery of consumption and exports. In the first quarter, the growth of GDP has been accompanied by a strong increase in business profits (31% interannual) and an improvement in the movements in non-agrarian employment. The maintenance of the rate of unemployment at 9.7% during the first three months of the year will enable private consumption to be sustained, while the rise in the value of the dollar could make the recovery of exports more difficult. The confidence indicators suggest continuity in the improvement in economic activity. This favourable movement in the first quarter has raised the forecasts of growth in GDP for the whole of 2010. In May, the principal international bodies placed the growth in GDP at 3% on average, between six and seven tenths above what was forecast between the end of 2014 and the beginning of 2010.

The prospects of lower world demand caused a fall in the price of a barrel of oil in May, but as the economic uncertainties dissipate the price of crude could rise. This possible rise in the price of oil and the depreciation of the euro will be the principal upward pressures on inflation in coming months. At the same time, at present, these inflationary pressures are being countered by weakness in demand. And it must be added that the freezing or reduction of public salaries approved by many European economies for this year will not be adding pressure on prices.

In short, the cyclical situation has improved significantly in recent quarters, due to the recovery of the emerging economies and the United States. World trade has grown by 27% in the first quarter > of 2010 and the IMF forecasts indicate growth in the world economy of much above 4% for 2010. Nevertheless, at the same time doubts arise over the capacity of the EMU to deal with the problem of the high levels of indebtedness of some countries. These doubts have given place to an increase in the differentials of sovereign debt and a new phase of financial instability. The rescue plan approved by the EMU reduces uncertainty in the short term, but not the risks in the medium and long term, and not the

negative impact that this could have on the incipient economic recovery in the euro zone, above all if Germany does not act as the motor of the recovery, on account of the austerity plan which it has decided to set in train. To this is added the high public debt which the United States economy also suffers and the impact that this could have on its future growth. Thus the economic situation at the time of closing this report is of a fragile recovery, without being able to discount a relapse in some developed economies.

THE MAIN FEATURES IN ECONOMIC DEVELOPMENT

The French economy, as with the rest of the developed economies, suffered in 2014 the deepest recession since the Second World War, caused by the financial crisis and the free fall in world trade, although not so deep as in Germany, Italy, the United Kingdom or Spain, due to the resistance of private consumption in France and the lower weight of the manufacturing sector in the French economy.

Over the year as a whole, the French GDP fell back by 2.5%, according to the French National Institute of Statistics (INSEE), but after the second quarter of 2014 there was positive quarterly growth, enabling the country to emerge from the recession earlier than most of the developed economies. In consequence, the French economy moved from showing a negative differential in growth with the euro zone of three tenths in 2008, to a positive differential of 1.6 points in 2014.

However, the GDP per capita in parity of purchasing power reduced slightly in 2014 for the fourth consecutive year, to 107% of the average for the EU-27.

For the first time in recent years domestic demand made a negative contribution to the GDP, 0.5 points, while the external sector and inventories continued the negative contribution of the previous year (-0.2 and -1.8%, respectively). This reduction in domestic demand was due to the fall in investment, in both capital goods and construction, while private consumption grew at a higher rate than in the previous year, contrary to what was happening in most of the European economies. Specifically, private consumption grew by 0.7%, two tenths more than in 2008, due to measures for economic stimulation, such as aid for the purchase of a motorcar and the payment of 200 euro to people on low incomes. The low interest rates also contributed to the growth of consumption as well as the fact that the fall in the price of financial and real estate assets had touched

ECONOMIC GROWTH AND PRIVATE CONSUMPTION IN FRANCE - Rate of interannual variation GDP Private consumption bottom. Public consumption, on the other hand, grew much above the level of the previous year, as the result of an expansive fiscal policy to combat the crisis.

On the other hand, investment suffered a strong contraction, especially intense in the case of investment in capital goods (-7.9% as against an increase of 2.2% in the previous year), as a result of the restriction on credit arising from the financial crisis, the fall in profits and the change of economic prospects. Investment in construction, however, experienced a fall of 8.7%, in line with the majority of European countries.

The negative contribution of the exterior sector to the growth of GDP was two tenths, caused by a more substantial contraction in exports than in imports (-12.2% and -10.6%, respectively). This fact is explained by the fall in the world economy and especially the European – to which 70% of French exports are directed – having been more intense than that of the French domestic demand, on which imports depend. This notwithstanding, the deficit balance on current account was reduced by four tenths, to 2.2% of the GDP in 2014, according to the OECD.

An analysis of supply shows that the fall in activity was broadly generalised. The sector which recorded the largest interannual fall was, for the second consecutive year, manufacturing industry (-11.8%), much affected by the fall in exports. The sectors of energy, construction, trade, transports and services to companies also recorded substantial falls in activity, between 3% and 5%. Only the branches of agriculture, the public sector (education, health and public administration), and financial and real estate activities recorded positive rates, but in no case above 3.5%.

This fall in activity was translated into a fall in the number of people employed for the first time since the crisis of the nineties, down by -1.3%, although it must be said that the impact of the current crisis on the French labour market was much less than in other countries, such as Ireland or Spain. It is notable that 70% of the jobs lost belonged to the sectors of industry and construction. The rate of unemployment, however, rose from 7.8% in 2008 to 9.1% in 2014, placed slightly below the average for the euro zone. In this context, salaried remuneration showed an increase of 1.8%, one point less than in the previous year, but much above the average annual inflation (0.1%). This rise in salaries was aggravated by the fall in apparent productivity of work, which fell back by 1% due to the limiting impact of the crisis on the labour market. In consequence, nominal unit labour costs (ULC) rose by 2.8%, the same percentage as for the previous year, which did not help to improve competitiveness in the French economy.

Precisely in order to boost the competitiveness of the French economy in the medium and long term, in December 2014 the French Government approved the grand emprunt national, a plan which defines the strategic priorities of public investment in order to guarantee more sustainable and lasting growth. The Government will allocate 35,000 million euro to finance five priorities: Higher teaching and training, with the aim of creating up to ten campuses of international excellence; Investigation, to revalue the results of research; Support to industry and SMEs, in order to boost the aeronautical, space, automobile, railway and naval construction industries; Sustainable development, to create the future nuclear reactor of the fourth generation; and, finally, to boost the transition to the digital economy, with the objective of extending broad band to the whole of the French territory.

With regard to prices, these have been kept practically stable during 2014 on annual average (0.1%) due to the fall in raw material prices and weakness in demand. For some months there was a risk of deflation, but this possibility was discounted because the underlying inflation, which best reflects the movements in central prices as it excludes volatile components, did not fall. In fact, the underlying inflation grew on annual average by 1.3%. On the other hand, the consumer price index did fall, continuously, between the months of May and October, but the recovery in the prices of raw materials and energy and the beginning of the economic recovery turned the situation round to positive rates by the end >of the year, which ended by closing with interannual growth in the harmonised price index at 0.9%.

The economic crisis notably accentuated the imbalance in public accounts. Specifically, the public deficit increased from 3.3% of the GDP in 2008 to 7.6% in 2014, in such a way that for the second consecutive year it exceeded the deficit limit permitted by the Stability and Growth Pact (SGP), at 3% of the GDP. The principal cause of this increased deficit was the rise in public spending as a result of the action of the automatic stabilisers and the measures set in train to fight against the crisis.

At the beginning of 2014 the French Government approved a plan of economic stimulus valued at 1.1% of the GDP, in line with the European Economic Recovery Plan, which envisages, among others, the following measures: acquisition by the State of more than 100,000 homes for social housing; investment of 11,500 million euro in transport infrastructures to accelerate the rate of execution of the four high speed lines being built in France; aid of 1,000 euro for the purchase of vehicles which emit less than 160 g of CO_2 per km; the creation of a credit line for the purchase of vehicles for a value of 1,000 million euro; and payments of 200 euro each to the 3.8 million people on low incomes who have a right to social subsidies, at a cost of 760 million euro.

As a result of all this, the weight of public spending on the French GDP has risen by nearly three points, to reach 55.6% of the GDP, the highest percentage in the euro zone. On the side of public income, the economic slowdown has caused a sharp fall in tax income, above all in VAT, the tax on real estate transactions and income tax, to which must be added the impact of the package of fiscal reductions put into operation, among which is the reduction in the local tax on businesses. The result was a reduction of the tax charge which was set at 48.1% of the GDP, although still one of the highest in the euro zone after Finland, and jointly with Belgium and Austria.

The increase in the deficit created a strong and rapid increase in public debt and made this the country in the euro zone with the highest debt ratio on GDP (77.5% in 2014 in contrast to 67% in 2008), after Greece, Italy and Belgium. In view of this situation, the French Government revamped its fiscal policy and made a commitment to implementing austerity measures in order to reduce the deficit and the public debt, with the intention of defending the AAA rating granted to it for the moment by the three big risk rating agencies.

PROSPECTS

In the first quarter of 2010, the French economy has slowed its rhythm of recovery as a consequence of the gradual withdrawal of the financial measures for the stimulation of private consumption. According to the first estimates made by INSEE, the French GDP has grown in inter-quarter terms by 0.1%, after progressing by 0.5% in the last quarter of 2014. This notwithstanding, the economy has returned to interannual growth, with a rate of 1.2%, after six consecutive quarters of fall.

By components, family consumption has remained stable for this quarter, against the increase of 0.9% recorded in the previous quarter, as a consequence of the drastic fall in the purchase of cars, due to the significant reduction, from 1 January, of help for difficulties in the vehicle industry, which will finally come to an end in December 2010. Gross capital formation, on the other hand, fell back but less than in the previous quarter. As a whole, domestic demand has made a negative contribution to the GDP of one tenth.

The positive note has been led by exports, which have accelerated their rate of quarterly growth from 0.4% to 3.9%, due to the recovery of world trade and plans for stimulation of the purchase of automobiles in force in other European countries. On the other hand, imports have been moderated, pulled down by the stagnation in domestic demand, and as a result the external sector has shown a positive contribution to the growth of the GDP of four tenths in this first quarter of 2010.

In this context, the rate of unemployment increased a little in the first quarter of the year, to 10%, and the harmonized inflation rate recorded a rise of 1.9% in May, pushed up by the recovery in energy prices and other raw materials, although the nucleus of inflation, called underlying inflation, remained below 1% and thus has distanced any indication of inflationary pressure.

The forecasts indicate that the French economy will continue its gradual recovery during 2010 on the basis of moderate growth in the world economy. It seems that production touched bottom at the end of 2014, mostly due to the temporary measures in favour of the automobile industry in France and in other European countries such as Germany and Spain. In parallel, credit conditions are beginning to soften, although the demand for credit by companies remains at minimal levels. The elimination of the tax on businesses could create growth in investment in the second half of 2010, while the delay in starting up public investment plans approved in 2014 will allow its effects to extend to 2010. In spite of this, it is expected that overall investment in construction will continue to be negative in 2010, although less so than in 2014.

As a result of the above data, the French GDP could return to growth of between 1.3% and 1.7% in 2010, according to forecasts by the European Commission and the OECD, respectively. This recovery in activity will take the form of a moderation in the rhythm of fall in employment, although the rate of unemployment could still increase slightly to around 10% in 2010. As a consequence of the loss of jobs, the rate of employment will fall again and will be somewhere under 64% in 2010, which will aggravate even more one of the main problems of the French economy, which is the under-usage of the labour force.

With regard to public accounts, a slight increase in deficit is forecast, up to 7.8% of the GDP, as a consequence of the growth in social spending associated with the increase in the rate of unemployment, and the rise in interest rates which will apply in the repayment of the debt. On the other hand, it is estimated that the balance of discretional measures for 2010 will be neutral: the reduction in the package of tax stimulation (from 1.1% of the GDP to 0.4% in 2010) will be set off by new measures included in the budget for 2010 and valued at 0.7% of the GDP (among which is the reform of local taxes on companies) and the measures of the grand emprunt national, valued at around 0.1% of the GDP. In parallel, the debt ratio on GDP will continue to rise and it is forecast to be around 83% in 2010.

The French authorities have announced that the strategy of tax consolidation – which seeks to reduce the public deficit progressively from 8% of GDP in 2010 to 3% in 2013 – will be based on a reduction in public spending of 45,000 million until 2013, and on a forecast of increased income of 50,000 million from the economic recovery and 5,000 million from the elimination of some tax exemptions. Among the austerity measures announced is the freezing of public spending until 2013 and, more specifically, the freezing of salaries for public officials, the replacement of only 50% of vacant places and the reduction of 10% in the state operating expenses over the next three years. France also has fixed as an objective putting the brakes on the growth of spending at territorial government levels and a reform of the health and pension systems

– in this latter case the Government has presented a reform which seeks to put back the retirement age from 60 to 62 years.

SPANISH ECONOMY

In 2014 the Spanish economy experienced the most profound recession in its recent history, in terms of activity and the loss of employment. It was also the longest recession, since the fall in the GDP extended over six consecutives quarters. The crisis was particularly intense in this country because, when the collapse of the international financial markets and the drastic reduction in world trade occurred, the Spanish economy was in an internal process of adjustment in the residential sector. The most intense phase of the recession was in the first half of the year, a point at which the fallback in activity exceeded 4% interannual. However, from the third quarter the fall in the GDP began to moderate, although there was no possibility of positive rates in 2014. This fact made Spain into one of the few developed countries, together with Italy and the United Kingdom, to end 2014 in recession.

In the year as a whole, the Spanish GDP reduced by 3.6% with respect to 2008, the first contraction of the Spanish economy since 1993 and the most intense for the last 60 years. However, although the fallback in the Spanish economy was substantial, it did not exceed the fall recorded for the whole of the euro zone (-4.1%). The positive differential of growth between Spain and the euro zone remained at the same level as in the previous year and, as a result, the GDP per capita in parity of purchasing power in relation with the average for the EU-27 remained at 103% in 2014.

The contraction of activity had a very dramatic impact on employment, since 1.2 million full-time jobs were lost during 2014, representing a fall of 6.7% in annual terms according to the National Accounting. But, undoubtedly, the most negative feature of the labour market was unemployment, which was placed at the end of the year at 4.3 million people, 1.1 million more than in the year before. In annual terms, the number of unemployed increased by 60%, a figure which was added to the increase of 40% recorded for 2008. The rate of unemployment escalated to 18.8% in the last quarter, nearly five points above the level arrived at in the previous year.

The fall in economic activity was the consequence of a marked weakness in national demand, which reduced growth by 6.4 points, in contrast with the 0.1 by which it rose in the previous year. On the other hand, net external demand showed a positive contribution (2.8 points) greater than in 2008 (1.4 points), as a consequence of a fall in imports (-17.9%) which was more intense than the decline in export (-11.5%), producing the corresponding improvement in the deficit on the balance on current account (which moved from almost 10% of the GDP in 2008 to 5.4% in 2014).

Private family consumption suffered a historic contraction, 5% annual, as a result of the drastic destruction of employment, deterioration of confidence, hardening of financial conditions and a reduction in home-based wealth due to the falling prices of financial and real estate assets. In this way, in spite of the fact that the disposable income of families had grown due to the fall in interest rates, a fall in the prices of imported raw materials and the measures of economic stimulation adopted by the public sector, the savings rate rose to a historic figure of close to 20% of the GDP. However, during the second half of the year, consumption ceased to fall in quarterly terms, encouraged by aids for buying cars and the recovery of confidence.

Investment also experienced a sharp fallback during 2014 of -15.3%, as a result of the weakness of its principal components, especially investment in equipment, which recorded a fall of 20.7%. The principal factors which inhibited the starting up of new investment projects by companies were the fall in profits, the restriction of access to credit and the deterioration of business prospects associated with the fall in activity. This notwithstanding, in the second half of 2014 investment recorded a slight advance in quarterly terms, associated with the slight easing of credit conditions and low interest rates. On the other hand, investment in construction worsened, to -11.2% in 2014, because of the deterioration in the residential sector, which could not be counteracted by the increase in public works.

Public consumption, however, was the only component of the GDP which continued growing in 2014, in line with the expansionist nature of the fiscal policy, although at a rate lower than in the previous year (3.8% as against 5.5%).

All the production sectors, except public services, experienced a fall in activity; among them industry was the sector recording the most acute fall (-14.7%). It must be said that the services sector of the market went into recession in 2014, with a fall of 2%, after having resisted during 2008 and shown with positive growth. The construction and agricultural sectors accentuated their fall during 2014 (-6.3 and -2.4%, respectively). The sector which lost most jobs was construction (-23%) – more than for industry (-13.3%) and has now suffered three consecutive years of falls in employment – while services recorded in 2014 the first reduction in employment since the crisis of 1993.

The reduction of employment began by affecting salaried employees with temporary contracts, but ended by also affecting salaried employees with open-ended contracts, which fell for the fist time since 1994, although less than for those temporary. As a consequence of this, the proportion of temporary employees reduced to 25.4% in 2014, the lowest since statistical data have been available, although it remains above that of the EU. It must be said, once again, that the adjustment in the Spanish labour market was the most intense of all the advanced economies, a fact which reflects the existence of structural problems in its functioning, as these encourage the adjustment for falling activity to be made basically by abolishing jobs.

Consumer prices in the Spanish economy fell for eight consecutive months, from March to October 2014, which had not happened since the start of the series in 1962, with a maximum fall recorded in July (-1.4%). In November prices recovered a positive trend and in December they rose by 0.8%. The downward trend in inflation was the consequence to a great degree of the movements in the prices of oil and foods, which set off the strong rises in the previous year. For this reason, underlying inflation – which excludes energy and unprepared foods – did not reach negative values during 2014, although showing a significant moderation due to the lesser pressure of demand, the reduction of prices of imported non-food consumables, and public aid to the automobile sector, among others. The inflation differential in relation with the euro zone remained at negative values throughout 2014, but gradually reduced to finish at just one tenth in December.

In spite of the fall in activity, the moderation in prices and the notable deterioration of the labour market, salaried remuneration, having discounted inflation, increased at a good rhythm in 2014, by over 4%, but with a clear trend to moderation during the year. This explains why, in spite of the fact that productivity grew strongly, business margins were reduced for the third consecutive year, by -0.5% in 2014. The growth of productivity per worker went up by 3.3% on annual average, largely because of the reduction in the less productive jobs. This increase in productivity, combined with a similar increase in labour costs, determined a growth of practically nil in unit labour costs (0.2%), very much in line with the average for the principal trading partners. For this reason, the positive differential between the harmonized indicator of labour cost per effective hour in Spain and in the euro zone remained almost the same as in the previous year, at 1.5 points.

In this context of recession, fiscal policy took a clearly expansionist direction during 2014, and as a result > created a considerable imbalance in public accounts. The Spanish economy has moved from achieving a surplus of 2.2% of the GDP in 2007, to a deficit of 4.1% in 2008 and 11.2% in 2014. The financing of this deficit caused strong and rapid growth in public debt, which reached 55.2% of the GDP in 2014, almost the maximum threshold of reference established in the Stability and Growth Pact (60%).

The State is the administration which showed a more substantial deterioration in its finances, due to the heavy fall in income and the increase in spending, associated with the increase in unemployment benefit and the economic stimulation measures put into effect by the Spanish Government. Among these measures are notable: the deduction of 400 euros in income tax for all workers; the creation of a State investment fund for local investment and a Special Fund for the revitalisation of the economy and employment, for an amount of 11,000 million euro, designed to promote investment in the municipal and strategic sectors throughout 2014; tax measures of support for liquidity (adjournment of tax obligations, monthly return of VAT, an advance on the deduction for a dwelling in Income Tax, etc.); and the 2000E Plan of aid for the purchase of an automobile. The estimated economic impact of these discretional measures, according to the calculations of the Spanish Government, was 1.5% of the GDP in 2014, and that of the automatic stabilisers, 0.6 additional points.

The Spanish Government also approved in March 2010 the Sustainable Economy Bill – currently in progress through parliament – which is for the purpose of introducing into the legal ordinance the structural reforms necessary to create conditions which encourage rational and lasting economic development. The result is a group of measures, very heterogeneous among themselves, varying from a reduction in the times of payment by the administration to a series of provisions to stimulate the restoration of homes and R&D&I.

PROSPECTS

The Spanish GDP returned to growth in the first quarter of 2010 after a year and a half in decline, although the advance is very discreet, just one tenth. This has led to moderation in the interannual fall in the GDP, from -3.1% in the fourth quarter to -1.3% in the first quarter of 2010. The growth has been encouraged by some more positive signs in consumption and by the visible recovery of external demand. In quarterly rates, home consumption has grown for the second consecutive quarter, while public consumption has risen by a notable 1.4%, after the contraction of the previous quarter. However, there is negative news on the side of investment, since investment in capital goods has fallen again after two consecutive rises, and investment in construction continues in a state of intense contraction, affected by the weakness of residential investment and the fall in public investment in infrastructures.

With regard to external demand, the positive contribution of this sector to the growth of the GDP has slowed because, although exports grew in interannual terms for the first time since the second quarter of 2008 (8.0 %), imports also returned to positive ground

(2.6 % interannual).

From the perspective of supply, the signs of recovery are concentrated in the branches of energy and industry and, to a lesser extent, in services, while in construction the fall has sharpened.

In this context of incipient economic recovery, but not free of risk, the rate of inflation has begun to rise – reaching 1.8% in May. Now, the inflationary pressures arising from the price of oil, at the moment, are being countered by the weakness in demand, which is demonstrated by the fact that Spanish underlying inflation is placed at historic minimums (0.2% in May). At the same time, neither the growth in salaries agreed in the collective bargaining process (1.27% up to April) and in line with inflation, nor the reduction in the salaries of civil servants which will apply this year (5% on average), will be adding inflationary pressures. What certainly will mean an increase in inflation is the rise in VAT from 1 July, which some estimates place at having an impact of three tenths. For this reason the forecasts place the average inflation for the year at around 1.5%.

The impact of the crisis in Spain is being felt intensely in the labour market – the rate of unemployment could exceed 19% in 2010, and with regard to public finances – the public deficit will reach 9.3% of the GDP in 2010 – and this negatively affects the credibility of a recovery in the Spanish economy in the financial markets. The high dependence on abroad to finance the Spanish debt (public and private) and the rising risk premium, which reached a historic maximum of 2% in June in relation with the German bond, has led the Spanish authorities to approve a substantial package of austerity measures to control the public deficit.

The first measures approved, before these financial tensions appeared, were tax increases. Thus, in June 2014 the special taxes on tobacco and hydrocarbons were increased and the budgets for 2010 approved the removal of the deduction of 400 euro in Personal Income Tax, an increase in the burden on income from capital (the first 6,000 euro are rated at 19% and the rest at 21%, as against the single rate of 18% which applied until 2014) and the rise in VAT from 1 July 2010 (from 16% to 18% for the general rate and from 7% to 8% for the reduced rate).

With regard to spending, the Spanish Government approved in May 2010 a plan for the reduction of public spending of 15,000 million euro between 2010 and 2011. The objective is to reduce the public deficit to 6% of the GDP in 2011 and then continue gradually until reaching 3% in 2013. The most important measures in this austerity plan are the reduction by 5% on average in public salaries in 2010; the freezing of pensions in 2011; the elimination of backdating in benefits for dependants; the suspension of the transitional regime in partial retirement; the elimination of the cheque for newborns from 1 January 2011; the cutback in pharmaceutical expenses, and the non-availability of credits for official aids to development and for public investment.

To the restrictions of the fiscal policy, which will affect above all consumption and public investment, are added other elements which will make the reactivation by way of consumption and private investment more difficult, such as the stagnation of credit, the problems in the construction and real estate sectors, and the gradual withdrawal of the measures for stimulation of consumption (aids for purchasing cars, the rise in VAT, etc.). Altogether this will take the form of a fall in the Spanish GDP in 2010, between the -0.2% forecast by the OECD and the -0.4% by the European Commission[1], and a feeble recovery for 2011, with a growth of GDP at around 1%, so that Spain will be one of the few OECD economies which will still register a fall in GDP in 2010, together with Greece, Iceland and Ireland.

1. Forecasts made before the Government presented its plan for the adjustment of public spending.

THE ANDORRAN ECONOMY - BASIC TRENDS

Andorra is a developed free market and economy with a low level of regulation and the country has a GDP per capita above the averages for Europe and Spain, and on a par with that of France. Like the rest of the European economies, Andorran economic activity is focussed mainly on services. This sector accounts for 89% of the country's companies and 79% of all employment, which is the highest level among all the countries of Western and Eastern Europe, with the sole exception of Luxembourg.

Trade and tourism account for almost half the people employed in the services sector in Andorra. The country receives close to 11 million visitors each year with most of them coming from Spain and France. As a result, the economic evolution of Andorra has depended largely on foreign trade, especially with Spain and France. The limited national production of manufactured goods is compensated for by the high level of goods imported to meet the internal demand, and, especially the demand from foreign visitors to the country. This fact has resulted in a very high ratio of imports per capita, and only Luxembourg, Belgium and the Netherlands have a higher level within Europe, which highlights the high degree to which the economy is open to foreigners.

The specific importance of the financial sector and the growing participation of the public sector in the economy deserve to be mentioned here, although the level of the latter is still lower than in other European economies. Furthermore, Andorra offers a wide range of professional services (lawyers, economists, consultants, engineers, etc.), to both companies and private individuals, and this has helped ensure the full development of the economic activity within the Principality. However and notwithstanding the preeminence of services, Andorra has managed to maintain its system of agriculture specialised in the production of tobacco and grazing land for livestock, and this is one of the bases of the attractiveness of the country for tourists, who in turn help maintain the strong services sector. The Andorran economy has undergone a process of opening up to overseas trade over the past number of years. In 1991 a customs union was established with the European Union, where 96% of exports are currently sold and from where 91% of Andorran imports come from. This step led to several agreements with other international institutions and economic bodies, such as the United Nations (1993), the Council of Europe (1994), the World Tourism Organization (1995), the Ibero-American Summits (2004), the International Francophone Organization (2006), etc. In addition to this, Andorra has enjoyed observer status at the World Trade Organization since 1997.

RECENT ECONOMIC DEVELOPMENT

The Andorran economy has experienced positive growth since 1997, and this has been favoured by the dynamism of the neighbouring countries, especially that of the Spanish economy, even though the rhythm of progress has slowed down significantly over the past two years. The average rhythm of growth in this activity was situated at about 4.5% in the period between 1997 and 2004, which was higher than the average progress of the Spanish economy (3.3%) and even higher than the French (2.4%) and European

(2%) averages. On the other hand, average annual growth during the period 2005- 2006, was less than 2%, falling below the Spanish (3.7%) and European (2.2%) averages and coming close to the average for France (1.6%).

This upward evolution in economic activity has translated into significant increases in the number of companies and the level of employment in the country, especially in the area of services and construction. As a result, the employment rate rose to 72.8% in 2006, more than eight points higher than the figure for the EU-25 group of countries taken as a whole. The intense economic growth has led to an ongoing demand for labour which, because of the limited offer from the indigenous population, has traditionally been covered by workers from other countries.

Tourism and construction are the driving forces behind Andorran growth and these have carried along activities in other related sectors, such as trade and industry. However, there has been a gradual slowing down in the growth of tourist and commercial activity in recent years while there has also been a reduction in building activity since 2006. These factors help to explain the more modest progress made by the Andorran economy in recent times.

At the same time, the Andorran economy has shown a high level of dynamism in terms of adapting to the new technologies over the past number of years, and the country has witnessed an important increase in the number of mobile telephones and very significant growth in the use of the internet and ADSL lines – reaching penetration levels similar to the European average. This ought to lead to a gradual improvement in productivity and should also contribute to boosting the competitiveness of the economy in the future.

Synthesis of activity indicators

Activity and demand	2006	Var. 06/05
Businesses (number)	8,555	3.3
Wage earners (number)	43,380	2.3
Industry	1,919	2.6
Construction	6,908	2.4
Services	34,409	2.2
New registrations with CASS	5,120	-12.5
Electricity consumption (MWh)	555,623	3.8
Vehicle registration (units)	5,769	-14.8
Bank credit (millions of euros)	5,628	18.1
Visitors (number)	10,736,722	-2.8

Foreign trade (millions of euros)	2006	Var. 06/05
Exports	119.99	5.1
Imports	1,415.68	-1.8
Imports of capital assets (1)	247.96	-9.1
Imports of building material (2)	72.30	12.0

(1) Includes chapters 84 and 85, according to the classification of the Andorran customs.
(2) Includes chapters 25, 68, 72 and 73, according to the classification of the Andorran customs.

POPULATION, EMPLOYMENT AND EDUCATION

POPULATION AND MIGRATORY FLOWS

Andorra has a population of 81,222 inhabitants although only 29,535 of these are from the native population. The remaining 51.687 inhabitants are foreigners with most coming from Spain (53%), Portugal (25%) and France (10%). The majority of these foreigners arrived between the start of the 1960s and 1993. Subsequently, there was a period of four years during which immigration all but ceased, although started to increase once again from 1998 onwards, albeit at a more moderate rate than during the previous migratory period, and the estimated average annual growth rate was situated at 1.8% until 2006. At the same time, the growth in native population figures has continued to contribute to the country's good rhythm of total demographic growth, with an average annual growth rate of 3.8% since 1998.

The birth rate in Andorra is quite similar to the average for Europe although the wedding rate is the lowest in all of Europe. On the other hand, the mortality rate is much lower than the European levels. The return of many immigrants to their countries of origin during the final part of their lives helps to explain this significantly lower death rate, while it also increases life expectancy to over 90 years, which is the highest level on the entire European continent.

The population pyramid shows the predominance of the males in all age groups, with the sole exception of the population above the age of 75. This predominance is especially notable in the 40 to 59 age group, because of the considerable presence of male labourers from abroad. This factor also marks the distribution of the population by age and nationality. Accordingly, more than three quarters of the foreign population is concentrated in the age group between 20 and 64. On the other hand, Andorrans represent the vast majority of inhabitants in the 0 to 9 (81.2%) and the 10 to 19 (65.5%), age groups, while their presence is limited to 22.9% in the case of persons older than 65.

Andorra has a surface area of 468 sq. Km. and a population density of 174 inhabitants per square kilometre, higher than the average for the EU-25 (116 inhab./sq. Km.), but lower that that of other small countries on the continent, such as Luxembourg (181 inhab./sq. Km.), Liechtenstein (218 inhab./sq. Km.) or San Marino (483 inhab./sq. Km.).

The Andorran population amounted to 84,082 people in 2014, a figure which represented the first reduction for nine years, being 0.5% below the figure for the previous year. In absolute terms, there were 402 fewer people in the country, a movement which contrasts with the increase of 1,347 in the year before. This fall comes after two consecutive years of slowdown in the growth of population and is the most severe recorded since 1995, when the population fell by 0.7%. This meant that the average rate of growth of the population for the period 1996-2014 was 2%, a figure which is still very significant.

By nationalities, the fall in the total population of Andorra was due exclusively to the movements of the foreign population, since the native population continued increasing. Specifically, the native population grew by 2.3% in 2014, seven tenths less than in the previous year and the lowest advance since 1987, when the native population recorded the only fall in the historical series (available since 1980). This showed a succession of five consecutive years in which the native population developed more favourably than the foreign. The number of foreigners reduced by 2.1%, a reduction which put an end to a stage of seven consecutive years of growth, beginning in 2003 with the process of regularisation, and which now is surely a consequence of the economic crisis.

Among the foreign groups, it is clear that the fall affected all the principal nationalities present in Andorra. The Spanish, the largest foreign population

group, recorded a fall for the fifth consecutive year, of 2.3%, thus continuing the downward trend which had already characterised this group during the decade before regularisation. In the same line, the French nationality group reduced by 2.2%, after three years of rather modest increases. The reduction in the Portuguese population was 3.1%, the most severe of the three large groups mentioned, halting the seven-year trend to strong growth which had doubled the number of Portuguese residents recorded in Andorra. To complete the picture, the group of other nationalities was the only one to show a positive movement, with an increase of 0.9%, although rather more modest than those recorded in recent years.

As a consequence of the data given, the weight of the total foreign population reduced by one point, to 61.8%, and continued moving away from the maximum value achieved in 1987 (78.7%). Conversely, during 2014 the Andorrans increased their weight by the same proportion – now showing at 38.2% – and thus continued the upward trend observed since 1988, only interrupted by the processes of regularisation in 2003 and 2004, as mentioned above.

With regard to the natural population movement, there was natural growth in 2014 of 566 people, less than in the previous year (-11.3%), a figure which represents a rate of 6.7 per thousand, also lower than in 2008. This natural movement in the growth of population was due to a reduction in the number of births (-4.2%) and an increase in the number of deaths (14.8%). In consequence, the birth rate fell to 10.0 per thousand, while the mortality rate increased to 3.2 per thousand, the highest level for the last four years. To these figures must be added the negative balance of 968 people resulting from migratory movements, for the first time since 2001.

For yet another year the distribution of population by parishes made it clear that 2014 had continued the trend for the higher and less populated parishes to gain in weight to the detriment of the lower parishes, a trend which has been in evidence since the start of the decade of the nineties, although at a slow rate of progress. Specifically, the parishes in which the population increased most during 2014 were, as in the previous eight years, Ordino (6.1%), Canillo (4.9%) and La Massana (1.4%), although in Ordino and La Massana it was at a slower rhythm than had been recorded during 2008. Escaldes-Engordany, Encamp and Sant Julià de Lòria also showed an increase in population, although rather more modest, and in the first two it was less than that recorded in the previous year. Finally, the only parish which showed a reduced population and which, therefore, suffered the whole of the fall in population, was Andorra la Vella (-5.3%).

Even so, it remains much the most populated parish, with 27.8% of the country's total population. However, it must be remembered that these results could have been influenced by the fact that during 2014 there was a change in the regulation criteria for the preparation of the population census, and that until then this had only been applied in the Commune of Andorra la Vella. As a result of this change, the population in the higher parishes increased in weight by one point to represent 40.6% of the total, against 29.1% at the start of the decade of the nineties; in contrast, the lower parishes lost positions, but still contribute 59.4% of the entire population. Altogether, this means that Andorra continues advancing slowly towards a more equal distribution of the population of the country.

The structure of the population by gender shows that the male population still dominates in all working age bands, with the sole exception of the population aged over 75 years. Thus, the weight of the total male population exceeds by 4.2 percentage points the weight of the female population, four tenths less than the difference recorded in 2008. The dominance of males is still more noticeable in the 40 to 64 age >

POPULATION, EMPLOYMENT AND EDUCATION 27

band, because of the higher proportion of foreign labour, traditionally mostly male. More specifically, 76.9% of the foreign population is concentrated in the age band between 20 and 64, while Andorrans in this age band are 53.8%. This shows that the presence of foreigners clearly exceeds that of Andorrans in all age bands above 20 years. In contrast, the proportion of Andorrans is much greater in the age bands from 0 to 9 (83.7%) and 10 to 19 (69.7%), while it is limited to 23.5% in the group of people aged over 65.

The distribution of population by ages shows that in 2014 the Andorran population continued ageing. Thus, the population band of up to 14 years showed a fall of 0.5%, equivalent to that of the total population, in contrast to the advance in the previous year. As a result of this circumstance, the proportion of this band on total population remained at 14.5%. Further, the group aged 65 and over grew at the fairly significant rate of 4.2%, although slightly less than in the previous year, and this brought the percentage represented by this group up to 12.9% of the whole Andorran population, the highest level since 2002. In parallel, the population aged from 15 to 64 years reduced for the first time since 2000 and did so at a rhythm of 1.3%, which reduced its weight over the total population – set at 72.7% – by six tenths.

EMPLOYMENT

In 2014, the employed population in Andorra showed a negative movement for the third consecutive year, in consonance with the fall in Andorran economic activity. According to data from Andorran Social Security (CASS), the annual average number of jobs fell by 4.1%, a larger reduction than in the previous year (-1%). This brought the total number of jobs down to 50,393. Further, new registrations with CASS were down for the seventh consecutive year, specifically by 27.9%, to 2,353, the lowest recorded in the historical series (available since 1991).

At the same time, salaried employment recorded a very significant fall of 2.8%, bringing the annual average down to 41,019 salaried employees. This fall represents the worst movement since 1993 and continues the falling trend which began in 2007, ending a period of thirteen years of sustained growth in employment. In consequence, the rate of employment – measured as the number of employees in relation to the population aged from 15 to 64 – reduced for the fourth consecutive year, by 1.1 points, to arrive at 67.1%, the lowest level for the last eleven years, although it is still higher than the average in the European Union (64.6%).

The distribution by large sectors showed that employment fell in construction and services, while it improved slightly in industry and agriculture. More specifically, the primary sector showed an increase in employment of 0.9%, in the context of a slight rise in the production of tobacco, in contrast to the reduction in the previous year (-0.3%). In any event, the movement in this sector has very little impact on the economy, as this is an activity with very little weight in the Andorran labour market, employing only 148 workers. The increase in employment in industry was a little more active, at 1.2%, thus linking two consecutive years of increases. The movement is explained by the rise in manufacturing industries, contrasting with the severe reduction of jobs in the ambit of the production and distribution of energy, gas and water.

In the contrary sense, services – the sector with the highest concentration of Andorran employment – recorded a fall of 1.6%, more severe than in 2008 (-1.3%), although a lower percentage than that of the total. However, undoubtedly the sector which lost most employment, as in the previous two years, was that of construction, both in percentage terms (-11.2%) and in absolute value. This movement continues the falling trend which began two years before, after the long, intense period of expansion between 1996 and 2006. All this produced an increase of one point in the weight of services in the figures for total employment, up to 81.8% of all workers, while construction lost 1.2 points in its weight, down to 13.2%. On the other hand, the weights of industry and agriculture showed a slightly upward movement, to reach 4.7% and 0.4%, respectively.

Making a more detailed analysis, the distribution of employment among the tertiary activities shows that >

the subsector of trade and motor vehicle repairs remains the most important service subsector, with a total weight of employees in Andorra of 25.3%, although reduced for the sixth consecutive year. In second place is hotels and catering, which takes up 12.5% of the employees, a percentage slightly above that of 2008, counteracting the falling trend of the last five years. Next came the public administration, defence and compulsory social security (11.5%), which continued gaining weight; real estate activities, rentals and business services (10%), and the heading of "other social activities and services provided to the community; personal services" – not including health and education – (6%). Finally, there were the financial sector (4.1%), health and veterinary activities (4.1%), homes employing domestic staff (3.3%) and transport, storage and communications (3%), with a lower volume of employees than manufacturing industries (4.3%). The rest of the tertiary activities have an employment weight of below 3%.

EDUCATION

During the academic year 2008-2014 the Andorran population in education, including schools, universities and non-university students abroad, amounted to 12,244 people. This figure cannot be compared with the previous year, because during the last three years no information was available for the population at university and in advanced professional training (FP). This is explained by a change of competences in managing the recording of the relevant data. A comparison in time could only be made, therefore, with the academic year 2004-2005, and this showed an accumulated increase of only 3% in four years.

If the university population and advanced professional training (FP) are excluded from the total, it emerges that the population in education in Andorra, not further education, was 11,061 students, 0.1% more than in the 2007-2008. This almost stability was the result of a slight reduction in the school population (-0.5%), combined with a very significant rise in the non-university population abroad (33.2%), for the second consecutive year. As a result, the percentage of the non-university population abroad, against the whole school-age population, rose by three tenths to reach 1.5%.

The distribution of the total population in education by countries in which they are studying showed that the number of students studying in Andorra amounted to 11,256, a figure representing 91.9% of the Andorran educational population, 0.9 points more than in 2004-2005, the last year with which it could be compared. Of the remaining 8.1%, Spain had the most important proportion (6.9%), while only 1.1% of Andorran students went to France. The distribution was completed by 15 students spread among other countries (0.1% of the total).

PRIMARY AND SECONDARY LEVELS

During the 2008-2014 academic year, the number of students in schools was 10,796. This figure represents a rate of schooling – calculated as the proportion of the school population on the overall population at this stage of life – of 44.7%, significantly lower than the 47.5% of the previous year, and even less than that for 2007 (50.3%).

The levels with the greatest number of students at this stage were kindergarten, primary and secondary, with 89.5% of the student body, six tenths less than in 2008. This reduction in weight was explained by the reduction in the number of students at all three levels, and especially at kindergarten (-3.9%), where it fell for the fourth consecutive year, in line with the gently descending trend in birth rate in recent years. The fall in students in primary and secondary education was less severe (-0.4% and -0.2%, respectively), although this represented a break in the sustained upward movement of recent years. For its part, the baccalaureate takes up 7.7% of students, three tenths more than in the previous year, due to an increase of 2.4% in their numbers, compared with the year before. Finally, professional training represented the remaining 2.9% of the population in education, half a point up on the previous year, after having recorded a strong increase of 19.1%, the most significant in the last nine years.

Finally, it must be pointed out that the movements in the population in education, by type of learning, continued to reflect the progressive implementation of the Andorran educational system, with an increase of 2.3%. This contrasted with the overall reduction of the total population in this stage and raised its weight by one point, to 37.1% of the whole of the student body. This showed that the school population in the Andorran educational system had grown uninterruptedly since the start of the decade of the nineties. It must be said that the advance in 2014 was evident both in the Andorran schools (1.9%) and in the professional schools (26.7%), although the little weight of the latter limits their contribution in absolute terms.

Conversely to the trend shown by the Andorran educational system, the number of students in the Spanish educational system reduced by 1.9%, a reduction which means that there have been five falls in the last six years. As a result, its weight over the total was reduced by four tenths to 30.8%, a figure which established a new historic minimum. This movement was explained by the sharp reduction of students in Spanish schools (-9.8%), compensated in part by the increase in congregational schools (3.2%), as also happened in the year before; students in private schools also showed a fall of 7%, after the stagnation observed in the year before.

As a consequence of these data, the traditional Spanish schools saw their weight cut back by one point, to 9.5% of the total Andorran school population, in contrast to the congregational schools, which increased their weight by seven tenths to reach 19.2% of students, while private schools only reduced their weight by one tenth, to 2.1% of the total. Finally, the French educational system recorded a reduction of students for the fourth consecutive year, of 2.3%, reducing its percentage on the total by six tenths to reach a historic minimum of 32.1%, although still above the weight of the Spanish educational system.

UNIVERSITY LEVEL

After three years without details, information was available in the 2008-2014 academic year relating to the university population in Andorra, amounting to 1,183 students, a figure exceeding by 10 students the numbers for four years ago. The distribution by gender showed that women still predominate, representing 59% of the total.

By countries of study, the University of Andorra accounted for 38.9% of the total, a percentage which set a historic record, keeping the country in second place in the ranking, but coming closer and closer to Spain (54.1% of university students). France was a long way behind, with 6.3% of the total, while 0.8% of the remaining students were spread about in other >

countries (Portugal, Germany, Belgium, Great Britain, Luxembourg and Puerto Rico).

With regard to the specific case of the Virtual Studies Centre, attached to the Open University of Catalonia (UOC), the number of students registered for diplomas and degrees was 209 for the year 20142010, to which must be added 39 students registered for courses leading to access for people aged over 25, the 28 registered to obtain advanced professional diplomas and the 621 who were in continuous training (postgraduate, updating courses and seminars).

Finally, an analysis by areas of study revealed that the area attracting most Andorran university students was that of legal and economic sciences, with 29.8% of the total of university students. The technical sciences came next (17.6%), followed by health sciences (17.5%). At the other extreme are the areas of tourism, communications and public relations, with only 33 and 47 students, respectively.

THE EVOLUTION IN ECONOMIC ACTIVITY

As shown by the historic falls recorded for most of the indicators of activity and demand available, 2014 was the worst year in the Andorran economy for decades. The depression of economic activity was part of an international context also at a historic low, suffering the worst recession since the Second World War, and this gravely prejudiced the economic development of Andorra. With regard to demand, the fall in activity is explained principally, as in the previous year, by the severe reduction in exports, tourist services and investment, to which 2014 added also the containment of consumption and public investment, breaking off the long stage of expansion, which in recent years had helped to moderate the containment of the Andorran GDP. With regard to supply, all the large sectors, except the primary, experienced a clearly unfavourable movement, with a particularly negative contribution from construction and services, both tourism and trade, and in the financial sector.

The worsening of the Andorran economic situation during 2014 was made clear by the movement, more negative than in the previous year, shown by the great majority of indicators of activity and demand in relation with 2008. In particular, there were heavy reductions in key indicators, such as total imports (-13.4%), down for the fourth consecutive year and shrinking at a record pace; salaried employment and bank lending, which fell at the fastest rate since 1993 (-2.8% and -2.2%, respectively), and the number of tourists (-4%), down for the eighth consecutive year, to which was added the reduction in the number of trippers (-4.6%), which has given as a result an aggregate fall in the total number of visitors of 4.4%.

To these facts were added the reductions in other indicators of activity, more serious than in the previous year, such as the registrations of industrial vehicles (-28.2%) and imports of building materials (-23.6%). Also falls were recorded, for the first time since the historical series became available, in the number of companies (-3%) and in the functioning expenses of the administration (-2%). On the other hand, imports of capital goods (-17.8%) and consumption of electricity (-2%) also fell, although less rapidly than in 2008. Overall, there is not one significant indicator which showed a positive movement, in such a way that the general balance sheet points to a further fall in the rhythm of activity, rather more severe than in the previous year.

By components, the indicators of domestic demand bring out, for yet another year, a distinctly negative behaviour. It seems that in 2014 private consumption continued weakening, following the trend of previous years, as is suggested by indicators such as a reduction in bank lending for the first time since 1993, a reduction in the registration of saloon cars and a lessening in the available income of Andorran consumers, the result of the sharp reduction in employment, to which was added a moderation in the growth of real salaries. The differential between the growth in the average nominal salaries of employees (1.8%) and inflation was reduced from 2.4 to 1.8 points, if inflation is measured in December (0%).

With regard to investment, the few indicators available also showed an unfavourable movement all round. Thus, a clearly descending trend was noted in investment in transport material, in accordance with the severe reduction of 28.2% in the registrations of trucks and vans, similar to that of the previous year, and in investment in capital goods, following the big reduction in the imports of these goods, at 17.8%, although this was a little milder than that recorded in the previous year. It must be taken into account, however, that this fall is very much conditioned also by the poor results for the trade in electronic goods for consumption and the big fall in re-exports. Similarly, the indicators on investment in construction showed a very negative movement, as can be understood from the very significant reduction of employment in the sector (-11.2%), imports of building materials (-23.6%) and bank lending, which in all three cases showed behaviour worse than that experienced in 2008.

In the public sector, the actions of the General Administration during 2014 were marked by a general cutback in spending, which particularly affected real investment (-16.3%), with a much bigger fall than in the previous year. Further, the functioning expenses were reduced (-1%) for the first time, but all this did not prevent the Government's public deficit from continuing to rise, since public income was reduced more than the expenses. On the other hand, the communes recorded a surplus overall, although less than in 2008, due to a sharper contraction in income than in expenses. In conclusion, the joint actions of the public sector were very much in a downward line, both with regard to public consumption with a reduction of 2% in >the functioning expenses, and with regard to public investment, with a 23.6% reduction in aggregated real investment, bigger than in the previous year. Therefore, the action of the public sector on the whole contributed to a lessening in the rhythm of Andorran economic activity in 2014, in contrast to what had happened in recent years, when fiscal policy was fairly expansive.

With regard to the foreign sector, during 2014 a reduction was recorded in the trade deficit for the second consecutive year, of 12.5%, more than in the previous year (-4.3%), so that its traditional negative contribution to the country's GDP was cut back once more. This movement is explained by the strong fall in imports (-13.4%), which fully off-set the effect of the fall in exports (-30.1%), since these are on a very much smaller scale. It must be taken into account that the Andorran economy is characterised by its heavy dependence on abroad, linking it very closely to the economic movements of the neighbouring countries, namely Spain and France, these being the principal customers and suppliers. Thus the serious worsening of the international context, with a historic fall in the GDP of the neighbouring countries, was a factor which deeply prejudiced economic movements in Andorra in 2014. This came out clearly in the numbers of visitors from both countries – Andorra's principal source of income – which were down by 4.4% in both cases, so that in the case of the French this made six consecutive years of falls, while Spanish visitors were reduced in four of the last five years. Thus the worsening of the current situation was added to certain other structural factors which for some years had been putting brakes on the tourist attraction of the country, such as, for example, the growing competition of other winter destinations. This has been indicated, for some years, by the results of questionnaires by the Chamber of Commerce, Industry and Services to the hotel sector, with a majority of business responses indicating an increase of competition, the loss of attraction of the area and an increase in the costs of exploitation, as being among the principal factors limiting business progress in the sector, in addition to the weakness of demand as the principal limiting factor.

The general reduction of visitors (-4.4%), combined with falls in the average degree of occupation, the average stay and hotel prices, suggested an unfavourable movement in income from tourist services and, in consequence, a negative contribution by this component to the growth in GDP. Therefore, in global terms, it can be said that the contribution from the foreign sector also deteriorated and was added to the negative trend in the rest of the fields in the Andorran economy.

An analysis of the movement of the principal economic sectors showed a new deterioration of activity in the construction sector, for the third consecutive year, after the long cycle of expansion between 1997 and 2006. Thus, there was a generalised and heavy fall in the principal indicators of activity in the sector, with a cutback in employment of 11.2%, more than in the year before, and reductions in imports of building materials (-23.6%) and in the number of companies (-9.8%) – also more intense than those recorded in 2008, while the consumption of energy in the sector moderated the rate of fall, although it continued being very significant (-11.5%). Further, the results of the Chamber's questionnaires showed a new deterioration in business progress – which is at the lowest levels since the questionnaires were started in 1997 – and a reduction in the sales turnover (-25.4%) and investment (-15.7%) and a serious diminution of works contracted and executed, falls which in all cases were bigger than those recorded in 2008. The modest increase in land authorised for building (3.7%) was the only indicator to buck the downward trend, although

EVOLUTION OF BUSINESS PROGRESS BY SECTORS - Balance between the percentage of positive and negative responses very moderated with respect to the advance recorded in the previous year.

With regard to services, the movement during 2014 was also very unfavourable, for the sixth consecutive year, principally due to the negative results for tourism, trade and financial activities. Tourism and trade were affected above all by the reduction in the entry of visitors, with a fall in both tourists (-4%), for the eighth consecutive year, and in trippers (-4.6%).

The deterioration in tourism and trade showed clearly, according to the results of the Chamber's questionnaires, a substantial reduction of business turnover in trade (-13.8%) and in hospitality (-14.2%), heavier than those recorded in 2008, and also in the clearly negative evaluation of business progress in both sectors, variables which in the case of trade established a new historic low in the series. Further, employment reduced more sharply than in the previous year in trade (-4.7%), while in the hotel sector it was also down, but more moderately (-2%).

To finish, other indicators which showed the falling activity were the number of companies, down by 10.1% in trade and 4.7% in the hotel sector; energy consumption, which also reduced in both sectors, and the number of skiing days sold (-0.5%). With regard to the financial sub-sector, its movement was very clearly conditioned by the international financial crisis, which resulted in a strong reduction in the volume of deposits (-18.9%) and bank lending (-2.2%) and was translated into a very small advance in profits (2.2%), after the depression of the previous year, with a fall of 44.3%.

In the same line, the industrial branches recorded a new deterioration in the rhythm of activity in relation with the previous year. Thus, the opinions collected in the questionnaires showed a very significant worsening of business progress, establishing a new historic minimum in the series, available since 1997, while the climate of confidence continued at very negative values. The questionnaires also showed a reduction in business turnover, investment and production over the year as a whole, on a record scale. Further, energy consumption in the sector was cut back by 7.8%. Notwithstanding this, the figures for employment were up by 1.2%, against the rise of 0.6% experienced in the previous year.

To finish the sectorial analysis, it must be noted that the primary sector was the only one to show a more favourable behaviour than in 2008, with an increase in tobacco production (2%), the number of companies (8.3%) and the numbers of employees (0.9%), percentages which contrast >with the reductions in these variables recorded in the previous year, while the livestock census showed a slight increase (1.6%), more modest than in 2008.

In conclusion, the evolution in the principal economic indicators and the opinions of companies enables it to be stated that the situation of recession into which the Andorran economy entered in 2007 worsened considerably in 2014, with a substantial fall in the GDP, of somewhere around 6%. This big fallback continued the trend to the loss of dynamism which began in 2005 and clearly exceeded in intensity the falls in activity recorded during the crisis during the first half of the 1990s. It must be added that the strong deterioration in the Andorran economy observed in 2014 fits into a very negative international and European context, immersed in the most serious economic recession of the last sixty years. However, the fall in the Andorran GDP was heavier than the falls in the European, French and Spanish GDP recorded in 2014, so that, once again, Andorra has lost relative position with respect to the neighbouring economies in terms of the level of wealth.

In this recessive context, the Andorran Government promoted a package of measures for economic reactivation, which came into effect at the beginning of 2014 (Law 31/2008, of 18 December, on measures for economic reactivation), following the line of the principal developed economies, and in which the global objective was to reduce spending and promote savings and/or increase the income of the citizens and the sectors involved, and also to encourage competitiveness in companies. The measures adopted included, among other provisions, measures for the containment of the functioning expenses of the General Administration, measures of administrative simplification and tax incentives for the creation of new companies, for the renovation of buildings and for energy savings.

With a view to 2010, business forecasts continue being pessimistic but they note a point of inflexion in the general movement of the economic activity. Construction will again take the lead in negative behaviour, with a business turnover which will continue to fall fairly sharply, while the rest of the sectors will maintain a weak rhythm of activity, especially in trade and hospitality, but with a tendency to moderate the deep contractions of 2014. Further, it is forecast that business investment will continue falling, above all in the construction sector, where the majority of the companies note an intention to revise their investment plans downwards. The improvement foreseen in the world economy, which was recorded during the first half-year of 2010, and the progressive normalisation of financial markets, have contributed to softening the recessive trend in Andorran economic activity. The evolution of the principal activity indicators available for the first months of 2010 seem to point in this direction, with a moderation in the rate of fall in the number of visitors and a return to growth in total imports, the consumption of electricity and registrations of saloon cars. On the other hand, the number of employees was still falling during the first quarter of the year, and this more strongly than in 2014. In conclusion, the prospects for 2010 are of moderation in the rate of fall in Andorran economic activity as a whole, although there is still no sign of a clear recovery of growth.

FOREIGN TRADE

In 2014, Andorra imported goods for a value of 1,137.4 million euro, a figure which represents a reduction, for the fourth consecutive year, of 13.4%, a record fall, which amply exceeded that recorded for the previous year (-5.9%). By chapters, the most negative contribution was that of fuels, oils and mineral waxes (-2.1 points), followed by machines and electrical appliances (-1.6 points) and automobiles (-1.6 points), falls which reflect the deterioration of the rhythm of consumption and investment in capital goods, and which also took the form of a contraction of re-exports of the goods corresponding to those last two chapters. The reductions in purchases of mechanical appliances and perfumery products also contributed significantly to the fall in imports. Again, tobacco imports recorded a bigger contraction than the average, so that imports without tobacco show a reduction (-13.2%) slightly below that of the total.

In the contrary sense, it is noted that there are very few chapters which recorded an increase, and of these the majority have a weight of little significance, so that their contribution to growth was minimal. This was the case of imports of coffee, tea, yerba mate and spices, and of soaps, organic products, waxes and candles.

Other chapters with a minimally significant weight in which imports were up were pharmaceutical products, various prepared foods and shoes and analogous articles. Altogether they contributed to a small increase in the sectorial concentration of Andorran imports, and thus halted the trend of recent years, in such a way that the first three groups (machinery and electrical material, food products and chemical industry products) represent 40.7% of the total, 1.3 points more than in the previous year.

With regard to Andorran exports, the evolution during 2014 was very negative for the third consecutive year, to the point that it showed the heaviest fall of the historic series available and exceeded the previous record fall recorded in 2008. Specifically, sales abroad amounted to 45.6 million euros, a figure which represents a fallback of 30.1%, and puts exports at the lowest value since 1999. At the same time, it must be noted that a significant part of this fall was concentrated in the chapters of machines and electrical appliances, and mechanical appliances. This, combined with the strong reduction in imports of these same chapters, suggested that a substantial contraction had occurred in the re-exports of these goods. >

The fall in exports being heavier than that in imports meant that the rate of cover fell for the third consecutive year, this time by one point, placing it at 4%, the lowest level since 1999. The analysis by sectorial groups showed a substantial fall in the high concentration of exports, in such a way that the first three groups represented 51.5% of the total sales, almost ten points less than in 2008, a figure which was far from the historic maximum reached in 2005 (69.2%) and represented the lowest level since 2000. It must be added that two of these three groups were also the first groups in imports, which showed that a significant part of Andorran imports are for the purpose of re-export.

GEOGRAPHICAL DISTRIBUTION OF FOREIGN TRADE

IMPORTS

During 2014 and for the second consecutive year, the European continent gained weight as the principal source of Andorran imports. In this period it took up 92.7% of the total, two tenths more than in 2008, a figure which established a new historic record, exceeding that reached in the previous year. This increase in geographical concentration was due to the fall in imports from the European Union being slightly less than for the total, combined with a much more modest reduction in purchases from European countries which are not part of the Union.

With regard to the other continents, imports from America were those which showed the biggest fall (-28.3%), much larger than the previous year (-8.9%), which meant a cutback in their weight of two tenths, to 1.1% of the total. Imports from Asia also fell, slightly more than the average, at a rate of 14.4% – which even so was less than in 2008 (-17%) – so that this participation was cut back by seven hundredths, to 5.96%. These falls were partly due to the trend to depreciation of the euro experienced in 2014, making products from outside the monetary union much more expensive. Against this, purchases from Africa showed a strong increase of 51.9%, thus linking four years of consecutive rises. In spite of this, their weight on the total remains very limited, at 0.3% – two tenths more than in the year before.

In the context of the EU-27, Spain has held onto its role as Andorra's principal supplier country, in spite of imports from the Spanish State having reduced, for the second consecutive year, by 11.3%, although this was less heavy than the average. As a result, Spain represented 59.5% of Andorran purchases from abroad, 1.4 points more than in the previous year. Imports from France were also down, at a higher rate, 14.8%, which meant a reduction of three tenths in the participation of the French State in the total, with a percentage of 19.1%. In spite of this, France was still easily the second supplier country to Andorra, although its weight was far from what it had been in the 1990s, when it was over 30%.

With regard to the rest of the EU-27 countries, Germany reduced, for the second consecutive year, its part in the total Andorran imports by four tenths, to 4.3%, the result of a fall of 19.6%, however even so it was still the third country in the ranking of suppliers. In the European context, next came imports from Italy, which were also severely down (-28.5%), so that their quota was cut by seven tenths, to 3.1%. After these were imports from the United Kingdom, which fell by 24.4% and reduced its weight to 1.3%, while imports from the Netherlands showed a progression of 2.9%, an increase which contrasted with falls for most of the countries, and which raised the Dutch participation in the total by one tenth, to 1%.

The movement was mostly negative for the other EU-27 countries with a minimally significant weight in the Andorran imports, such as Belgium (-4%), Portugal (-16.2%), Austria (-33.9%), Ireland (-36.4%) and Sweden (-46.3%), a trend which broke with the increases recorded in the previous year for the majority of these countries. Only Denmark and some countries of the East, such as Romania, the Czech Republic and Poland were outside this trend, with increases of 22.8%, 22%, 18.9% and 16%, respectively. Thus, purchases from the twelve new member states incorporated into the EU in 2004[2] and 2007[3], considered as a whole, recorded an increase of 6%, and so raised their relative weight to 0.8%, although this was much more moderate than that experienced in the previous year (49.2%). Outside the European Union, imports from Switzerland halted the descending trend observed for the last eight years, with a rise of 5.2%, so that its quota increased to 1.1% of the total, the same level as that recorded in 2006. On the other hand, there was a notable fall in imports from Turkey (-26%), where the quota was limited to 0.2%.

With regard to imports from countries in the rest of the world, it must be remembered that only those from the United States and from some countries in Asia had any importance. In the first case, the movement was negative, with a contraction of 17.6%, influenced by the depreciation of the euro with respect to the dollar during 2014, but it was more moderate than that recorded in the previous year (-25%). As a result, its weight on the total was kept at 0.7%, very close to the lowest level of the historical series (0.6% in 2006). In the case of imports from Asian countries, the first point to be noted was the reduction of imports from China, down by 7.4%, a movement which broke with the trend of substantial growth recorded during the period 2000-2007. However, this was a containment more moderate than the average, so that its weight on the total rose by three tenths to a maximum of 3.5%, which consolidated China as the top Asian supplier to Andorra and put it in fourth place in the global ranking, thus overtaking Italy for the first time. On the other hand, Japan continued losing weight, due to a heavy fall in imports for the second consecutive year, of 33.2%, which placed its participation in the total at a historic minimum of 1%. South Korea also reduced heavily its contribution to Andorran imports (0.1%) and ceased to be the third most important Asian supplier. In contrast, other countries such as Vietnam, India and Indonesia gained positions as suppliers to Andorra, with increases of 37.1%, 21.8% and 21.4%, percentages which placed their weights at between 0.3% and 0.2%.

EXPORTS

In 2014 Andorran exports recorded a heavy fall for the third consecutive year, of 30.1%, a circumstance which contrasted with the rising trend which characterised >

1. Slovakia, Slovenia, Estonia, Hungary, Latvia, Lithuania, Malta, Poland, Czech Republic and Cyprus.

2. Bulgaria and Romania.

the period 2000-2006. The distribution by geographical areas showed that the reduction was explained mostly by the deterioration in sales to the EU-27 – the principal destination of Andorran exports – which were cut back by 29.2%. Even so, this reduction was slightly less than the average, so that the weight on the total was up by 1.3 points, at 96.8%.

By countries, Spain was still the leading consumer of Andorran products in 2014, with a contraction in exports of 29.5%, a little less than the average. This lifted its weight on the total by seven tenths, to 70.2%, a historic record which exceeded by a small amount the former record, for 2006. Thus, the fall in sales to Spain explained 68.1% of the total fall in exports. Sales to the second big Andorran market, France, also recorded a fall for the fifth consecutive year, although considerably more moderate than that for Spain and for the previous year, of 9.8%, a movement which meant an increase in its participation on the total of 4.5 points, to 20.1%. This meant that the behaviour of exports to France only accounted for 5.1% of the total fall. However, the balance between Andorra's two principal partners continued to be clearly in favour of Spain, in contrast to the similar participations which both countries had at the start of the 1990s.

For the rest of the EU-27 countries, it must be noted that exports sent to Italy reduced by 18.5%, below the total, which increased its weight by three tenths to 2.1%. Thus, this country became the third European market in importance for Andorra, after eight consecutive years when it had been Germany. The fourth country in the ranking was the Netherlands, with a weight of 1.1%, three tenths more than in 2008, the result of a fall in exports rather more moderate than the average (-11.9%). Next came Belgium, with a weight of 0.9% and a heavy reduction of 67.7%. In the same line, Germany fell from third to sixth position, taking a nosedive of 86.1%, after having already reduced heavily in the previous year (79%), which placed its proportion of the total at only 0.9%, as against the maximum of 15.9% which it had achieved in 2007. For its part, the weight of Portugal in Andorran exports was similar to that of Germany (0.9%) and four tenths up on the previous year, as it was one of the few European countries to which sales had increased (26.5%). With regard to the rest of the EU countries with a minimally significant weight (at least 0.1%), strong falls were noted in Andorran exports to the United Kingdom, Austria and Slovakia, while for Denmark and Malta the movement was significantly positive.

In contrast to the EU-27, sales to the rest of Europe experienced growth, specifically of 4.6%, so that their weight increased for the second consecutive year, to arrive at 1.4%. This movement was explained fundamentally by the rising behaviour of exports to Switzerland (281.8%), which multiplied its weight on the total by more than five, to reach 1.4%, while the rest of the countries in this group had a minimal participation.

With regard to exports to the rest of the world, their quota on the total reduced by half, to 1.8%, as a result of the strong fall in sales to Asia (-88.8%), after being multiplied by eighteen in 2008, which placed the weight of that continent at 0.4% as against the 2.8% in 2008. This fall was explained by the intense contraction of sales to India, of 98.4%, after having multiplied by 49 in 2008, cutting back its weight from 2.6% to a mere 0.1%. Further, there was a noted fall in sales to Japan, of 71.2%, a movement which also contrasted with the big increase recorded in the previous year, so that this country ceased to have a minimally significant weight (not as much as 0.1%). On the other hand, Andorran exports to America (19.7%) and Africa (8.5%) increased, favoured by the fall in the value of the euro in 2014. At the same time, in the case of Africa, it must be noted that the only countries which individually represented 0.1% of the total were Algeria and Angola, with increases of 31.7% and 2.9%, respectively, raising the weight of the continent as a whole to 0.3%.

With regard to the American continent, exports showed three consecutive years of increase, which lifted its weight on the total to 1%, the highest level since 2002. This progress was principally aided by the rise in sales to the United States – multiplied by 56, to represent 0.4% of the total – and, to a lesser degree, by sales to Chile (46.7%), a country which jointly with Argentina, Nicaragua and Guyana, were the only ones with a minimally significant weight – of 0.2%, 0.1% and 0.1%, respectively.

Finally, there was also a notable increase in exports to Oceania, which were multiplied by more than six, a behaviour which showed a fairly erratic record of movement, appropriate to the very low values represented (less than 0.1% of the total).

SECTOR COMPOSITION OF FOREIGN TRADE

IMPORTS

The reduction in Andorran imports in 2014 (-13.4%) was motivated above all by the negative contributions of machinery and electrical material, mineral products and transport materials. The rest of the groups also recorded falls, of varying degrees, although their contribution to the total was not so great as in the case of the three groups mentioned.

In more detail, imports of "machinery and electrical material" recorded a reduction for the fifth consecutive year, of 17.8% in 2014, slightly less heavy that that experienced in the previous year (-19.1%), which on its own accounted for 20% of the total fall in Andorran purchases from abroad. In consequence, its weight on the total reduced by eight tenths to 14.2%, which was the lowest level since 1997, although still, even only by a very little, the most important group of imports to Andorra. This negative movement was above all the result of the reduction in purchases of mechanical appliances (-21.1%), which thus completed five years of consecutive falls. In the same way, the chapter of machines and electrical appliances continued the falling trend begun in 2008, with a cutback in imports of 16%, which took 1.6 points off the total growth.

In the same line, the imports of "foods, beverages and tobacco" recorded a fall of 6.2%, which contrasted with the increase in 2008, but was less than the reduction in total imports. As a result, its weight over the total increased by 1.1 points, to 14.2%, a level which left it still as the second most important group of imported products, but very close to the first. The chapter which stood out in this movement was tobacco, with a reduction in imports of 19.1%, which halted two years of increases of over 30%, and meant a drop of two tenths in its weight on the total imports, to 2.4%. Further, the chapter of beverages, alcoholic liquids and vinegars – the most important of the group, with a weight of 4.8% on the total of Andorran imports

– recorded a fall (-4.2%), which also contributed to explaining the fall for the group as a whole.

The third group in the ranking continued being "chemical products", although purchases were reduced for the second consecutive year, at a rate of 5.7%, lower than that of the total, placing its proportion on the overall figure of imports at 12.3%, one point above that for 2008 and the highest level of the historic series, available since 1991. This movement was very much conditioned by the negative behaviour of perfumery products (-11%), the most important chapter of the group, with a weight of 7.6% on the total imports. On the other hand, the purchases of pharmaceutical products

– the second chapter in the group in importance – rose by 4.3% and lifted its participation by half a point to > 2.6% of the total. There was also a strong increase in the imports of soaps, organic products, waxes and candles (19.2%), which had a weight of 0.9%.

However, purchases of "textiles" from abroad recorded a fall of 7.3% during 2014, greater than that of the previous year, but less than for the total. Thus, its weight increased by six tenths to 9.9%, a movement which raised it from fifth to fourth position in the ranking. In this group, the falls in imports were relatively modest in the case of the two most important chapters: clothing and accessories other than knitwear (-9.7%) and knitwear (-1.7%), which set their weights at 6.3% and 2.9% of the total, respectively.

The purchases of "mineral products" were those which made the second most negative contribution to the variation in imports in 2014, with a strong fall of 22.4%, due fundamentally to the fall in imports of fuels, oils and mineral waxes (-22.4%), the most important chapter in the group – with a weight of 8.5% on total imports. The fallback in this chapter contrasted with the rising trend shown in the prices of oil during the year under study and was the result of a reduction both in the litres of fuel imported and in the prices, driven down by the process of liberalisation applied since February 2014. Also purchases of salt, sulphur, earth and stone, gypsum, lime and cement recorded a heavy reduction of 22.2%, more intense than in 2008, because of the continuing deterioration in the rhythm of activity in construction. In consequence, the participation of the group of mineral products on the total fell, for the first time in five years, by 1.1 points, to 9.5%, so that it dropped one place in the ranking of imports, to fifth place.

After these were imports of “transport material”, which remained in the same position as for the year before, but which also lost weight, from 7.8% to 7%, through falling for the fourth consecutive year, this time by 22%. This behaviour meant that it was the group which made the third most negative contribution to the fall in Andorran purchases from abroad, thus accounting for 12.8% of the total reduction, after machinery and electrical material and mineral products. The explanation of this movement was found fundamentally in the reduction of imports of the chapter of automobiles, tractors, motorbikes and bicycles (-21.4%), the most important of the group, in sympathy with the heavy fall in registrations in the Andorran market and the big reduction in re-exports of vehicles, as also happened in the year before.

The reduction in imports of live animals and animal products was more modest (-7.8%), although it halted a trend of eight years of uninterrupted growth. In consequence, its weight over the total rose by four tenths, to 5.5%. In this group, there were notable reductions in the imports of milk and milk products (-9.3%) and of meat and combustible offal (-6.1%), the two most important chapters of the group.

Also the group of “sundry goods and products” experienced a fall in imports of 15%, which continued the downward trend begun the previous year (-13.6%). As a result, the group fell to eighth position in the ranking of import groups, with a participation on the total of 5.3%, one tenth less than in 2008. This contracting movement was explained, in the first place, by the reduction in purchases of toys and sports articles (-21.9%) and, to a lesser degree, in furniture and light fittings (-10.1%), which are the chapters which have the most considerable weight in the group.

To finish, with regard to the principal groups of products with a participation of below 5% of purchases from abroad, it must be said that the movement was negative in every case. The most substantial falls were in objets d'art and antiques (-41%), which was the group that fell most in 2014 for the second consecutive year; manufactures of stone, cement and ceramic products (-27.1%); furs and leather (-24.5%); optical, photographic and precision equipment (-20.9%); base metals (-19.2%); timber and cork (-18.3%) and fats and oils (-16.2%). The rest of the groups also recorded reductions but less severe than the average, oscillating between -11.7% for arms and ammunitions and -0.8% for footwear, headgear, umbrellas and feathers, which was the group which fell the least.

EXPORTS

The heavy fall in Andorran exports, 30.1%, experienced in 2014 was explained mostly, and in the same way as in the previous year, by the negative contribution of the machinery and electrical material group, at 13.6 points. This group was also the one which contributed most to the fall in imports, a coincidence which showed that a significant proportion of the purchases of these products was destined to re-export. Well behind, there were also the negative contributions by the groups of food products, beverages and tobacco, and of base metals and their manufacture (-9.5 and -4.5 points, respectively). In the contrary sense, there was a positive contribution by exports of footwear, headgear, umbrellas and feathers, which added one point to the growth in exports, and in optical, photographic and precision apparatus, which added eight tenths more. In more detail, the movement of the principal groups of products exported was as explained below.

The most important exporting group in 2014 was “transport material”, a position which it had not held since 2003, with a weight of 20.2%, 4.1 points more than in the year before. This progress was the result of a fall in exports (-12.4%) substantially less than that of the total, thus representing a moderation with respect to the heavy fall recorded in 2008 (-40.2%). It must be said that this behaviour was determined by the relatively moderate reduction in the chapter of automobiles (-7.4%), which took up 98% of the exports of the group, a movement which continued the falling trend observed since 2005.

In second place was the group “machinery and electrical equipment” – especially electronic material, after two years in which it had led the ranking. This loss of position was explained by the big reduction experienced, of 55.3%, similar to that of 2008 (-53.7%), which was the second largest for all the groups, second only to objets d'art and antiques. As a result of these falls in the last two years, its weight was cut to 15.8%, as against the record level reached in 2007 (38.1%). This big contraction was explained both by the sales of machines and electric appliances, the principal chapter of this group, being down – by 54.6% – and by the reduction in sales of mechanical appliances – which were down by 56.4%.

In the same line, exports of “food products, beverages and tobacco” fell in 2014 from second to third place in the ranking, with a weight of 15.5%, 4.8 points less than in the previous year. This movement was the consequence of a fall in exports of the chapter “various prepared foods” (-48.6%), after having been multiplied in 2008 almost by ten. > On the other hand, the group of “textiles” improved by one position in the ranking, due to an increase of 1.9%, which halted two years of falls and pushed its quota up to 7.6%, the highest level since 1998. In this group there was an increase, for the second consecutive year, in sales to abroad of clothing and accessories other than knitwear (9.8%) – the most important chapter of the group – while exports of knitwear clothing and accessories – the second chapter in importance – reduced by 13.9%.

Also, exports of the group of “chemical industry products” experienced a slight fall of 0.6% in 2014, clearly milder than that of the total, which raised its weight on the total by 2.1 points, to 7%, a value which placed it as the fifth exporting group in Andorra. This progress was explained fundamentally by the moderate fall in sales of perfumery and toiletry products, of 1.3%, the most important chapter of the group.

The reduction in exports of “base metals” was much more severe, at 49.2%, the third most important of all the groups and more severe than in the year before. As a result, its weight on the total was down by 2.5 points, to 6.6%. This contraction was principally due to the reduction in sales of the chapters of castings, iron and steel (-47.8%) and manufactures of castings, iron and steel (-64.4%), which are the two most important in the group.

On the other hand, there was notable growth in the exports of paper and graphic arts, up by 12%, which lifted their participation in the total from 3.8% to 6%. The chapters which produced this increase were those of paper and cardboard (80%) and publishing products and graphic industries (9.7%). This last chapter was the most important of the group.

To finish, the movement of the rest of the groups, with a proportion of below 5% of total exports, varied substantially during 2014. On the positive side increases were noted in the sales of footwear, headgear, umbrellas and feathers; in precious stones, pearls and metals; in optical, photographic and precision apparatus and in fats and oils, all with increases of two digits, which raised their weight on the total and as a whole contributed 2.4 points to the growth of exports. The movement of sales of furs, leather and their manufacture, live animals and animal products, and plastic, rubber and manufactures were also positive, but relatively more moderate and with a minimal contribution to growth. The rest of the groups with a minimally significant weight recorded reductions, in some cases substantial. In particular, it must be noted that the fall in sales of objets d'art and antiques, which was 98.7%, subtracted 1.9 points from the growth of exports and reduced the group's weight on the total to practically 0%, as against the 1.9% of the year before. Other groups of exports which reduced substantially were mineral products; wood, cork and their manufacture, and manufactures of stone, cement and ceramic products, groups which, for their weight on the total of Andorran exports, each reduced the total growth of exports by some tenths.

CONSUMER PRICES

During 2014, the progress of inflation was very much affected by depressed demand, linked to the climate of economic recession and the behaviour of oil prices, as for the rest of the developed economies. In this context, consumer prices showed an increasingly downward trend during the first eight months of the year, coinciding with the worst moments of the world crisis, with a record interannual fall of 2.3% in August. This fall was less acute in the last months of the year, due to the upward pressure of oil prices, finally closing the year at a historic minimum of 0%, as against the 2% of the year before. This stagnation

in price levels was in contrast with the increases recorded in Spain (0.8%), the source of the major proportion of consumer goods, in France (0.9%) and the average for the euro zone corresponding to the same period (0.9%).

By components, the majority trend once again was for moderation. First, there was a significant reduction in the prices of the component "entertainment and culture" (-3.2% in December), which continued the downward trend started in the previous year. The second most reduced component was that of housing (-0.8%) – in spite of the increase in the price of fuels during the year, which was also the first time that this had happened since data on the index became available. The other components which recorded falls in prices were those of food, beverages and tobacco (-0.3%), also for the first time, and diverse goods and services (-0.2%), a development which contrasts in both cases with the increases experienced in 2008.

Furthermore, the increases in prices were very modest and less than in the previous year for the cases of hotels, cafes and restaurants (0.4%), certainly affected by the weakness of demand, due to the falling numbers of visitors, and education (0.8%). Moderation also typified the movements in the prices of health (1.1%) and furniture, domestic goods and chattels and home services (1.6%), in contrast to the acceleration seen in 2008, although this last was the second most inflationary component. Finally, the only components which recorded a higher rise in prices than in the previous year were transport (0.6%) – a component very dependent on the consumption of fuels – and clothing and footwear (3.6%), which was the most inflationary component of the year.

With regard to the analysis of prices for special groups, it was noted that the energy group experienced a big reduction of 3%, more severe than in the previous year (-0.7%), a fact which contrasts with the increase in oil prices recorded during 2014, and is explained by the entry into effect in February of the Law 27/2008 on special taxes, which freed the setting of fuel prices. Prices also fell, although more modestly, in the case of food, with a fall of -1%. It must be said that this was the first time that a negative movement in food prices had appeared since the historic series has been available, making clear the degree to which weakness of demand had depressed prices. This fact also contributed to a considerable moderation in prices for services other than rentals, from 2.9% to 0.1%, motivated by the slowdown and fall in prices for both the services most linked to tourism and basic services such as health and education.

On the whole, if considering only the nucleus of inflation, measured by the underlying inflation – which excludes energy and food, for the third consecutive year a very significant slowdown was observed, from 2.3% to 0.3%, with an intensity similar to that experienced by the general index, placing it in line with the underlying inflation rate recorded in Spain (0.3%). Again, among the factors contributing to this notable moderation was the contraction in demand which characterised 2014.

WAGES

According to data supplied by Andorran Social Security (CASS), average salaries in Andorra rose by 1.8%, an advance rather more moderate than the 4.3% experienced in 2008 and the most modest progression since the historical series became available (1992). Notwithstanding this, the increase continues to exceed that of inflation, so that the improvement in purchasing power of the average salary was fairly significant, at 1.8 points, although less than in 2008

(2.4 points).

It must be noted that this pattern of salary rises clearly exceeding inflation, which has been repeated in recent years in Andorra, represents a significant and continuous increase in costs for Andorran companies, and in consequence will become a persistent factor in the loss of competitiveness of the Andorran economy. Furthermore, the minimum national hourly wage was increased, as is normal, in proportion to the consumer price index for the previous year (2%) and was established at 5.28 euro per hour in 2014 (for workers aged 18 or over).

By sectors, the movement in pay was once again very divergent. The most notable increase was in foreign organisations, where the increase was spectacular (40.8%), and much higher than in the previous year, when there were also very significant increases (10.6%), and well above the average. Next came voluntary declarations without activity (40.6%) and domestic work for the community, with a very notable increase of 8.6%, contrasting with the fall recorded in 2008. Pay rises were also very significant in the case of agriculture, livestock, hunting and forestry (4.8%), health and veterinary activities (4.7%) and transport, storage and communications (4.6%), although in all three cases they were more moderate than those recorded in the previous year. On the other hand, salary rises accelerated in the production and distribution of electricity, gas and water and in manufacturing industry, with increases of 3.4% and 3.2%, respectively. Other sectors where the salary increase was above average were real estate and rental activities and business services (2.7%) and education (2.3%), although in both cases they were less than in the previous year.

The rest of the activities were placed below the average growth and also below the increase recorded in the previous year. Within this group, the most significant salary rises were in the financial sector (1.5%), the public administration (1.2%) and homes employing domestic personnel (1.2%). The most modest increases in remuneration were recorded in trade and motor vehicle repairs (0.8%), other social activities and services to the community (0.6%) and hospitality (0.3%). Finally, it must be noted that the only sector in which a fall in average salary was recorded was construction (-0.3%), which emphasises the weakness of activity in that sector.

An analysis of salary levels also brings out fairly significant differences between sectors, a situation of imbalance which eased a little during 2014, with a reduction in the difference between the highest and the lowest salaries in relation with the previous year. This shows that the highest salaries were paid in the financial sector, where the remuneration doubled the average salary. As has been said, this level contrasts with domestic work for the community, with a salary 41.4% below the average, this being the sector with the poorest pay. The second sector in the salary ranking is that of the production and distribution of electricity, gas and water, with salaries some 67.6% above the average. Somewhat behind, but also above the average, were foreign organisations, with salaries 31.2% above; extraction industries (23.4% above); the public administration – which paid 20.6% more; health, veterinary and social services activities; transport, storage and communications; education, the manufacturing industries and construction – with salaries which were between 20% and 0.5% above the average.

The rest of the branches were placed below the average salary level, in percentages varying between 4% for real estate and rental activities and business services, and the 41% less paid for domestic work for the community. Within this group of sectors were the cases of trade and hospitality, which employ a good proportion of the Andorran population (37.8% of the total employees), with pay at 13% and 24% below the average, respectively. Also it is noted that during 2014 both sectors slightly increased their distance from the average salary, which in the case of hospitality was for the fifth consecutive year.

ENERGY COSTS

In 2014 the Law 27/2008 on special taxes came into force, in accordance with which the sales price of fuels could be established freely (sixth additional provision). In consequence, from February 2014, the Government ceased fixing the maximum retail prices of fuels and no longer publishes official details on price movements, so that it is no longer possible to make a detailed analysis of those variables, as was done in the reports for previous years. In any event, the movement in the energy component of the CPI, which was commented on in section 1 of this chapter, showed that the prices of energy products had experienced a fairly significant fall during 2014 (-3%), the fruit precisely of this process of liberalisation, and that it easily compensated for the upward pressures arising from the increase in oil prices recorded during the year.

PUBLIC SECTOR

CENTRAL GOVERNMENT PERFORMANCE

According to the provisional settlement of the Government accounts, the year 2014 closed with a non-financial cash deficit for the twelfth consecutive year, at 116.6 million euro. This figure represented an increase of 17.6% with respect to the deficit for 2008 and established a new historic maximum, both in absolute terms and in those relative to the scale of the Andorran economy, as it surpassed the record established in the previous year (-99.2 million euro). This high level of deficit is far from the slight surplus initially budgeted of 0.2 million euro. On the other hand, the final budget result, obtained by the incorporating the movements in financial assets and liabilities during 2014 into the cash deficit, showed a positive balance of 2.6 million euro, although very much below that recorded in the year before, when it was 33.1 million euro. This development is basically the consequence of an increase of 119.3 million euro in the balance drawn down on credit lines between 31 December 2008 and 31 December 2014, so that the short-term indebtedness of the General Administration rose to 361.6 million euro, while the live balance of public debt has remained at 260 million euro since 31 December 2005.

The increase in the Andorran deficit in 2014 was the result of a reduction in income greater than the reduction in expenses, the latter not having fallen for the last ten years. In its turn, the reduction in spending is explained fundamentally by a sharp contraction in capital expenditure of 12.6%, continuing the downward trend started in the previous year, plus a reduction, also for the first time in eleven years, in current expenses, although on a much more modest scale (-2.1%). In parallel, the fall in income affected all items, without exception, with a particularly negative contribution from the collection of indirect taxes, with its high weight on the total (85.6%).

With regard to fiscal novelties, approval was given in 2014 to Law 3/2014 on the exchange of information in tax matters on prior application, through which a new modulation of banking secrecy was established. This Law regulates cooperation in the exchange of fiscal information, following the principles established by the OECD, with the objective of taking the country off the list of tax havens.

INCOME

During 2014, the non-financial income received came to a total of 271.2 million euro, a figure which represents a rate of implementation of 75.8% on the budgeted item and an interannual reduction of 14.4%, much more severe than the 1.6% fall recorded in 2008.

This reduction was explained principally by the unfavourable behaviour of direct and indirect taxes and patrimonial income, which recorded very substantial falls, with the addition also of a fall in current transfers and in dues and other income. In more detail, the collection of direct taxes, which were first obtained in 2007, with the entry into force of the tax on capital gains on real estate capital transfers, experienced a spectacular reduction, for the second consecutive year, of 37.2%, which is explained by the deep depression which the real estate sector is suffering. This movement placed the rate of budgetary implementation at a poor 27.7% and reduced its weight over total income by two tenths to reach 0.6%.

The income from indirect taxes also recorded a substantial fall, of 10.7%, worse than that experienced in 2008, although less severe than for the total non-financial income. In consequence, the degree of implementation of this item was placed at 74.3% of the figure budgeted, while its weight on total non-financial income rose by 3.6 points with respect to the value for 2008, after two years of falls, being placed at 85.6%.

As in the previous year, this negative movement in indirect taxes is explained by the falling collections of the principal taxes. Income from the indirect tax on the supply of services (ISI) – the first tax levied in Andorra – reduced sharply, by 21.5%, the movement thus continuing the steeply downward trend started in 2008, when it fell by 14.3%, and placing its budgetary rate of implementation at a scarce 69.7%. In turn, this reduction is explained fundamentally by the fall in income from banking and financial ISI, due to the poor results for 2008 in the banking entities, faced with the deep financial crisis which has affected the whole world.

The reduction in the collections of taxes on the consumption of goods (IMI, IAC and the variable rate) and on foreign trade was even more severe (-48.8% and -46.6%, respectively) than for services, as a result, on the one hand, of the clear reduction of income from IMI (-29.8%) and the tax on commercial activities (-29.6%), which fell more than in the previous year and, on the other hand, a reduction of 89.5% in the collection of the variable rate and also a reduced tax on consumption (-48%). It must be noted, however, that these data are not comparable with those of the previous year, due to the entry into force at the beginning of 2014 of the Law 27/2008 on special taxes, since a part of these taxes was included in 2008 in both IMI and IAC and in the concept of taxes on consumption (variable rate and foreign trade). Thus, if the amount collected during 2014 in concept of special taxes is added to the total collections on consumption and foreign trade, the reduction of income is limited to 11.5%, with a budgetary implementation rate of 72%. It must be added that, with regard to the tax on consumption, the most important concepts refer to imports of beverages and tobacco, which showed significant reductions, of -11.6% and -13.7%, respectively.

On the other hand, the collection of the tax on capital transfers showed an increase of 65.8%, thus breaking the sequence of falls recorded in the two previous years and placing the budgetary implementation at 115.2%. However, it is important to note that this amount includes one single real estate transfer on which the State received 7.5 million euro. Not taking into account this particular transaction, the collection would have been 21.1% below that of 2008, a situation which would have reflected the climate of recession which continues to affect the real estate sector.

In the same line, the collection of dues from the para-public entities (FEDA and STA) increased, in contrast to the previous year, by 20.6%, a development which brought the degree of budgetary implementation to 101%. However, this variation has not been calculated with homogeneous data, as the collection in 2014 included the dues from the para-public STA for the fourth quarter of 2008 and the first three quarters of 2014, while in 2008 it only included the dues for the first three quarters of 2008. Therefore, to obtain a true comparison, the dues from STA for the fourth quart quarter of 2007 need to be added to the budgetary settlement of 2008. The result is that the increase in the collection of dues from the para-public entities is limited to 3.7%.

To complete the analysis of movements in indirect taxes, it should be mentioned that the collection for the tax on the game of bingo reduced by 6.4%, two points less than in the previous year, while the collection of taxes on internal production reduced by 5.6%, as against the increase in 2008 (10.9%). For these, the degree of budgetary implementation was 77.6% and 74.1%, respectively.

With regard to the collection of rates and other income, the movement in 2014 was slightly negative for the first time in four years, with a fall of 0.5%, compared with the increase of 4.4% in the previous year, placing the degree of budgetary implementation at 97.7%. This was clearly less unfavourable than the movement for the total income, and therefore meant an increase in its weight, of 1.3 points, up to 9%.

A detailed analysis showed that the slight fall in 2014 was the result of fairly divergent movements in the various items. On the one hand, there was continuity in the expanding development of income for the supply of services (7%), although at a slower rate than due particularly to income from withholdings on savings income, in compliance with the Agreement between the Principality of Andorra and the European Community established in 2005. This item was improved by the fact that during the second half-year of 2014 the withholdings applied rose from 15% to 20%. Collections also increased a touch (0.1%) in the case of the item listed as "other income", as against the previous year, as a result of the combination of more income for damage and contingencies and for surcharges, with less resources obtained from sanctions, the most important item in this section. On the other hand, there was a fall in income from dues (-5%), among these a fall in collection for dues on trade marks (-42.1%), on work permit applications (-20.9%) –closely linked to the economic cycle, which continued to be recessive – and judicial taxes (-12.2%). The reduction was much more modest in the case of the tax on vehicles (-0.5%) and mildly positive in the case of the notarial tax (0.5%) and economic activities (0.9%), behaviour evidencing that the economic situation remained weak. Another component which recorded a reduction in income was the sale of goods (-4.9%), principally in the headings of the sale of own publications, forms, cartography and photography and health products. Further, a steep fall was recorded in receipts from repayments (-61%), although the reduced weight of this item limited its impact in absolute terms.

To finish with income, current transfers experienced an appreciable reduction of 15.2%, but the fall in patrimonial income was even more severe, at 56.1%, thus becoming the item of income which fell the most. The repercussions of the first of these on total income are very small, because of its minimum weight (0.02%). On the other hand, the heavy fall in patrimonial income, which contrasts with strong growth in the previous year, was more important because this income represented a more appreciable proportion on the total and was cut back by half, to 4.8%. This movement is explained because no patrimonial income was obtained in 2014 from real investments, as opposed to 2008, when 14.5 million euro of income was allocated for this concept, a figure which represented almost half of the patrimonial income for that year. Therefore, leaving aside this item, which showed very volatile behaviour, the most important item in patrimonial income was the distribution of results by the para-public entities (96% of the total in 2014), which recorded a reduction of 10.1%. Also the income for interest on deposits and bank accounts was reduced (-77.3%), because of the fall in market interest rates which forced the central banks to supply liquidity to the system, and in real estate income (-1.5%), while income obtained as a result of trading transactions (dues from ITV and Bus Exprés shelters) recorded an increase of 7%.

EXPENDITURE

The total of non-financial expenses settled in 2014 was 387.8 million euro, showing a significant reduction of 6.8%, which ended nine years of consecutive growth at an average rate of 9.9%. This figure represented a degree of implementation on budgeted expenses in the final budget (the initial budget plus amendments and changes approved during the year) of 75.8%, higher than in the previous year and identical to the percentage implementation of income.

The fall in expenses noted in 2014 was explained above all by the reduction in capital expenditure (-12.6%) and, to a lesser degree, by the fall, for the first time since 1998, in current expenses (-2.1%). This decreasing trend in current expenses was principally due to the big reduction in financial expenses (-34.6%), after four years of sharp increases, and this in its turn was explained by the reduction in interest rates, which fully compensated for the effect on expenses of the increase in the Government level of indebtedness. As a result, the weight of this item on the total was cut back by 1.7 points to 3.9%, the lowest level for the last three years. The other item of current expenses which was reduced, for the second consecutive year, was that of consumption of current goods and services (-5.5%), although to a lower degree than the total of non-financial expenses, so that its weight increased by one tenth, to 11%.

On the other hand, the personnel expenses – the most important item in current expenditure, with a weight of 23% – continued growing, at a rate of 1.4%, although this advance represented an appreciable moderation in comparison with the previous year (5.1%) and was the lowest recorded since the historical series became available (1991). Current transfers (to autonomous and administrative bodies, private and public companies, local corporations, families and non-profit-making institutions and also to abroad) also rose, by 6%, but at a more modest rate than that recorded in the previous year (32.3%), thus placing the weight of this item on the total at 20.2%, 2.4 points more than in 2008. Overall, current expenses represented 58.2% of the Government's non-financial expenses, 2.8 points more than in the previous year, and the degree of implementation fell by nearly 7 points to 88.5%.

With regard to capital expenditure, movements in 2014 were very negative for the second consecutive year, with a fall of 12.6%, the worst result for the last ten years. This fall put the amount at 162.1 million euro, with a weight on the total of 41.8%, 2.8 points less than in 2008, and a budget implementation level of 63.1%, a very low record compared with that of current expenses. By chapters, the reduction in capital expenditure was due, firstly, to the fall in real investments (-16.3%), which was in addition to the fall in >the previous year (-1.8%). This placed the total amount at the lowest level of the last four years, with a degree of budget implementation of 52.7% and a weight on total non-financial expenses which was reduced by 2.9 points, to 25.6%. The unfavourable movement in capital expenditure was also contributed to by the fall in capital transfers (-6%), after the stagnation which had typified the behaviour of this item in the previous year. This placed the level of budget implementation for capital transfers at 91.6%, and its weight on the Government's total non-financial spending during 2014 at 16.2%, one tenth less than in the year before.

COMMUNES (LOCAL GOVERNMENT) PERFORMANCE

According to the data on budget settlements in the commune administrations, prepared by the Government's Statistics Department, the total income obtained by the communes during 2014 was 182.78 million euro, higher than the final figure of 172.11 million euro for expenses. In consequence, the commune administrations as a whole ended the year with a budget surplus, for the second consecutive year, of 10.67 million euro, although less than that recorded for the previous year (22.39 million). This reduction in the fiscal surplus of the communes was the result of the combination of substantial reductions in income, which affected five of the seven communes, and were more intense than the cutbacks applied to expenses.

A detailed analysis of the data showed that four communes – Ordino, Andorra la Vella, Sant Julià de Lòria and Escaldes-Engordany – recorded a surplus which improved their budgeted forecasts on fiscal balance, while the other three recorded a deficit which worsened their forecasts on budgeted balance. In addition, in five communes, all except Sant Julià de Lòria and Escaldes-Engordany, the balance obtained represented a worsening with respect to the fiscal balance recorded in 2008. Escaldes-Engordany was the Commune which obtained the highest surplus

(6.60 million euro), much above that of 2008 (2.54 million euro). In second place was Andorra la Vella, with a surplus of 5.37 million euro which, in contrast to Escaldes-Engordany, was less than that recorded in the previous year. Next were Sant Julià de Lòria and Ordino, with surpluses of over two million euro, which for the first meant an improvement with respect to the deficit which it had shown in 2008 and, for the second, a worsening with respect to the situation of surplus also recorded in 2008. The deficits shown by the other three communes, La Massana, Canillo and Encamp, also represented poorer progress than in the previous year, when the last two had ended the year with surpluses. Further, it must be said that Encamp was the Commune which recorded the worst imbalance.

INCOME

During 2014, the total income received by the communes reduced by 11.9% in relation to the previous year, in contrast to the trend to accelerated growth which had typified the previous three years. In spite of this fall, income exceeded the budgeted figure, with a degree of implementation of 117%. This meant that the income of the communes represented 21.9% of the entire income of the public sector (understood as General Administration plus the communes) in Andorra,

9.7 points less than in 2008. It must be said, however, that this movement is considerably distorted by the big increase in the financial liabilities of the General Administration, the result of its borrowing needs, which considerably raised its total income, artificially reducing the participation of the communes in the total.

By parishes, the most significant fall in income was in Ordino (-64.6%), which was precisely the commune which had increased its income most in the previous year (74.9%). Next came Encamp, with a reduction of 29.5%, after a sharp rise of 64% in 2008, making this the Commune with the highest deficit. These were followed by La Massana (-25.2%), Andorra la Vella (-22%) and Canillo (-17.5%), where reductions also contrasted with the increases which they had recorded in the previous year and explained the deterioration in their fiscal balance. As a consequence, Canillo became the Commune with the lowest volume of income in Andorra, equivalent to 12.40 million euro (6.8% of the total).

On the other hand, Escaldes-Engordany and Sant Julià de Lòria recorded strong increases in income, of 92.3% and 12.8%, respectively, as against the falls which characterised their movement in 2008. This placed Escaldes-Engordany in first place in the ranking of the communes by volume of income, with 58.77 million euro (32.2% of the total), overtaking Andorra la Vella, which had not happened since 2004.

EXPENDITURE

In 2014 the total expenses of the communes showed a reduction for the second consecutive year, of 7%, which constituted the worst result since 2002. In spite of this fall, the percentage implementation in relation with the budget was 110%, more than 7 points above 2008. In parallel, the weight of commune expenses on total spending in the public sector (understood as General Administration plus the communes) in Andorra fell by 9.8 points, to 21%, a percentage lower than the participation in income, as had happened the year before. It must be added that this severe fall in the participation of the communes in the total income of the public sector was artificially conditioned, as has been mentioned above with regard to income, by the variations in the Government's financial liabilities, linked to borrowing needs. Thus, if only non-financial expenses are taken into account, the weight of the commune expenses on total expenses in the public sector fell by only 1.5 points to reach 25.7% in 2014.

By chapters, a strong cutback in capital expenditure can be observed, of 37.2%, more than was applied to current expenses (-5%), although less than in the previous year. The decline in capital expenditure is exclusively the result of a contraction in real investments (-45.1%), down to an amount of 22.2 million euro, the lowest since 1994, while capital transfers, less important in volume – 4.9 million euro – increased by 84.6%, after having nearly tripled in 2008. With regard to current expenses, the rise in expenses for current transfers (13.3%) is notable, thus linking together three years of substantial increases. The rise in personnel expenses was more modest, at 3.9%, which was fairly moderate in comparison to the increases, often of two digits, recorded in recent years. On the other hand, expenses for the consumption of goods and services fell for the first time in nine years, at a rate of 11.2%, while financial expenses were reduced by 31.9%, after three years of sharp increases, a movement which was very much conditioned by the behaviour of interest rates.

With respect to the development by parishes, it must be noted that all the communes, except Escaldes-Engordany, showed reductions in expenses. The sharpest fall was recorded in Ordino (-60.7%), making this the Commune with the lowest expenses in 2014 (6.4% of the total), after being in 2008 the Commune had increased its expenses the most (26.6%). The second largest cutback was recorded in Andorra la Vella (-22.9%), thus making two years of substantial reductions. This circumstance has lost it first position in the ranking of the communes, now taken by Escaldes-Engordany, where expenses increased by 86.2%, to 30.3% of the total. La Massana and Sant Julià de Lòria also recorded falls in expenses, of 22% and 17.4%, respectively, while Encamp (-6.8%) and Canillo (-2.9%) applied more modest reductions, which contributed to their being the communes with the largest deficits in 2014.

OFFSHORE SECTOR

Jurisdiction	Income Tax	Social Taxes	Capital Gains tax	Property Tax	Stamp Duty	Other Taxes
Andorra Currency: Spanish Peseta (SPA) US$1 = SPA 180	N/A	Employer pays 13% of salary. Employee pays 5 %. Self-employed pays 18%	N/A	Acquisition tax is in the range of 1-2%	N/A	Municipal Rates, SPA15-20,000 per year per household

All foreigners wanting to work in Andorra need work permits. These are obtained by employers, whether Andorran individuals or companies, on behalf of employees. Self-employment is not allowed until after 10 years' residence.or trade in Andorra.

Annual quotas are established for new issues of renewable work permits. In 1998 the quota for EU and EFTA was for 900 semi-skilled workers and 150 highly-qualified workers. The quota for other nationals was 25.

There are separate types of non-renewable work permit for temporary and seasonal workers, to which the quotas don't apply. The holder of such a work permit must leave the country within one month of expiry of the permit.

Renewable work permits are issued first for 6 months, extensible for a further year; then a temporary residence card is issued valid for a renewable 2 years; then, a 5-year ordinary residence card is issued; and finally a 10-year privileged residence card is issued. Fees are modest, except that the employer must pay SPA25,000 when first applying for a permit.

Applications for work permits must include photographs, home police certificate, cv, passport, property ownership or rental details and marital status certificate. The CASS will conduct a medical examination.

Tourist visas are issued freely, but for longer-term stay it is necessary to have either a work permit (which will ensure issue of a residence permit) or a Passive Residence Permit (PRP). Permanent residence means a stay of more than 183 days in the year.

Work permits are not easy to get. In principle they are issued only to EU and EFTA nationals, and then only if there is no Andorran national available for the job. They are issued only to individuals working for an Andorran person or company, and not to self-employed foreigners. It may be possible to form an Andorran company and then employ yourself and others.

The Law on Passive Residence Permits 1996 allows 200 new residence permits per year. Passive residents do not work or carry out professional activity in the principality. New entrants must:

- show minimum annual income of 4 m pesetas (24,000 euros) for the
- head of the family and 1 m pesetas for each dependent family member;
- prove good conduct in their previous domicile;
- produce health insurance and a pension plan;
- own or rent a house or apartment in the principality;
- pay a non-interest-bearing deposit of 4 m pesetas (plus 1 m for each dependant) to the Government, which is refundable on departure.

All businesses in Andorra, if they are going to trade in the principality, whether constituted as companies, individual proprietorships of partnerships, need to obtain a trading license, or in other words to register for a particular type of trading, and this must be done at the Registre de Comerc in the commune (Comu) where they are based. The annual cost of this registration is SPA100,000. A holding company, not involved in business activity as such, does not require a trading license.

BASIC LAWS AFFECTING OFFSHORE ACTIVITY

This is a non-exhaustive list of the main Andorran statutes affecting offshore and non-resident business. The statutes are listed in alphabetical order – click on the statute for a fuller description of the statute or the legal regime it forms part of.

Corporations Act 1983
Law on Passive Residence Permits 1996
Law of Protection of Banking Secrecy and of Prevention of Laundering of Money or of Assets Deriving from Crime 1995
Law Regulating the Financial System 1993

BANKING LAW

Banks and other financial institutions in Andorra are regulated by the Andorran National Financial Institute (INAF) under the Law Regulating the Financial System 1993.

Andorran banks are all members of the Agrupacio de Bancs Andorrans, which operated a system of self-regulation until the regulatory law was passed in 1993. The banks have very conservative policies, and high solvency ratios: depositors' funds are guaranteed under a 2003 law, but no Andorran bank has ever defaulted on its depositors.

The over-riding characteristic of Andorran banks that attracts foreign depositors and investors, apart from the absence of taxes, is secrecy. Numbered accounts, made available only to top-quality clients, are said to be known only to 'the customer, the banker and God'. General accounts, also secret under the law, are highly protected as well.

The Andorran Penal Code includes specific provisions against disclosure of details of a bank account to anyone, including the authorities. Only a court order (judge's warrant) can force disclosure.

In response to international concern over money-laundering, Andorra introduced the 'Law of Protection of Banking Secrecy and of Prevention of Laundering of Money or of Assets Deriving from Crime' in 1995. This law requires financial institutions to report any suspicious money movements to the INAF; and the INAF is then entitled to pass on such information to foreign countries if an Andorran judge orders it. However, this will only be done if there is prima facie evidence of a crime (which in Andorra definitely does not include tax avoidance or evasion), and even then is only permitted to countries which have banking secrecy laws, thus excluding, for instance, the UK and the US. In most circumstances, the effect of the law is to strengthen secrecy, not weaken it.

The Law is quite explicit about wanting to balance the attack on money-laundering on the one hand against the need to preserve banking secrecy on the other. Article One reads: 'The present law has as its object the protection of banking secrecy and the prevention of the laundering of money or assets deriving from drug trafficking and other criminal activities'.

The Law defines money-laundering (and offences against banking secrecy) in terms of the existing Penal Code: this provision clearly excludes tax matters from the ambit of the Law.

The Law imposes 'know-your-customer' rules on financial institutions and intermediaries ('fiduciaries').

The Law permits disclosure only in the context of judicial proceedings and in response to an Order from a 'Batlle' (Andorran court).

The Law doesn't just impose a passive duty on financial institutions and intermediaries; there is a positive requirement to report what appear to be suspicious transactions (preferably in advance) to the duty Batlle. The Batlle then either takes appropriate action, or authorises the transaction; the financial authorities are kept informed in either case.

The Law specifically prohibits any person who is reporting a suspect transaction from giving any information about it to the subject of the suspicions, or to any third party.

Financial institutions or intermediaries which infringe the Law are subject to penalties depending on the severity of the infringement:

- Minor infractions are punished with a fine between SPA10,000 and 50,000;
- Serious infractions receive up to six months' suspension and a fine between SPA50,000 and 2m;
- Very serious infractions receive suspension up to 3 years, or permanent suspension, and a fine between SPA2m and 50m.

The Penal Code provides imprisonment up to 4 years for malicious infraction of the privacy law, and 7 years if done for gain.

FORMING A COMPANY IN ANDORRA

The Corporations Act 1983 governs corporations formed in Andorra. There are three types of company, the Societat de Responsabilitat Limitada and the Societat per Accions both having shareholders with limited liability, and the Societat Colectiva, whose partners have unlimited liability.

Companies with commercial or profit-seeking goals must be owned at least two-thirds by Andorran citizens; this means, people born in Andorra, or Privileged Residents - those with more than 20 years' residence. In practice, the Andorran majority owner of a business (called a 'titular' in Catalan) can be an Andorran individual or professional adviser who is willing to cede operational control of the business to the foreign 'owner', and sign a share transfer in blank, in return for a fee (called 'prestanom' in Catalan). In practical terms the titular is a nominee; but not in legal terms. Although this system is in everyday use in thousands of companies, and even though formal contracts are entered into between the parties, the inescapable legal fact remains that the titular can wield considerable power if he wants to. Presumably one is on fairly firm ground with a established, professional titular.

SOCIETAT LIMITADAD (SL)

The Societat Limitadad (SL) is commonly used for local trading and requires a minimum paid up share capital of ESP1,000,000 (Spanish Pesetas), with a minimum of two shareholders. In order to set up an SL, the first step is to obtain approval of the proposed name (some generic words are banned). The name, once approved and registered, will have local protection.

The company's Memorandum and Articles ('estatuts' and 'rao social') are then presented to the Government ('Andorra Govern') in a petition ('suplica') for incorporation. This step is straightforward when a holding company is being created for local assets, but if local trading or complex external financial situations are involved, the Government may look closely, particularly if the foreign party (who is being given 'rights' by the titular) is a newcomer or non-resident.

Once the Government's approval is given, the capital can be deposited and a notary will formalise the incorporation, along with the 'nominee' paperwork.

If there is to be actual trading or other tangible activity in Andorra, the company will need to apply via a 'suplica' to the Commercial Register in the appropriate commune for a trading license, or 'Registre de Comerc' permission. Finally, the Commune has to approve the premises proposed to be used, which requires further paperwork . . .

Once everything is in place, the Government becomes involved once more (another suplica) to approve the formal opening of the business.

It can be imagined that this whole process will take some months even if everything goes smoothly; if not, it can take a year or more. However, for a straightforwad holding company, it may be only two or three months.

The Government's annual fee (tax) for the registration of an SL is ESP100,000, and if a Registre de Comerc is needed, a further ESP100,000 is due annually. It can be imagined that professional fees will add substantially to these costs due to the formality and complexity of the process.

SOCIETAT ANONIMA (SA)

The Societat Anonima (SA) is usually created for larger types of company, or those with many shareholders, and must have a minimum paid up share capital of ESP5,000,000.

The formation procedures for an SA are the same as for a Societat Limitada (see above) except that Governmental checks will be more stringent; and the annual fee (tax) for registration is ESP150,000.

SOCIETAT COLECTIVA

The Societat Colectiva is a company whose capital is shared between partners with unlimited responsibility. Its formation procedures are similar to those of the SA and SL.

PARTNERSHIP

There are no limited partnerships in Andorra. Civil companies can be created by two or more persons to incorporate a partnership with unlimited liability by private contract or deed. In order to trade, it will need a Registre de Comerc permission from its local commune, at a cost of SPA100,000 annually. This is a form that can be used by a foreigner wanting to set up in business locally, say as a restaurant; the usual rules about 67% local ownership will apply, and the Andorran titular will need to sign contracts giving the foreigner day-to-day management rights, and control over finances. It suffers from the obvious difficulty that the unlimited liability of a partner under the law cannot be signed away so easily.

Sole Proprietorship

A citizen or an individual who has exceeded ten years residency is permitted to establish a business as a sole trader, however he will need a trading license from his local Registre de Comerc, at an annual fee of SPA100,000.

This form also could be the basis of a foreign/Andorran business relationship; the Andorran in this case owning 100% of the business, but signing away operating and cash-flow rights to the foreigner. The difficulties are obvious; the advantage is that the Government doesn't have to become involved.

BASIC CONTACTS

Offshore Company Formation
Servissim SL
P O Box 133 La Massana Principality of Andorra
Telephone +376 837836
Fax +376 837879
Summit International
103 Kingsway, London, WC2B 6AW
Telephone +44 207 813 9152
Fax +44 297 813 9153

TAXATION IN THE PRINCIPALITY OF ANDORRA

PRESENTATION OF THE ANDORRAN TAXATION SYSTEM

The law dated 19 December 1996 governing taxation in Andorra governs the general taxation framework and organises the establishment as well as the development of the taxed sectors.
As a result, this law provides for a mechanism of implementing tax legislation, but does not define the various categories of taxation existing in the Principality of Andorra.

This law stipulates that various categories of taxation in Andorra can only be established on the basis of law, which comes within the competence of the Andorran General Council (parliament).

Regional organs called "Comuns" are competent as regards developing and regulating taxes at parish level (local taxes).

At present, there is no direct income tax, corporation tax or wealth tax in the Principality of Andorra.

Nonetheless, the Government plans to implement an inheritance tax, indirect taxation on services and an environmental tax to protect the environment.

The Andorran system has adopted an indirect tax regime which represents approximately 12.6 % of the Gross National Product.

Sectors affected by taxation at national level:

1. **The law on Taxation on Indirect Goods (IMI)** sets up a general indirect taxation system on the **production, manufacture and import of all products** (physical goods) found on Andorran territory, i.e. the merchandise described in **Sections 1 to 97** of the harmonised Community system.
The law provides for four different rates which apply to the value of goods. These rates vary from 1 to 12 % according to the products concerned.

Other taxes are added to this sum depending on the type of products considered, e.g. Comsumption Tax which applies solely to the import of agricultural products

2. **The law on Consumption Tax dated 30 December 1985** provides for a consumption tax which, since the Trade Agreement signed with the European Community in 1990, only applies to the **import of agricultural produce** described in Sections 1 to 24 of the harmonised system.
The percentage for this tax ranges from 2 to 60 % depending on the goods concerned.

3. Other government taxes apply to:
- electricity consumption and telephone bills
- vehicle owners
- individuals wishing to register a brandname.

4. Furthermore, persons involved in a business activity must pay an inclusive tax which is payable on their entry into the Register of owners of a business activity and in each civil year from 1 April to 30 June of that year.

This tax affects three professional categories:

- persons with title to a Public Limited Company or Private Limited Company entered into the Register of Commercial Companies,
- persons who carry out a commercial activity and are entered into the Commercial and Industrial Register,
- persons authorised to carry out a professional activity.

Persons in the Register of Commercial Companies must pay 75,000 pesetas (in the case of Public Limited Companies or Share-based companies) or 50,000 pesetas for any other type of company (e.g. Private limited company) at the time of registration and in each civil year.

Traders entered in the Commercial and Industrial Register only have to pay 25,000 pesetas for each premises registered.

If registration on the Commerical and Industrial Register does not follow within three months of registration in the companies register, 110,000 persetas must be paid by Public Limited Companies and 100,000 pesetas by all other types of company at the time of registration and in each civil year.

Professionals must pay a tax of 50,000 pesetas from the third year following entry into the register of professionals ; nonetheless, they only pay 25,000 pesetas from the time when they are entered into the Commercial and Industrial Register.

5. The law on judicial taxes dated 20 December 1995, has set up a taxation system in the form of fiscal stamps for proceedings launched in the courts.
The value of these stamps varies according to the estimated value of the case submitted to the competent Court.

6. Finally, a law dated 28 November 1996 taxes the organisations authorised to organise lottery games.

7.**The Law on the patrimonial properties transfers of the 15th of December 2000** , published in the Official Bulletin of the Principality of Andorra n° 3 year 13 of the 10th of January 2001 sets up a taxation on property acquisition.The due imports will be decided according to the regulation.

LOCAL TAXES:

- The local authorities ("Comuns") in each parish have been authorised by the General Council to raise general taxes as well as to establish, administer and raise supplementary taxes.

Even though taxes are not uniformly regulated in the various parishes, the most important taxes can be identified:

1. Taxes on provision of services: sewage, lighting, drinking water, rates, etc.
2. Taxes on construction licences and authorisation, changes of commercial names and address registration, installation of signs, etc.
3. Taxes on commercial and industrial activities, rent, property or acquisition of real estate, transfer of patrimony, etc.

OFFSHORE TAXES

The term 'offshore' is not used in Andorran legislation or in describing company forms. Indeed there is no 'offshore' sector as such, since there is no significant direct taxation of Andorran entities in any event. See Direct Corporate Taxation for details of the few taxes that impinge on business; see Personal Taxation for details of taxes impinging on individuals.

Forms of Offshore Operation

The corporate forms available for external operations in Andorra are the same as those available for internal operations

Fees Payable by Companies

The annual fee (tax) payable to the Government by a Societat Limitadad is SPA100,000; and by a Societat Anonima is SPA150,000.

Taxation of Foreign Employees of Offshore Operations

This section refers to the taxation of foreign employees in Andorra. The general principles of individual taxation in Andorra, which also apply to the resident employees of foreign entities. There are in fact no personal taxes as such in Andorra and there is no distinction between the employees of resident or non-resident operations, because all employers have to be Andorran and resident.

Exchange Control

There are no exchange controls in Andorra; indeed there is no national currency. Most of the important world currencies are accepted freely.

Offshore Activities in Andorra

Since there is no offshore sector as such in Andorra, and all trading or business activity has to be carried on by entities which are majority-owned by Andorran nationals or long-stay residents. Other than the rules concerning ownership, there is very little legislation to restrain business activity, which takes place in a liberal environment. However, the Penal Code and the Law of Protection of Banking Secrecy and of Prevention of Laundering of Money and Assets Deriving from Crime 1995 contain severe penalties for criminal activity; and the Government is very watchful in this respect. (Tax avoidance and evasion do not count as crimes.)

EMPLOYMENT AND RESIDENCE

All foreigners wanting to work in Andorra need work permits. These are obtained by employers, whether Andorran individuals or companies, on behalf of employees. Self-employment is not allowed until after 10 years' residence.or trade in Andorra.

Annual quotas are established for new issues of renewable work permits. In 1998 the quota for EU and EFTA was for 900 semi-skilled workers and 150 highly-qualified workers. The quota for other nationals was 25.

There are separate types of non-renewable work permit for temporary and seasonal workers, to which the quotas don't apply. The holder of such a work permit must leave the country within one month of expiry of the permit.

Renewable work permits are issued first for 6 months, extensible for a further year; then a temporary residence card is issued valid for a renewable 2 years; then, a 5-year ordinary residence card is issued; and finally a 10-year privileged residence card is issued. Fees are modest, except that the employer must pay SPA25,000 when first applying for a permit.

Tourist visas are issued freely, but for longer-term stay it is necessary to have either a work permit (which will ensure issue of a residence permit) or a Passive Residence Permit (PRP). Permanent residence means a stay of more than 183 days in the year.

The Law on Passive Residence Permits 1996 allows 200 new residence permits per year. Passive residents do not work or carry out professional activity in the principality. New entrants must:

- show minimum annual income of 4 m pesetas (24,000 euros) for the head of the family and 1 m pesetas for each dependent family member;
- prove good conduct in their previous domicile;
- produce health insurance and a pension plan;
- own or rent a house or apartment in the principality;
- pay a non-interest-bearing deposit of 4 m pesetas (plus 1 m for each dependant) to the Government, which is refundable on departure.

CORPORATE TAXES

In Andorra there are no taxes on profits, dividends or income; there is no capital gains tax, no withholding tax and no sales tax. The taxes impinging on companies are business license fees, social security contributions,and property taxes. Corporate entities pay registration fees to the GovernmentBUSINESS LICENSE FEES

All businesses in Andorra, if they are going to trade in the principality, whether constituted as companies, individual proprietorships of partnerships, need to obtain a trading license, or in other words to register for a particular type of trading, and this must be done at the Registre de Comerc in the commune (Comu) where they are based. The annual cost of this registration is SPA100,000. A holding company, not involved in business activity as such, does not require a trading license.

PAYROLL TAXES

There is a health and social security system in Andorra known as the CASS (Caixa Andorrana de Seguretat Social) which applies to all employees of Andorran individuals or companies. The rates of contribution are 13% of salary by the employer, and 5% by the employee. In practice, the employer often pays the lot.

PROPERTY TAXES

Property taxes are levied by the municipality in which a business is located; a business renting its premises will be liable only for business rates; a business owning or constructing property for its own use will pay taxes on the acquisition of property and its construction in addition to business rates. The actual rates of municipal property taxes vary with the municipality (Comu). In most municipalities, the rate of acquisition tax is in the range 1-2%. Business rates are charged on a square metre basis. There are also small percentage charges on rental income.

PERSONAL TAXES

In Andorra there is no income tax, capital gains tax, gift, inheritance or capital transfer taxes. Employees pay national insurance contributions, and there are municipal taxes on property. There are customs duties on some imported goods (Andorra applies the common external tariff of the EU), and a number of sales taxes on various classes of goods, typically at single digit rates' although higher on alcohol, tobacco and cars.

RESIDENCE AND LIABILITY FOR TAXATION

Andorran residents as such do not have liability to Government taxation, other than to municipal property taxes (see below).

Permanent residence means a stay of more than 183 days in the year. Non-Andorran nationals can become resident only by having a work permit (which will ensure issue of a residence permit) or by obtaining a Passive Residence Permit.

Employees of an Andorran enterprise (which means all employees since there is no provision for foreign companies to operate other than through an Andorran entity) must pay social security contributions (see below). The self-employed (only possible with more than 10 years' residence) also pay social security contributions.

Other Andorran taxes or duties are related to events, rather than residence status.

PAYROLL TAXES

There is a health and social security system in Andorra known as the CASS (Caixa Andorrana de Seguretat Social) which applies to all employees of Andorran individuals or companies. The rates of contribution are 13% of salary by the employer, and 5% by the employee. In practice, the employer often pays the lot. Self-employed individuals pay 18% of earnings.

'Employers', ie individuals who own companies or who register as traders and employ others, cannot join the CASS.

MUNICIPAL TAXES

A resident of Andorra registers with the parish (Comu) where he rents or owns the property in which he lives. This entails liability to taxes and property rates imposed by the parish. Percentages charged vary according to the parish.

There are a number of headings under which charges are imposed:

- 'Foc i Lloc' (meaning hearth and home) and 'Serveis' (services) rates are general rates payable by heads of household, may vary according to the size of the household, and may be more for absentee owners; on average, they amount to SPA15-20,000 per year;
- Property ownership tax is levied on each property owned (flat, house or chalet) and averages around SPA20,000 per property;
- Rental tax is levied by some parishes on rental income received at around 3%;
- Property acquisition tax is payable when property is bought (not inherited) and varies quite widely: often it is 1% or 2% of acquisition cost, but is sometimes levied per square metre.

DECREE AMENDING THE DECREE ANNOUNCES THE GENERAL NOMENCLATURE OF PRODUCTS.

By agreement of the Government on 27 May 2010, and pursuant to Article 30, paragraph 3) of Law 5 / 2004 of 14 April, the Customs Code, modifying the decree of 31 December 2008 and January 14, 2014, by which it communicates the general classification of products, to take into account the categories of sugar depending on your conditioning as if intended for industrial or intended for sale as provided Law 10/2010, of April 22, modifying the overall rate of consumption rates.

For practical reasons of legal certainty and is published in full the General Nomenclature of products applicable to the Principality of Andorra, which corresponds to that provided for in Regulation (EEC) number 2658/87 on the tariff and statistical nomenclature and the Common Customs Tariff, recently amended by Regulation (EC) number 948/2014 of the Commission on 30 September 2014 and Regulation (EU) number 33/2010 of the Commission on 12 January 2010 and the number 211 / 2010 of the Commission on March 11, 2010, except for the following positions:

(1) When the chapter number is preceded by an "ex" means that only refers to part of the chapter

This Decree shall enter into force the day after being published in the Official Gazette of the Principality of Andorra.

Which is published for general knowledge.

Andorra la Vella, 27 May 2010

James Bartumeu Cassany.

Head of Government

Code	Appointment
ex Chapter 17	
At 1701.11.90	- - - - In packages of 50 kg
B 1701.11.90	- - - - Presented otherwise than in packages up to 50kg
At 1701.12.90	- - - - In packages of 50 kg
B 1701.12.90	- - - - Presented otherwise than in packages up to 50kg
At 1701.91.00	- - - - In packages of 50 kg
B 1701.91.00	- - - - Presented otherwise than in packages up to 50kg
At 1701.99.10	- - - - In packages of 50 kg
B 1701.99.10	- - - - Presented otherwise than in packages up to 50kg
At 1701.99.90	- - - - In packages of 50 kg
B 1701.99.90	- - - - Presented otherwise than in packages up to 50kg
Chapter 24	
2401	Tobacco raw or unprocessed, tobacco waste:
2401.10	- Tobacco not esporgats:
2401.10.35	- - Light air cured Tobacco
2401.10.35.1	- - - Ros
2401.10.35.2	- - - Black
2401.10.60	- - Tobacco sun cured Oriental type
2401.10.60.1	- - - Ros
2401.10.60.2	- - - Black
2401.10.70	- - Dark air cured tobacco
2401.10.70.1	- - - Ros
2401.10.70.2	- - - Black
2401.10.85	- - Flue cured Tobacco
2401.10.85.1	- - - Ros
2401.10.85.2	- - - Black
2401.10.95	- - Other tobacco
2401.10.95.1	- - - Ros
2401.10.95.2	- - - Black
2401.20	- Tobacco partly or wholly esporgats:
2401.20.35	- - Light air cured Tobacco

2401.20.35.1	- - - Ros
2401.20.35.2	- - - Black
2401.20.60	- - Tobacco sun cured Oriental type
2401.20.60.1	- - - Ros
2401.20.60.2	- - - Black
2401.20.70	- - Dark air cured tobacco
2401.20.70.1	- - - Ros
2401.20.70.2	- - - Black
2401.20.85	- - Flue cured Tobacco
2401.20.85.1	- - - Ros
2401.20.85.2	- - - Black
2401.20.95	- - Other tobacco
2401.20.95.1	- - - Ros
2401.20.95.2	- - - Black
2401.30.00	- Waste of tobacco
2401.30.00.1	- - Residues from manufacturing, tobacco "trunk"
2401.30.00.2	- - Other
2402	Cigars (including those with the ends cut) and "little cigars", containing tobacco:
2402.10.00	- Cigars (including those with the ends cut) and "little cigars", containing tobacco:
2402.10.00CE	- - Cigars (including those with the ends cut) and "little cigars" that contain tobacco. EC
2402.10.00DC	- - Cigars (including those with the ends cut) and "little cigars" that contain tobacco. DC
2402.20	- Cigarettes containing tobacco
10/20/2402	- - Containing carnations species
2402.20.10.1CE	- - - Ros EC
2402.20.10.1DC	- - - Ros DC
2402.20.10.2CE	- - - Black EC
2402.20.10.2DC	- - - Black DC
2402.20.90	- - Other
2402.20.90.1CE	- - - Ros EC
2402.20.90.1DC	- - - Ros DC
2402.20.90.2CE	- - - Black EC
2402.20.90.2DC	- - - Black DC
2403	Other tobacco and tobacco substitutes, manufactured, tobacco "homogeneïzats" or "reconstituted" tobacco and sauces and extracts:
2403.10	- Tobacco smoking, even if containing tobacco substitutes in any proportion:
10/10/2403	- - In immediate packings of a net content not exceeding 500 g
2403.10.10.1	- - - Ros, for the industrial manufacture of tobacco products
2403.10.10.2	- - - Black, for the industrial manufacture of tobacco products
2403.10.10.3CE	- - - Other, solely dedicated to the EC market

2403.10.10.3DC	- - - Other, solely dedicated to the commercialization DC
2403.10.90	- - Other
2403.10.90.1	- - - Ros, for the industrial manufacture of tobacco products
2403.10.90.2	- - - Black, for the industrial manufacture of tobacco products
2403.10.90.3CE	- - - Other, solely dedicated to the EC market
2403.10.90.3DC	- - - Other, solely dedicated to the commercialization DC
	- Other:
2403.91.00	- - Tobacco "homogenized" or "reconstituted"
2403.91.00.1	- - - Tobacco "homogenized" or "reconstituted"
2403.91.00.2	- - - Tobacco "homogenized" or "reconstituted" for production of the coat or cloak of cigar
2403.99	- - Other:
2403.99.10CE	- - - Tobacco for chewing or sniffing EC
2403.99.10DC	- - - Tobacco for chewing or sniffing DC
2403.99.90	- - - Other
2403.99.90.1	- - - - Designed for the industrial manufacture of tobacco products
2403.99.90.2CE	- - - - Other EC
2403.99.90.2DC	- - - - Other DC
ex Chapter 27 (1)	
	- - - Heavy oils:
	- - - - Diesel:
2710.19.31	- - - - - Destined to receive a specific process
2710.19.35	- - - - - Destined to undergo a transformation to another chemical treatment that is defined for subposició 271019.31
	- - - - - Intended for other uses:
2710.19.41.1	- - - - - - Diesel oil (by weight of a sulfur content below 0.05%)
2710.19.41.2	- - - - - - Heating oil (a by weight sulfur content less than 0.05%)
ex Chapter 87	
8701	Tractors (except truck-tractors no. 8709):
8701.10.00	- Motocultors
8701.20	- Road tractors for semi-trailers:
8701.20.10	- - New
8701.20.10.C1	- - - They have the distinctive Euro V
8701.20.10.C2	- - - Other
8701.20.90	- - Used
8701.20.90.C1	- - - They have the distinctive Euro V
8701.20.90.C2	- - - Other
8701.30.00	- Tractors chenille
8701.30.00.A	- - Emitting less than 120 g / km CO2
8701.30.00.B	- - Emitting less than 150 g / km CO2
8701.30.00.C	- - Other
8701.90	- Other:
	- - Agricultural tractors and forestry tractors with wheels (excluding motocultors)

	- - - New, with an engine power:
8701.90.11	- - - - Not exceeding 18 kW
8701.90.11.A	- - - - - Emitting less than 120 g / km CO2
8701.90.11.B	- - - - - Emitting less than 150 g / km CO2
8701.90.11.C	- - - - - Other
8701.90.20	- - - - Exceeding 18 kW but not exceed 37 kW
8701.90.20.A	- - - - - Emitting less than 120 g / km CO2
8701.90.20.B	- - - - - Emitting less than 150 g / km CO2
8701.90.20.C	- - - - - Other
8701.90.25	- - - - Exceeding 37 kW but not exceeding 59 kW
8701.90.25.A	- - - - - Emitting less than 120 g / km CO2
8701.90.25.B	- - - - - Emitting less than 150 g / km CO2
8701.90.25.C	- - - - - Other
8701.90.31	- - - - Exceeding 59 kW but not exceeding 75 kW
8701.90.31.A	- - - - - Emitting less than 120 g / km CO2
8701.90.31.B	- - - - - Emitting less than 150 g / km CO2
8701.90.31.C	- - - - - Other
8701.90.35	- - - - Exceeding 75 kW but not exceeding 90 kW
8701.90.35.A	- - - - - Emitting less than 120 g / km CO2
8701.90.35.B	- - - - - Emitting less than 150 g / km CO2
8701.90.35.C	- - - - - Other
8701.90.39	- - - - Exceeding 90 kW
8701.90.39.A	- - - - - Emitting less than 120 g / km CO2
8701.90.39.B	- - - - - Emitting less than 150 g / km CO2
8701.90.39.C	- - - - - Other
8701.90.50	- - - Used
8701.90.50.A	- - - - Emitting less than 120 g / km CO2
8701.90.50.B	- - - - Emitting less than 150 g / km CO2
8701.90.50.C	- - - - Other
8701.90.90	- - Other
8701.90.90.A	- - - Emitting less than 120 g / km CO2
8701.90.90.B	- - - Emitting less than 150 g / km CO2
8701.90.90.C	- - - Other
8702	Motor vehicles for the transport of ten or more persons (including the driver):
8702.10	- With piston engines and compression ignition (diesel or semi)
	- - Of a cylinder capacity exceeding 2500 cc:
8702.10.11	- - - New
8702.10.11.A	- - - - Emitting less than 120 g / km CO2
8702.10.11.B	- - - - Emitting less than 150 g / km CO2
8702.10.11.C	- - - - Other
8702.10.19	- - - Used
8702.10.19.A	- - - - Emitting less than 120 g / km CO2
8702.10.19.B	- - - - Emitting less than 150 g / km CO2

8702.10.19.C	- - - - Other
	- - Of a cylinder capacity not exceeding 2500 cc:
8702.10.91	- - - New
8702.10.91.A	- - - - Emitting less than 120 g / km CO2
8702.10.91.B	- - - - Emitting less than 150 g / km CO2
8702.10.91.C	- - - - Other
8702.10.99	- - - Used
8702.10.99.A	- - - - Emitting less than 120 g / km CO2
8702.10.99.B	- - - - Emitting less than 150 g / km CO2
8702.10.99.C	- - - - Other
8702.90	- Other:
	- - With piston engines and spark ignition:
	- - - Of a cylinder capacity exceeding 2800 cc:
8702.90.11	- - - - New
8702.90.11.A	- - - - - Emitting less than 120 g / km CO2
8702.90.11.B	- - - - - Emitting less than 150 g / km CO2
8702.90.11.C	- - - - - Other
8702.90.19	- - - - Used
8702.90.19.A	- - - - - Emitting less than 120 g / km CO2
8702.90.19.B	- - - - - Emitting less than 150 g / km CO2
8702.90.19.C	- - - --Other
	- - - Of a cylinder capacity not exceeding 2800 cc:
8702.90.31	- - - - New
8702.90.31.A	- - - - - Emitting less than 120 g / km CO2
8702.90.31.B	- - - - - Emitting less than 150 g / km CO2
8702.90.31.C	- - - - - Other
8702.90.39	- - - - Used
8702.90.39.A	- - - - - Emitting less than 120 g / km CO2
8702.90.39.B	- - - - - Emitting less than 150 g / km CO2
8702.90.39.C	- - - - - Other
8702.90.90	- - Other
8702.90.90.A	- - - Emitting less than 120 g / km CO2
8702.90.90.B	- - - Emitting less than 150 g / km CO2
8702.90.90.C	- - - Other
8703	Cars and other tourist vehicles principally designed for transport of persons (other than no. 8702), including cars such as "break" and race:
8703.10	- Vehicles specially designed for moving over snow, special vehicles to transport people to the land of golf and similar vehicles:
8703.10.11	- - Vehicles specially designed for moving over the snow, with piston engines and compression ignition (diesel or semi-) or with piston engines and spark ignition)
8703.10.11.A	- - - Emitting less than 120 g / km CO2
8703.10.11.B	- - - Emitting less than 150 g / km CO2
8703.10.11.C	- - - Other

8703.10.18	- - Other
8703.10.18.A	- - - Emitting less than 120 g / km CO2
8703.10.18.B	- - - Emitting less than 150 g / km CO2
8703.10.18.C	- - - Other
	- Other vehicles, with alternative piston engine ignition sparks:
8703.21	- - Of a cylinder capacity not exceeding 1000 cc:
8703.21.10	- - - New
8703.21.10.A	- - - - Emitting less than 120 g / km CO2
8703.21.10.B	- - - - Emitting less than 150 g / km CO2
8703.21.10.C	- - - - Other
8703.21.90	- - - Used
8703.21.90.A	- - - - Emitting less than 120 g / km CO2
8703.21.90.B	- - - - Emitting less than 150 g / km CO2
8703.21.90.C	- - - - Other
8703.22	- - Of a cylinder capacity exceeding 1000 cc but not exceed 1500 cc:
8703.22.10	- - - New
8703.22.10.A	- - - - Emitting less than 120 g / km CO2
8703.22.10.B	- - - - Emitting less than 150 g / km CO2
8703.22.10.C	- - - - Other
8703.22.90	- - - Used
8703.22.90.A	- - - - Emitting less than 120 g / km CO2
8703.22.90.B	- - - - Emitting less than 150 g / km CO2
8703.22.90.C	- - - - Other
8703.23	- - Of a cylinder capacity exceeding 1500 cc but not exceeding 3 000 cc:
	- - - New:
8703.23.11	- - - - Automotive Caravans
8703.23.11.A	- - - - - Emitting less than 120 g / km CO2
8703.23.11.B	- - - - - Emitting less than 150 g / km CO2
8703.23.11.C	- - - - - Other
8703.23.19	- - - - - Other
8703.23.19.A	- - - - - Emitting less than 120 g / km CO2
8703.23.19.B	- - - - - Emitting less than 150 g / km CO2
8703.23.19.C	- - - - - Other
8703.23.90	- - - Used
8703.23.90.A	- - - - Emitting less than 120 g / km CO2
8703.23.90.B	- - - - Emitting less than 150 g / km CO2
8703.23.90.C	- - - - Other
8703.24	- - Of a cylinder capacity exceeding 3000 cc:
8703.24.10	- - - New
8703.24.10.A	- - - - Emitting less than 120 g / km CO2
8703.24.10.B	- - - - Emitting less than 150 g / km CO2
8703.24.10.C	- - - - Other
8703.24.90	- - - Used
8703.24.90.A	- - - - Emitting less than 120 g / km CO2

8703.24.90.B	- - - - Emitting less than 150 g / km CO2
8703.24.90.C	- - - - Other
	- Other vehicles, with engine alternative reciprocating compression ignition (diesel semi)
8703.31	- - Of a cylinder capacity not exceeding 1500 cc:
8703.31.10	- - - New
8703.31.10.A	- - - - Emitting less than 120 g / km CO2
8703.31.10.B	- - - - Emitting less than 150 g / km CO2
8703.31.10.C	- - - - Other
8703.31.90	- - - Used
8703.31.90.A	- - - - Emitting less than 120 g / km CO2
8703.31.90.B	- - - - Emitting less than 150 g / km CO2
8703.31.90.C	- - - - Other
8703.32	- - Of a cylinder capacity exceeding 1500 cc but not exceeding 2 500 cc:
	- - - New:
8703.32.11	- - - - Automotive Caravans
8703.32.11.A	- - - - - Emitting less than 120 g / km CO2
8703.32.11.B	- - - - - Emitting less than 150 g / km CO2
8703.32.11.C	- - - - - Other
8703.32.19	- - - - Other
8703.32.19.A	- - - - - Emitting less than 120 g / km CO2
8703.32.19.B	- - - - - Emitting less than 150 g / km CO2
8703.32.19.C	- - - - - Other
8703.32. 90	- - - Used
8703.32.90.A	- - - - Emitting less than 120 g / km CO2
8703.32.90.B	- - - - Emitting less than 150 g / km CO2
8703.32.90.C	- - - - Other
8703.33	- - Of a cylinder capacity exceeding 2500 cc:
	- - - New:
8703.33.11	- - - - Automotive Caravans
8703.33.11.A	- - - - - Emitting less than 120 g / km CO2
8703.33.11.B	- - - - - Emitting less than 150 g / km CO2
8703.33.11.C	- - - - - Other
8703.33.19	- - - - Other
8703.33.19.A	- - - - - Emitting less than 120 g / km CO2
8703.33.19.B	- - - - - Emitting less than 150 g / km CO2
8703.33.19.C	- - - - - Other
8703.33.90	- - - Used
8703.33.90.A	- - - - Emitting less than 120 g / km CO2
8703.33.90.B	- - - - Emitting less than 150 g / km CO2
8703.33.90.C	- - - - Other
8703.90	- Other:
8703.90.10	- - Vehicles with electric motors
8703.90.10.A	- - - Emitting less than 120 g / km CO2

8703.90.10.B	- - - Emitting less than 150 g / km CO2
8703.90.10.C	- - - Other
8703.90.90	- - Other
8703.90.90.A	- - - Emitting less than 120 g / km CO2
8703.90.90.B	- - - Emitting less than 150 g / km CO2
8703.90.90.C	- - - Other
8704	Motor vehicles for the transport of goods:
8704.10	- Tombarella motor designed to be used off-road network:
8704.10.10	- - With piston engines and compression ignition (diesel semi-egg) or sparks
8704.10.10.A	- - - Emitting less than 120 g / km CO2
8704.10.10.B	- - - Emitting less than 150 g / km CO2
8704.10.10.C	- - - Other
8704.10.10.C1	- - - - They have the distinctive Euro V
8704.10.10.C2	- - - - Other
8704.10.90	- - Other
8704.10.90.A	- - - Emitting less than 120 g / km CO2
8704.10.90.B	- - - Emitting less than 150 g / km CO2
8704.10.90.C	- - - Other
8704.10.90.C1	- - - - They have the distinctive Euro V
8704.10.90.C2	- - - - Other
	- Other, with piston engines and compression ignition (diesel semi-egg):
8704.21	- - Of a maximum laden weight not exceeding 5 tonnes:
8704.21.10	- - - Specially designed for the transport from highly radioactive products (Euratom)
8704.21.10.A	- - - - Emitting less than 120 g / km CO2
8704.21.10.B	- - - - Emitting less than 150 g / km CO2
8704.21.10.C	- - - - Other
8704.21.10.C1	- - - - - They have the distinctive Euro V
8704.21.10.C2	- - - - - Other
	- - - Other:
	- - - - With engine displacement exceeding 2500 cc:
8704.21.31	- - - - - New
8704.21.31.A	- - - - - - Emitting less than 120 g / km CO2
8704.21.31.B	- - - - - - Emitting less than 150 g / km CO2
8704.21.31.C	- - - - - - Other
8704.21.31.C1	- - - - - - - They have the distinctive Euro V
8704.21.31.C2	- - - - - - - Other
8704.21.39	- - - - - Used
8704.21.39.A	- - - - - - Emitting less than 120 g / km CO2
8704.21.39.B	- - - - - - Emitting less than 150 g / km CO2
8704.21.39.C	- - - - - - Other
8704.21.39.C1	- - - - - - - They have the distinctive Euro V
8704.21.39.C2	- - - - - - - Other

	- - - - With engine displacement not exceeding 2500 cc:
8704.21.91	- - - - - New
8704.21.91.A	- - - - - - Emitting less than 120 g / km CO2
8704.21.91.B	- - - - - - Emitting less than 150 g / km CO2
8704.21.91.C	- - - - - - Other
8704.21.91.C1	- - - - - - - They have the distinctive Euro V
8704.21.91.C2	- - - - - - - Other
8704.21.99	- - - - - Used
8704 21 99 A	- - - - - - Emitting less than 120 g / km CO2
8704.21.99.B	- - - - - - Emitting less than 150 g / km CO2
8704.21.99.C	- - - - - - Other
8704.21.99.C1	- - - - - - - They have the distinctive Euro V
8704.21.99.C2	- - - - - - - Other
8704.22	- - Of a maximum laden weight exceeding 5 tons but not exceeding 20 tonnes
8704.22.10	- - - Specially designed for the transport of highly radioactive products (Euratom)
8704.22.10.C1	- - - - They have the distinctive Euro V
8704.22.10.C2	- - - - Other
	- - - Other:
8704.22.91	- - - - New
8704.22.91.C1	- - - - - They have the distinctive Euro V
8704.22.91.C2	- - - - - Other
8704.22.99	- - - - Used
8704.22.99.C1	- - - - - They have the distinctive Euro V
8704.22.99.C2	- - - - - Other
8704.23	- - Of a weight above 20 tons maximum load:
8704.23.10	- - - Specially designed for the transport of highly radioactive products (Euratom)
8704.23.10.C1	- - - - They have the distinctive Euro V
8704.23.10.C2	- - - - Other
	- - - Other:
8704.23.91	- - - - New
8704.23.91.C1	- - - - - They have the distinctive Euro V
8704.23.91.C2	- - - - - Other
8704.23.99	- - - - Used
8704.23.99.C1	- - - - - They have the distinctive Euro V
8704.23.99.C2	- - - - - Other
	- Other, with piston engines and spark ignition:
8704.31	- - Of a maximum laden weight not exceeding 5 tonnes:
8704.31.10	- - - Specially designed for the transport from highly radioactive products (Euratom)
8704.31.10.A	- - - - Emitting less than 120 g / km CO2
8704.31.10.B	- - - - Emitting less than 150 g / km CO2

8704.31.10.C - - - - Other
8704.31.10.C1 - - - - - They have the distinctive Euro V
8704.31.10.C2 - - - - - Other
- - - Other:
- - - - With engine displacement exceeding 2800 cc:
8704.31.31 - - - - - New
8704.31.31.A - - - - - - Emitting less than 120 g / km CO2
8704.31.31.B - - - - - - Emitting less than 150 g / km CO2
8704.31.31.C - - - - - - Other
8704.31.31.C1 - - - - - - - They have the distinctive Euro V
8704.31.31.C2 - - - - - - - Other
8704.31.39 - - - - - Used
8704.31.39.A - - - - - - Emitting less than 120 g / km CO2
8704.31.39.B - - - - - - Emitting less than 150 g / km CO2
8704.31.39.C - - - - - - Other
8704.31.39.C1 - - - - - - - They have the distinctive Euro V
8704.31.39.C2 - - - - - - - Other
- - - - With engine displacement not exceeding 2800 cc:
8704.31.91 - - - - - New
8704.31.91.A - - - - - - Emitting less than 120 g / km CO2
8704.31.91.B - - - - - - Emitting less than 150 g / km CO2
8704.31.91.C - - - - - - Other
8704.31.91.C1 - - - - - - - They have the distinctive Euro V
8704.31.91.C2 - - - - - - - Other
8704.31.99 - - - - - Used
8704.31.99.A - - - - - - Emitting less than 120 g / km CO2
8704.31.99.B - - - - - - Emitting less than 150 g / km CO2
8704.31.99.C - - - - - - Other
8704.31.99.C1 - - - - - - - They have the distinctive Euro V
8704.31.99.C2 - - - - - - - Other
8704.32 - - Of a maximum laden weight exceeding 5 tons:
8704.32.10 - - - Specially designed for the transport from highly radioactive products (Euratom)
8704.32.10.C1 - - - - They have the distinctive Euro V
8704.32.10.C2 - - - - Other
- - - Other:
8704.32.91 - - - - New
8704.32.91.C1 - - - - - They have the distinctive Euro V
8704.32.91.C2 - - - - - Other
8704.32. 99 - - - - Used
8704.32.99.C1 - - - - - They have the distinctive Euro V
8704.32.99.C2 - - - - - Other
8704.90.00 - Other
8704.90.00.A - - Emitting less than 120 g / km CO2

8704.90.00.B	- - Emitting less than 150 g / km CO2
8704.90.00.C	- - Other
8704.90.00.C1	- - - They have the distinctive Euro V
8704.90.00.C2	- - - Other
8705	Motor vehicles for special uses other than those that have been designed primarily to transport persons or goods (cranes, crane trucks, fire engines, concrete mixer trucks, cars broom, espargidors cars, car workshop, cars radiology, for example) :
8705.10.00	- Truck crane
8705.10.00.C1	- - They have the distinctive Euro V
8705.10.00.C2	- - Other
8705.20.00	- Core drilling towers with cars or drilling
8705.20.00.C1	- - They have the distinctive Euro V
8705.20.00.C2	- - Other
8705.30.00	- Car Fire
8705.30.00.A	- - Emitting less than 120 g / km CO2
8705.30.00.B	- - Emitting less than 150 g / km CO2
8705.30.00.C	- - Other
8705.30.00.C1	- - - They have the distinctive Euro V
8705.30.00.C2	- - - Other
8705.40.00	- Truck mixers
8705.40.00.C1	- - They have the distinctive Euro V
8705.40.00.C2	- - Other
8705.90	- Other:
8705.90.10	- - Cars for fault repairs
8705.90.10.A	- - - Emitting less than 120 g / km CO2
8705.90.10.B	- - - Emitting less than 150 g / km CO2
8705.90.10.C	- - - Other
8705.90.10.C1	- - - - They have the distinctive Euro V
8705.90.10.C2	- - - - Other
8705.90.30	- - Cars injection pump concrete
8705.90.30.C1	- - - They have the distinctive Euro V
8705.90.30.C2	- - - Other
8705.90.90	- - Other
8705.90.90.A	- - - Emitting less than 120 g / km CO2
8705.90.90.B	- - - Emitting less than 150 g / km CO2
8705.90.90.C	- - - Other
8705.90.90.C1	- - - - They have the distinctive Euro V
8705.90.90.C2	- - - - Other
8711.20.93	- - - Exceeding 80 cc but not exceeding 125 cc
8711.20.93.D1	- - - - Of a cylinder capacity of 125 cc
8711.20.93.D2	- - - - Other
8711.90.00	- Other
8711.90.00.D1	- - Other of a cylinder motorcycles of 125 cc

8711.90.00.D2	- - Other
ex Chapter 94 (1)	
9499	Changes of residence in accordance with Article 5 of Law of the indirect taxation of goods:
9499.99.99	- Changes of residence in accordance with Article 5 of Law of the indirect goods tax

Correlation table ARANZALÀRIES AND TAX (in relation to amending the Decree codes)

Code NPM	New Code NPM	Tax rate			
		Consumption rate		IMI	IAC
		Specific	Ad valorem		
1701.11.90	At 1701.11.90		2%	1%	0%
1701.11.90	B 1701.11.90	23.45 euros per 100 kg / net		1%	0%
1701.12.90	At 1701.12.90		2%	1%	0%
1701.12.90	B 1701.12.90	23.45 euros per 100 kg / net		1%	0%
1701.91.00	At 1701.91.00		2%	1%	0%
1701.91.00	B 1701.91.00	23.45 euros per 100 kg / net		1%	0%
1701.99.10	At 1701.99.10		2%	1%	0%
1701.99.10	B 1701.99.10	23.45 euros per 100 kg / net		1%	0%
1701.99.90	At 1701.99.90		2%	1%	0%
1701.99.90	B 1701.99.90	23.45 euros per 100 kg / net		1%	0%

ECONOMY

Tourism, the mainstay of Andorra's economy, accounts for roughly 80% of GDP. An estimated 13 million tourists visit annually, attracted by Andorra's duty-free status and by its summer and winter resorts. The banking sector, with its "tax haven" status, also contributes substantially to the economy. Agricultural production is limited by a scarcity of arable land, and most food has to be imported. The principal livestock activity is sheep raising. Manufacturing consists mainly of cigarettes, cigars, and furniture. Andorra is a member of the EU Customs Union; it is unclear what effect the European Single Market will have on the advantages Andorra obtains from its duty-free status.

National product: GDP - purchasing power equivalent - $760 million (1992 est.)

National product per capita: $14,000 (1992 est.)

Budget:
revenues $138 million
expenditures $177 million (1993)

Exports: $30 million (f.o.b., 1993 est.)
commodities electricity, tobacco products, furniture
partners France,Catalonia, Spain

Electricity:
capacity 35,000 kW
production 140 million kWh
consumption per capita 2,570 kWh

Industries: tourism (particularly skiing), sheep, timber, tobacco, banking

Agriculture: sheep raising; small quantities of tobacco, rye, wheat, barley, oats, and some vegetables

INVESTING IN THE PRINCIPALITY OF ANDORRA

The Embassy of the Principality of Andorra is at your disposal for information about the steps to be taken to import products to Andorra, to establish a company or to buy a business.

To obtain a list of Andorran companies in a particular industry, please contact the Chamber of Commerce, Industry and Services

CCIS (http://www.andorra.ad/ccis/index.html)
Prat de la Creu, 8
Edifici les Mans - Despatx 204-205
Andorra la Vella
Tel. : (00 376) 863 232
Fax : (00 376) 863 233
E-mail: ccis@correu.andorra.ad

BUSINESS REPRESENTATIVES WISHING TO VISIT ANDORRA

The Principality of Andorra signed the ATA Convention in June 1998. Business representatives can therefore bring their promotional products to the Principality of Andorra if they hold an ATA card – issued by the Chamber of Commerce of their region – listing the products and samples they wish to promote.

Business representatives may also enter the territory of the Principality to promote their products without holding an ATA card. But in this case they must complete a T2L form covering temporary imports, available from Andorran customs.

They will have to pay to the Andorran Custom Office a security equivalent to the IMI_ – the tax on merchandise – due on their samples. This security will be refunded on their departure from the Principality of Andorra, if they leave the country with all the samples they brought.

FINANCIAL SECTOR AND LIST OF BANKS

http://www.aba.ad or http://www.andorra.ad/inaf

The Andorran financial system is, contrary to appearances, highly regulated. Several laws have been introduced to provide a solid legal framework for the system.

Various legal documents regulate the system, such as the « law on payments made by financial institutions » of 27 November 1993, the « law on the regulation of the coefficient of mandatory investments» of 22 August 1994, the « law on the protection of banking secrecy and the prevention of money-laundering or products derived from crime » of 11 May 1995 or the « law on the regulation of criteria for the solvability and liquidity of financial institutions » of 29 February 1996.

In 1998, all banks were approached and very high standards set to ensure compliance with the regulations.

For more detailed information about Andorran banks please contact the Banking Association or visit the web page mentioned below.

ASSOCIATION DES BANQUES ANDORRANES – ABA (http://www.aba.ad)
C/ Ciutat de Consuegra 16
Escala A - 2cn 4a.
Andorra la Vella
Tel. : (00 376) 866 845 or (00 376) 824 955
Fax : (00 376) 866 847

Winter Office Hours : Monday to Friday from 9:00 to 13:00 and from 15:00 to 19:00;
Summer Office Hours: Monday to Friday from 8:00 to 15:00

LIST OF BANKS:

Banc Agricol i comercial d'Andorra
http://www.banc-agricol.ad
Av. fiter i Rossell, 4 bis
Escaldes Engordany
Tel: 00 376 873 345 Fax: 00 376 873 350 E-mail: internacional@banc-agricol.ad

Banc Internacional i Banca Mora - (http://www.bibm.ad)
Av. Meritxell, 96 (Andorra la Vella)
Tel: 00 376 884 488 Fax: 00 376 884 499 E-mail: bibm@bibm.ad

Banca Privada d'Andorra - (http://www.bpa.ad)
Av. Carlemany, 119 (Escaldes-engordany)
Tel: 00 376 873500 Fax: 00 376 873 517 E-mail: bpa@bpa.ad
Banca Reig
Av. Meritxell, 79 (Andorra la Vella)
Tel: 00 376 872 872 Fax: 00 376 872 875

Banc Sabadell d'Andorra - (http://www.bsa.ad)
Av. del Fener, 7 (Andorra la Vella)

Tel: 00 376 735 600 Fax: 00 376 735 601 E-mail: info@bsa.ad

Caixabank - (http://www. caixabank.ad)
Plaça Rebés, 3 (Andorra la Vella)
Tel: 00 376 874 874 Fax: 00 376 862 762 E-mail: info@caixabank.ad

Crèdit Andorrà - (http://www.creditandorra.ad)
Av. Meritxell, 80 (Andorra la Vella)
Tel: 00 376 888 035 Fax: 00 376 888 881
http://www.andorraonline.ad/pages/bancs/bancs.

RESIDENT STATUS IN ANDORRA

There are two main categories of residence in the Principality of Andorra :

- Active residence, i.e. the residence status granted to people wishing to work in Andorra and already having an employment contract.

- Passive residence , i.e. the residence status granted to people wishing to live in Andorra without carrying out professional or gainful activities.

WORKING IN ANDORRA

The indispensable condition for obtaining a residence permit in Andorra as an employee is to have found a job.

Job offers in the Andorran market can be found in the local newspapers or in EURES, the European research service.

Daily newspapers :

Diari d'Andorra (http://www.DiariAndorra.ad)
C/ Bonaventura Riberaygua 39 4art.
Andorra la Vella
Tel. : (00 376) 863 700
Fax : (00376) 863 800

El Periòdic d'Andorra (http://www.elperiodico.es)
Andorrana de Publicació
C/ Sant Salvador 10
Andorra la Vella

Weekly magazines :

7 Dies
C/ Bonaventura Riberaygua 39 4art.
Andorra la Vella
Tel. : (00 376) 863 700
Fax : (00 376) 863 800

Informacions
C/ de la Unió 2, 3°pis
Andorra la Vella
Tel. :(00376) 821 134
Fax : (00 376) 860 839
Monthly magazines :

Actual
Av. Princeps Benlloch 68
Andorra la Vella
Tel. : (00 376) 865 776
Fax : (00 376) 867 771

Andorra Magazine
C/ Verge del Pilar 5 3er pl. Desp. 12
Andorra la Vella
Tel. : (00 376) 867888
Fax : (00 376) 867887

EURES
European Commission
DG Employment and Social Affairs- EURES Service
Rue Joseph II, 27
1040 Brussels
E mail : http://www.europa.eu.int/comm/dg05/elm/eures/fr/indexfr.htm

If you have found employment you must register with the Immigration Service at the Department of the Interior in order to legalise your stay in the Principality.
Different documents will be required for your dossier, depending on the type of employment contract signed.

1) If you have a contract for seasonal work :

- The following documents are required for the authorisation of your stay and permission to carry out temporary work :
- Certificate of good character
- Original and photocopy of your current passport or identity card
- Certified copy from the Civil Registry Office and marriage certificate
- Rental agreement, ownership deed or evidence of accommodation and living conditions
- Three passport photos
- Curriculum vitae and a certified copy of a document confirming your occupation.

2) If you have an employment contract for an indefinite period :

Work permits are valid for 6 months and can be renewed for 1 year.
The following documents are required for the authorisation of your stay and permission

to work :

- Certificate of good conduct
- Original and photocopy of your current passport or identity card
- Certified copy from the Civil Registry Office and marriage certificate
- Rental agreement, ownership deed or evidence of accommodation and living conditions
- Three passport photos
- Curriculum vitae and a certified copy of a document confirming your occupation

3) If you are on temporary assignment in Andorra on behalf of a foreign company :

These permits concern temporary foreign workers in Andorra who are on a mission for a foreign company under contract with an Andorran company. Maximum validity is 6 months.

You will need to submit the following documents when registering :

- Certificate of good character
- Original and photocopy of your current passport or identity card
- Certified copy from the Civil Registry Office and marriage certificate
- Rental agreement, ownership deed or evidence of accommodation and living conditions
- Three passport photos
- Document confirming that you are insured with your Regional Health Board.

4) Conditions for the issue of a permit to carry out a profession :

- In the Principality of Andorra a profession is deemed to be any occupational activity requiring a specialised qualification satisfying the criteria of the relevant professional association.

- If there are no Andorran qualifications for a particular specialisation the Andorran authorities will recognise the diplomas issued in the neighbouring countries, i.e. France and Spain.
Diplomas issued by specialised educational centres in other countries may also be recognised in Andorra if they will be accepted in France or Spain or if the holder has his/her diploma validated by the Andorran authorities.

- In principle, a foreign national wishing to exercise a profession independently must have lived in the Principality of Andorra for 20 consecutive years. The Government may adapt this condition depending on the needs of the Principality's labour market.

- People employed in a profession but having signed an employment contract will be deemed to be employees whose status is regulated under the heading « employees».

The permit to exercise a profession remains valid for 10 years, if the nature of the work does not justify a shorter period. Renewed permits remain valid indefinitely. If a request fo renewal is turned down, the person concerned may continue in his/her profession for a period of 2 years to enable him/her to put an end to his/her activities.

DAILY LIFE IN ANDORRA

HOUSING

Please contact the relevant Association to obtain information about estate agents in the Principality of Andorra.

Association of Estate Agents in the Principality of Andorra - AGIA -(http://www.agia.ad)
-Sant Salvador, 7
Despatx 45
Andorra la Vella
Principality of Andorra
Tel. and fax : (00 376) 826 142
Office Hours : 9:30 to 13:00 and 15:30 to 19:30

1) If you wish to rent a house or apartment :

- Urban residential properties must have been approved for human habitation; tenants may demand the relevant certificate. The number of people living in the property must not exceed the maximum number mentioned in the certificate.

- Rental agreements run for a minimum of three years, except if the tenant is a resident holding a residence permit for less than that period. If so, the maximum duration of the rental agreement must not exceed the validity of the residence permit.

- In principle a security is required, which may not exceed three months' rent.

- If the rented accomodation is furnished or if special fixtures have been installed these should be listed in an appendix to the contract.

- The tenant may unilaterally cancel the rental agreement prior to the end of the agreed period. If he does, he must compensate the owner by paying the equivalent of one month's rent for each year he had agreed to stay.

- A review of the rent may only be carried out once a year when the contract is renewed; such a review must be based on changes in the general index of consumer prices.

- On termination of the rental agreement the tenant must leave his accomodation in the state it was in on the day when the contract was signed.

2) If you wish to buy land, a house or an apartment :

- Under Andorran law foreign nationals may buy land in the Principality not exceeding an area of 1000 m2, on which they may build an individual house or other accomodation, which must not occupy more than 33% of the land.
- In addition, a decree of the General Council of 8 July 1965 authorises the purchase of apartments in the Principality by non-nationals.
- Before buying it is advisable to enquire from the government of Andorra if the property you have chosen may be sold
- Each purchase of a property, a building or land by a foreigner must be authorised by the government of the Principality of Andorra. It is therefore necessary to make a request to the Andorran government; the request must be accompanied by a file containing the exact data of the property - -size, area, plan, etc.
- The government will study the request and, if approved, will publish a decree authorising the purchase. The price of the certificate of purchase is 15 975 pesetas (approx. 92.23 euros).
- The prospective buyer must submit the decree to a notary in the Principality for the purpose of registering the acquired property. Registration must take place in the presence of the seller.
- Finally, the new owner must inform the parish (administrative division) where the transaction took place of the event and pay the local taxes.

IMPORTING A MOTOR VEHICLE IN ANDORRA

- Anyone wishing to import a motor vehicle in Andorra must submit an Administrative Importation Document (DUA) and the original invoice of the vehicle to Andorran customs.

- In case of a second-hand vehicle the Traffic Division of the Department of Economy of the Principality must be asked for an estimate of the value of the vehicle.

- Owners of vehicles put on the road in Andorra must pay the IMI – Indirect tax on merchandise, which amounts to 7% of the value of the vehicle.

- People residing in Andorra are not allowed to import vehicles of more than 3 years old. Exceptionally, someone intending to take up residence in Andorra may be allowed to import a vehicle not older than 5 years in the Principality of Andorra.

REGISTRATION OF VEHICLES

1) Conditions

- You must have been resident in the Principality of Andorra for at least 6 months. If you have been resident in Andorra for more than a year and own a vehicle you must register it and obtain Andorran registration plates.

- A dossier containing the documents indicated below must be submitted to the Motor Vehicle Division of the Government of the Principality of Andorra - C/ Prat de la Creu 62 64 - ANDORRA LA VELLA Telephone (00 376) 87 57 00. (http://www.tramits.ad)

2) Required Documents

- Passport

- Residence Certificate

- Original invoice of the vehicle

- Documentary evidence that the owner has submitted the vehicle to a technical inspection by the Motor Vehicle Technical Inspectorate - Carretera d'Os - Edf. Govern - Aixovall – (00 376) 841 666 - Office Hours 9:00-13:00 and 15:00-17:00.

- A motor insurance policy with an insurance company in the Principality of Andorra (please contact the Chamber of Commerce, Industry and Services for a list of addresses : -ccis@correu.andorra.ad)

- Technical Certificate of the vehicle

3) Steps to be taken

- Insure your car. Your insurance agent will tell you what to do to pass the technical inspection.

- Submit all documents to the Motor Vehicle Division of the Government of Andorra, who will give you the documents for your car - carta groga – (yellow card = grey card).

- Buy a tax certificate. Its price varies depending on your car's power and its consumption of diesel or petrol.

- The registration plates are available from the Automobil Club of Andorra - Carrer Babot -Camp 13 - ANDORRA LA VELLA - Telephone (00 376) 820 890 -. They cost 4,650 pesetas -(approx. 28.01 euros).

EDUCATIONAL SYSTEM IN ANDORRA

http://www.netdays99.ad

- The Andorran educational system is pluralistic. It consists of an Andorran system, a Spanish system, a French system and a private English system (Elians).There is also a church-controlled system that neither financially nor institutionally depends on the Spanish system (it is financed by the Andorran state), but offers the same educational programme.

-School attendance amounts to 100%, as education in three of the systems - Andorran, Spanish and French - is compulsory and free until the age of 16. Only the private English school charges fees.

- The educational system has three distinct levels : kindergarten, primary school and secondary school (comprehensive and grammar school).

- The educational system also contains a special branch for vocational training, specialised education and adult education.
There is also an infrastructure in place for higher education. (A training college for nurses, a college for information technology, and the Virtual University of Andorra.)

1) See here for a list of schools:

Vocational and higher education
Pre-school, primary and secondary education

2) School holidays 1999-2000

- **Beginning of the school year** : 12 September 2000

- **All Saints**: from Saturday 28 October to Sunday 5 November 2000 (both dates included).

- **Armistice Day** (Only observed in the French system) : 11 November 2000.

- **Immaculate Conception**: Friday 8 December.

- **Christmas** : from Saturday 23 December 2000 to Sunday 7 January 2001 (both dates included).

- **Mardi Gras** : from Saturday 24 February 2001 to Sunday 4 March 2001 (both dates included).

- **Constitution Day**: Wednesday 14 March 2001.

- **Easter** : from Saturday 7 April 2001 to Sunday 22 April 2001 (both dates included).

- **Labour Day** : Tuesday 1 May 2001.

- **Whitsun** : Monday 4 June 2001

- **End of the school year** : Saturday 30 June 2001.

In addition another holiday will be determined independently by each of the educational systems.

Each school also celebrates the feast day of its parish - parròquia -.

3) Free courses in Catalan

Adult education includes a programme for free courses in Catalan, dealing with both the spoken and the written language and enabling participants to improve their knowledge of Andorran culture and the country's social and political background.
This programme facilitates the integration of new residents in the Principality of Andorra.

The courses in Catalan are given during the equivalent of one school year, i.e. from September to January or from March to June. They are available in all the parishes of the Principality and are taught by qualified teachers. Students should enrol at the Department in charge :

Department of Education, Youth and Sport
Avinguda Meritxell, 80. Edifici Crédit Center
Andorra la Vella
Tel. : (00 376) 866 585

Office Hours: from 9:00 to 17:30.

CULTURAL PROJECTS IN THE PRINCIPALITY

If you are planning a cultural project in the Principality of Andorra, and if you need support to realise it, do not hesitate to contact us !

To facilitate the realisation of your project, please find below information about some public and private bodies in the Principality linked to the world of culture.

Museums, exhibitions, art galleries, conference halls, and other essential information to acquaint yourself with the cultural infrastructures and the cultural programme of the Principality.

http://www.andorraonline.ad/pages/cultura/cultura.htm

PRESENTATION OF ANDORRA ABROAD

Diplomatic missions of the Principality of Andorra abroad

- Embassy of the Principality of Andorra in Brussels (covering the Benelux, Germany and Denmark) : http://www.andorra.be
10, rue de la Montagne

1000 Brussels
Tel. : (0032) 2 513 28 06
Fax : (00 32) 2 513 07 41
E-mail: ambassade@andorra.be
Office Hours: 9:00 to 17:30

- Andorran Mission to the EU: http://www.andorra.be
10, rue de la Montagne
1000 Brussels
Tel. : (0032) 2 513 28 06
Fax : (00 32) 2 513 07 41
E-mail: ambassade@andorra.be
Office Hours: 9:00 to 17:30

- Embassy of the Principality of Andorra in France : http://www.amb-andorre.fr
30, rue d'Astorg
75008 PARIS
Tél. : (00 33) 1 40 06 03 30
Fax : (00 33) 1 40 06 03 64
E-mail : ambaixada@andorra.ad
Office Hours: 9:00 to 17:30

- Permanent Delegation of Andorra to UNESCO
30, rue d'Astorg
75008 PARIS
Tel. : (00 33) 1 40 06 03 30
Fax : (00 33) 1 40 06 03 64
E-mail : ambaixada@andorra.ad
Office Hours: 9:00 to 17:30

- Representation of Andorra to the Council of Europe
Bureau 2027
Palais de l'Europe
67075 Strasbourg
Tel. : (00 33) 3 88 41 29 62
Fax : (0033) 3 88 41 37 50
E-mail: rpand@andorra.ad
Office Hours: 9:00 to 17:30

- Embassy of the Principality of Andorra to Spain, Switzerland, the United Kingdom and Finland
Embajada del Principado de Andorra
C/ Alcalà, 73
28001 Madrid
Tel. 91 431 74 53/91 431 78 35
Fax 91 577 63 41
E-mail: ambaixada@emb-principado-andorra.es
Office Hours: 9:00 to 14:00 and 16:00 to 19:00

- Mission of Andorra to the United Nations, Embassy of Andorra to the United States and Canada
Permanent Mission of Andorra to the United Nations
Two, United Nations Plaza 25th floor New York. NY 10017
Tel. : (00 1 212) 750 80 64
Fax : (00 1 212) 750 66 30
E-mail : andorra@un.int
Office Hours: 9:00 to 17:30

- Ministry of Foreign Affairs and non resident Embassies (covering OSCE, Austria, Greece, Italy, Morocco, Holly See, Ireland, Portugal, Sweden, Iceland and Norway)
C/ Prat de la Creu 62-64
Andorra la Vella
Tél: 00 376 875704
Fax: 00 376 869559
E-Mail: epalacios.gov@andorra.ad
Office Hours: 9h00 to 17h30

ANDORRAN MEMBERSHIP OF INTERNATIONAL ORGANISATIONS

Permanent International Association of Road Conferences 17/11/1989
International Association of Francophone Parliaments 1988
Work Community of the Pyrenees - CPT- 04/11/1993
International Red Cross 02/05/1994
CNUCED (http://www.unicc.org/unctad) 28/07/1993
Council of Europe (http://coe.fr) 10/11/1994
Convention on the Creation of a Cooperative Customs Council 03/09/1998
EUTELSAT (http://www.eutelsat.org/) 01/12/1994
ICCROM (http://www.iccrom.org) 05/06/1998
INTERPOL 23-27/11/1987
WIPO (http://www.wipo.int) 28/10/1994
WHO (http://www.oms.ch) 15/01/2003
World Tourism Organisation (http://www.world-tourism.org) 10/05/1996
UN (http://www.un.org/) 28/07/1993
OSCE (http://www.osce.org) 25/04/1996
UNESCO (http://www.unesco.org) 20/10/1996
UNICEF (http://www.unicef.org) 28/07/1993
ITU (http://www.itu.int) 12/11/1993
Instrument for Amending the ITU Constitution and Convention 1992 08/10/1998
Conference of ITU Plenipotentiaries - Kyoto 1994 08/10/1998
Interparliamentary Union 16/02/1995
ICAO - International Civil Aviation Organisation, or "Chicago Convention" - 19/01/2001

Council of Europe (http://coe.fr)	signed	ratified

- Adhesion to the Statutes of the Council of Europe	10/11/1994	10/11/1994
- European Cultural Convention	10/11/1994	22/11/1995
- Convention for the Protection of Human Rights and Fundamental Liberties	10/11/1994	22/12/1995
Protocol 11	10/11/1994	02/11/1995
Protocol 6	22/11/1995	
- Convention for the Prevention of Torture	28/10/1996	01/05/2003
Protocol no.1	04/11/1999	
Protocol no.2	04/11/1999	
- European Convention for the Protection of our Archeological Heritage	14/05/1998	27/12/1998
- General Agreement on Privileges and Immunities	08/10/1998	24/11/1998
- Additional Protocol to the General Agreement on Privileges	08/10/1998	24/11/1998
- Sixth Additional Protocol to the General Agreement on Privileges	08/10/1998	25/12/1998
- European Agreement concerning People Participating in the Procedures of the European Tribunal of Human Rights	08/10/1998	01/01/1999
- European Centre for Living Languages	02/02/1996	
- Convention on the Transfer of Convicted Criminals	04/11/1999	
- Convention concerning Money Laundering, the Discovery, Seizure and Confiscation of Products of Crime	22/04/1999	
- European Convention for the Protection of our Architectural Heritage	22/04/1999	
- European Convention on Extradition	11/05/2000	13/10/2000
- Additional Protocol European Convention on extradition	11/05/2000	13/10/2000

Convention on the conservation of European wildlife and Natural Habitats date	11/05/2000	13/10/2000
-European social Charter	04/11/2000	
WHO (http://www.oms.ch)		
- Basic Agreement between the WHO and the Government of Andorra	28/10/1996	15/01/2003
- Acceptance of the two amendments art. 24 and 25 of the constitution of the WHO.	04/01/1998	
World Tourism Organisation (http://www.world-tourism.org)		
- Administrative Convention for the Establishment of an Institution to Promote Quality and Effectiveness in Tourism Education and Schooling	03/06/1998	
UN (http://www.un.org/)		
- Convention on Children's Rights	22/11/1995	02/02/1996
- Convention on the Elimination of Discrimination towards Women	28/10/1996	14/02/2003
- Treaty for the Non-Proliferation of Nuclear Weapons	25/04/1996	
- Convention against the Illegal Traffic in Drugs and Narcotic Substances	22/04/1999	
- Convention against the use of Antipersonnel Mines	14/05/1998	01/03/1999
Agreements deposited with the UN		
- Convention of Vienna on Consular Relations	02/08/1996	
- Convention of Vienna on Diplomatic Relations	02/08/1996	

- AETR - Transport	12/08/2003	
- Convention of Good Neighbourship between Andorra France and Spain	3/06/1993	01/07/1993
WCO (World Customs Organisation)		
- ATA Customs Convention + appendixes	02/09/1998	02/12/1998
- Convention concerning Temporary Admission (Conv. of Istanbul)	02/09/1998	02/12/1998
EU (http://www.europa.eu.int)		
- Trade Agreement including a Customs Union for the products of 25 to 97 of the SH (JO L374-31/12/1990)	28/06/1990	01/07/1991
- Protocol of Agreement in the form of an Exchange of Letters with the EEC (free market)	16/10/1996	01/12/1996
- Protocol on Veterinary Issues	15/05/2003	01/03/1998
UNESCO (http://www.unesco.org)		
-Convention for the Protection of our Heritage in Case of Armed Conflict	1954	
-International Copyright Convention	31/12/1952	
-Protocol 2 annexed to the International Copyright Convention concerning the Works of Certain International Organisations	31/12/1952	
-Protocol 1 annexed to the International Copyright Convention concerning the Application of this Convention to Works by Refugees and Displaced Persons	22/01/1953	
-Convention for the Protection of our Cultural and Natural Heritage	03/01/2003	03/04/2003

-Adhesion to the Statutes of the International Study Centre for the Conservation and Restoration of Cultural Objects ICCROM	16/03/1998	
OTHERS		
-Convention of The Hague	12/05/1996	31/12/1996
-Convention for the Creation of an International Bureau for Epizootic Diseases	28/10/1996	03/01/2003
-Appendix to the Convention	03/01/2003	
-Cooperative Arrangement for keeping Roads Accessible in Winter	16/12/1996	
-Protocol of Entente between the Government of Canada and Andorra	04/12/1996	
-Hispano-Andorran Convention on Educational Matters	11/01/1993	
-Convention between the Government of the Principality of Andorra and the French Government on Educational Matters	19/03/1993	19/04/1993
-Cooperative Agreement between the French and Andorran Governments concerning the Cross-Frontier Transport of Waste	05/11/1996	
-Convention on Social Security between the Portuguese Republic and Andorra	11/03/1988	
-Arrangement concerning the Coordination of French and Andorran Social Security Provisions	09/06/1970	
-Convention with France on the Recognition of Diplomas	08/10/1996	18/05/2003
-Convention with Spain on the Recognition of Diplomas	09/10/1995	
-Convention about Children protection and cooperation relating to International Adoption	28/10/1996	
-Agreement between Letland and Andorra about the	21/05/1998	

Suppression of Visas		
-Agreement between the Principality of Andorra and the Kingdom of Morocco concerning Assistance to Detainees and Convicted Criminals	30/09/1999	
-Agreement between the Principality of Andorra and Portugal concerning international transport of persons and goods	08/11/2000	
-Cooperative convention between Portugal and the Principality of Andorra in the field of education	08/11/2000	
-Agreement between the Principality of Andorra and France concerning international transport of goods	03/11/2000	
-Protocol of Entente between the Andorran and the USA Governments about exchange programme "Fulbright"	29/11/2000	
-Trilateral Conventions between France, Spain and the Principality of Andorra concerning the circulation and the residence in the Principality of other States citizens, and entry, circulation, residence and settling of their own citizens	04/12/2000	
-Social Security Convention between the Principality of Andorra and France	12/12/2000	
-Safeguards Agreement, Small Quantities Protocol and Model Protocol Additional to the Safeguards Agreement with the International Atomic Energy Agency	09/01/2001	
-Convention between the Government of the Principality of Andorra and the French Government on administrative cooperation	15/02/2001	

TRAVELING TO ANDORRA

ANDORRA FOR TOURISTS

Andorra offers you a large variety of activities for your holidays, 3000 shops with a very wide range of goods, a thermal centre where you can relax, mini-golf, trekking, excursions, mountaineering, an ice-rink.

The country's medieval history has left marvellous traces, including more than thirty churches and monuments ! Andorra also offers historical tours, visits to picturesque sites ...and you can combine this programme with very intresting cultural events ! ! !

All information for a successful and enjoyable stay is available from the Tourist Office

- Andorran Tourist Office in Brussels
10, rue de la montagne
1000 Brussels
Telephone : (00 32) 2 502 12 11
Fax : (00 32) 2 513 39 34

Office hours: Monday to Friday from 9:00 to 17:30

Manager : Mr Serge de BEHR

E-mail address: tourisme@andorra.be

US STATE DEPARTMENT SUGGESTIONS FOR SPAIN AND ANDORRA

COUNTRY DESCRIPTIONS: Spain and Andorra are both highly developed and stable democracies with modern economies. Additional information may be obtained from the Tourist Office of Spain, telephone (212) 265-8822

Entry Requirements: A passport is required. A visa is not required for tourist or business stays of up to 90 days. For further information concerning entry requirements for Spain, travelers should contact the Embassy of Spain at 2375 Pennsylvania Avenue N.W., Washington, D.C. 20037, telephone (202) 728-2330, or the nearest Spanish consulate in Boston, Chicago, Houston, Los Angeles, Miami, New Orleans, New York, San Francisco, or San Juan. Further information on Andorra should be obtained from the Andorran Mission to the U.N., 2 U.N. Plaza, 25th Floor, New York, N.Y. 10018, telephone (212) 750-8064.

MEDICAL FACILITIES: Good medical care is available. U.S. medical insurance is not always valid outside the United States. Serious medical problems requiring hospitalization and/or medical evacuation to the United States can cost from approximately 200 dollars a day to 10,000 dollars to 40,000 dollars or more.

MEDICAL INSURANCE: Doctors and hospitals often expect immediate payment for health services, and U.S. medical insurance is not always valid outside the United States. U.S. Medicare and Medicaid programs do not provide payment for medical services outside the United States. Please check with your insurance company to confirm whether your policy applies overseas, including provision for medical evacuation. Please ascertain whether payment will be made to the overseas hospital or doctor or whether you will be reimbursed later for expenses that you incur. Some insurance policies also include coverage for psychiatric treatment and for disposition of remains in the event of death. Useful information on medical emergencies abroad, including overseas insurance programs, is provided in the Department of State, Bureau of Consular Affairs brochure *Medical Information for Americans Traveling Abroad*, available via the Bureau of Consular Affairs home page (http://travel.state.gov) or autofax service at (202) 647-3000.

OTHER HEALTH INFORMATION: Information on vaccinations and other health precautions may be obtained from the Centers for Disease Control and Prevention's international travelers hotline at 1-877-FYI-TRIP (1-877-394-8747); fax: 1-888-CDC-FAXX (1-888-232-3299), or by visiting the CDC Internet home page at http://www.cdc.gov.

CRIME INFORMATION: While most of Spain has a low rate of violent crime, the principal tourist areas are experiencing increasing crime directed against tourists. Madrid and Barcelona, in particular, have reported a growing incidence of muggings by gangs brandishing weapons and/or using force. Travelers using public transportation should be alert to the potential for muggings or pickpocketings. Crimes such as pickpocketing, robbery, and theft from cars are frequent, and scams are often employed.

For example, thieves often attempt to distract their victims by squirting mustard on their clothing, asking for directions on the street, or otherwise diverting attention from an accomplice. Thefts of small items like radios, luggage, cameras or briefcases from parked cars are a common problem. Roadside thieves posing as "Good Samaritans" to persons experiencing car and tire problems typically attempt to divert the driver's attention by pointing out a mechanical problem, and then steal items from the vehicle while the driver is looking elsewhere. Drivers should be extremely cautious about accepting help from anyone other than a uniformed Spanish police officer or Civil Guard. Travelers who accept unofficial assistance are advised to protect their valuables by keeping them in sight or locking them in the vehicle. Andorra has a low rate of crime.

Travelers are urged to keep a photocopy of their passport, driver's license, train or airline tickets, and credit cards in a safe place to facilitate replacement should these items become lost or stolen. The loss or theft abroad of a U.S. passport should be reported immediately to the local police and the nearest U.S. embassy or consulate. U.S. citizens may refer to the Department of State's pamphlet *A Safe Trip Abroad* for ways to promote a more trouble-free journey. It is available from the Superintendent of Documents, U.S. Government Printing Office, Washington, D.C. 20402, or on the Bureau of Consular Affairs home page at http://travel.state.gov.

SAFETY/SECURITY: The ETA Basque terrorist organization remains active in Spain. ETA efforts have historically been directed against police, military, and other Spanish government targets. On November 27, 1999, ETA announced the end of the fourteen-month cease-fire, stating that after December 3, ETA would tell its commandos when to begin to carry out actions. In 1999, a smaller Marxist group, GRAPO, mounted several attacks resulting only in minor property damage. Americans have not specifically been targets of the attacks of either of these groups. In summer 1996, several small, homemade bombs exploded in areas frequented by tourists, including a bus station, regional airport, water amusement park and tourist hotels. In most cases, the size and location of the bombs indicate that they were not meant to cause serious injury, but rather to frighten the throngs of summer tourists visiting Spanish monuments and resorts. However, in one incident, several tourists were injured. These anti-tourism attacks had occurred every summer for the past several years prior to the cease-fire.

TRAFFIC SAFETY AND ROAD CONDITIONS: While in a foreign country, U.S. citizens may encounter road conditions which differ significantly from those in the United States. The information below concerning Spain is provided for general reference only, and may not be totally accurate in a particular location or circumstance.
Safety of Public Transportation: Good
Urban Road Conditions/Maintenance: Excellent
Rural Road Conditions/Maintenance: Good
Availability of Roadside Assistance: Good

Traffic in Madrid and Barcelona is faster-paced than in U.S. cities. Night driving on Fridays and Saturdays in urban areas may be dangerous due to drivers under the influence of alcohol. Night driving in isolated rural areas can be dangerous because of farm animals and poorly marked roads. Traffic is usually heavier in July and August, as well as during the Christmas and Easter seasons.

Public transportation in large cities is generally excellent. Taxi services are relatively inexpensive, although taxi drivers occasionally overcharge tourists coming from the airport. Travelers are advised to use registered cabs only.

AVIATION SAFETY OVERSIGHT: The U.S. Federal Aviation Administration (FAA) has assessed the Government of Spain's Civil Aviation Authority as Category 1 -- in compliance with international aviation safety standards for oversight of Spain's air carrier operations. For further information, travelers may contact the Department of Transportation within the U.S. at telephone 1-800-322-7873, or visit the FAA's Internet web site at http://www.faa.gov/avr/iasa.htm. The U.S. Department of Defense (DOD) separately assesses some foreign air carriers for suitability as official providers of air services. For information regarding the DOD policy on specific carriers, travelers may contact the DOD at telephone 618-256-4801.

CUSTOMS REGULATIONS: Spain's customs authorities encourage the use of an ATA (Admission Temporaire/Temporary Admission) Carnet for the temporary admission of professional equipment, commercial samples, and/or goods for exhibitions and fair purposes. ATA Carnet Headquarters, located at the U.S. Council for International Business, 1212 Avenue of the Americas, New York, N.Y. 10036, issues and guarantees the ATA Carnet in the United States. For additional information, please call (212) 354-4480, or send an e-mail to atacarnet@uscib.org, or visit http://www.uscib.org for details.

It is advisable to contact the Embassy of Spain in Washington, D.C. or one of Spain's consulates in the United States for specific information regarding customs requirements.

This is especially important if you are attempting to send any medications to Spain through postal channels.

CRIMINAL PENALTIES: While in a foreign country, a U.S. citizen is subject to that country's laws and regulations, which sometimes differ significantly from those in the United States and may not afford the protections available to the individual under U.S. law. Penalties for breaking the law can be more severe than in the United States for similar offenses. Persons violating Spanish law, even unknowingly, may be expelled, arrested or imprisoned. Penalties for possession, use, or trafficking of illegal drugs in Spain are strict, and convicted offenders can expect jail sentences and fines.

REGISTRATION/EMBASSY AND CONSULATE LOCATIONS: Americans living in or visiting Spain or Andorra for more than a few weeks are encouraged to register at the Consular Section of the U.S. Embassy in Madrid or at the U.S. Consulate General in Barcelona where they may obtain updated information on travel and security within Spain or Andorra. The U.S. Embassy in Madrid, Spain is located at Serrano 75; telephone (34)(91) 587-2200, and fax (34)(91) 587-2303. U.S. citizens who register in the Consular Section at the U.S. Embassy or Consulate listed below can obtain updated information on travel and security within Spain or Andorra. Additional information is also available through the U.S. Embassy's Internet home page at http://www.embusa.es/indexbis.html.

There is a U.S. Consulate in Barcelona, at Paseo Reina Elisenda 23-25; telephone (34)(93) 280-2227 and fax (34)(93) 205-5206.

There are also Consular Agencies in the following locations:

Malaga, at Centro Comercial "Las Rampas", Fase 2, Planta 1, Locales 12-G-7 and 12-G-8, Fuengirola, telephone (34)(952) 474-891 and fax (34)(952) 465-189, hours 10:00 a.m. to 1:00 p.m.;

La Coruna, at Canton Grande 16-17, telephone (34)(981) 213-233 and fax (34)(981) 222-808, hours 10:00 a.m. to 1:00 p.m.;

Las Palmas, at Edificio Arca, Calle Los Martinez de Escobar 3, Oficina 7, telephone (34)(928) 222-552 and fax (34)(928) 225-863, hours 10:00 a.m. to 1:00 p.m.;

Palma de Mallorca, Ave. Jaime III, 26 Entresuelo, 2-H-1 (97), telephone (34)(971) 725-051 and fax (34)(971) 718-755, hours 4:00 p.m. to 7:00 p.m.;

Seville, at Paseo de Las Delicias 7, telephone (34)(954) 231-885 and fax (34)(954) 232-040, hours 8:30 a.m. to 1:30 p.m.;

Valencia, at Cl. de La Paz 6-5, Local 5, telephone (34)(96)-351-6973 and fax (34)(96) 352-9565, hours 10:00 a.m. to 1:00 p.m.

For Andorra, please contact the U.S. Consulate in Barcelona.

TO ANDORRA FROM SPAIN

By plane: Airports at Barcelona (200 km. from Andorra) and Girona.

By train: From Barcelona to Puigcerdà, thereafter by bus or car to Seu d'Urgell and Andorra. From Madrid to Lleida, thereafter by car to Seu d'Urgell and Andorra.

By road: Barcelona-Andorra via Puigcerdà and Seu d'Urgell. Barcelona-Andorra via Igualada, Calaf, Ponts and Seu d'Urgell. Barcelona-Andorra via the tunnel of El Cadí. Daily bus service from Barcelona at Ronda Universidad. From Madrid daily bus service going through Zaragoza, Lérida and Seu d'Urgell.

TO ANDORRA FROM FRANCE

By plane: Airport at Toulouse-Blagnac (180 km. from Andorra).

By train: To Ax-les-Thermes, L'Hospitalet or La Tour de Carol (lines from Toulouse to Perpignan). From all three railway stations, by bus or car to Andorra.

By road: From L'Hospitalet or La Tour de Carol to Pas de la Casa (on the Andorran border). Port d'Envalira (altitude 2,407 meters, the highest pass in the Pyrenees) and thence a gradual and continuous descent to the Valleys.

VISA REGULATIONS

Passports: A valid passport is required by all except for nationals of France and Spain, providing they hold a valid ID card.

Visa: There are no visa requirements for entry into Andorra, however, the relevant regulations for France or Spain should be followed, depending on which country is transited to reach Andorra. Visitors wishing to have their passport stamped with the Andorran coat of arms should apply to the Sindicat d'Initiativa in the capital.

Validity: Stays of up to 3 months are allowed without a visa.

Temporary residence: Apply in person at the Immigration Office, Edifici Rebés, C/ Joan Maragall, Andorra la Vella.

ACCOMMODATIONS

HOTELS

There are over 350 hotels and guest houses, principally catering for the summer months, although some stay open all year round. Rooms during the summer months (July to August) should be booked well in advance. Hotels (and restaurants) are registered with the Sindicat d'Initiativa and are bound to keep to the registered prices and services. Information on hotels can be obtained from the Andorran Hotel Association: Unio Hotelera de les Valls d'Andorra, Antic Carrer Major 18, Andorra la Vella, Tel: 820 625.

MOUNTAIN REFUGES

These offer cheap and basic accommodation; normally they will have one room available for visitors, and may or may not have a hearth and bunk beds. Enquire locally concerning locations and prices.

CAMPING

There are 25 campsites in Andorra, most of which are close to the main towns and well sign posted. Several have shops and other facilities. There are also facilities for caravans

RECREATION

The Principality also has the largest warm water treatment center in Europe - CALDEA. Caldea, a unique glass structure with a distinguished decor at an altitude of 1,100 m, is a water palace designed for the visitor to enjoy the pleasures, virtues and the beauty of water.

CALDEA, which covers 25,000 sq.m. and contains many plants and rocks, has a wide range of activities for relaxation, amusement and the care of the body for which no effort is required.

It is open throughout the year - in winter after skiing its facilities are most welcome, while in summer its freshness makes it ideal for resting and relaxation.

WINTER SPORTS

One of the most specific natural traits of Andorra is snow, that generous winter-long companion of the mountains which allows, thanks to well-equipped ski stations, to practice skiing as well as other winter sports in perfect snow conditions for six months out of the year.

There are several ski stations in the Principality of Andorra are, here are some of tham: Pas de la Casa-Grau Roig, Soldeu-Tarter, Arinsal, Pal and Arcalís. They all have excellent ski runs as well as other zones suitable for other winter activities or simply for rest and relaxation. Each station is well equipped with state of the art equipment that helps to facilitate the winter sporting activities.

The Andorran National Ski School (E.N.A.D.E.) which is internationally recognized as a member of the International Ski Instructors' Association (A.I.M.S.) and "Interski" offers its specialized services in the form of private or group ski classes, cross country skiing, nordic skiing and "snow garden". They have a highly qualified professional staff of a hundred and eighty instructors.

The Principality has the highest and the largest area for skiing in the Pyrenees. Its 6 stations cover 2,522 hectares and have 155 runs totalling 255 km, all in an area of only 468 sq. km. 872 snow cannons ensure that skiing is possible throughout the season, while there are 86 ski lifts and 530 professional instructors on the staff of all the stations.

THE SKI STATIONS

Arinsal, in the North-West of the country with a maximum altitude of 2,560 m, has 28 km of Alpine ski runs which can accommodate 14,000 skiers per hour, who can practice mono-skiing, snowboarding and helicopter skiing. The station has 73 snow cannons, 14 ski lifts and 60 Alpine ski instructors.

Pal, South of Arinsal, which rises to 2,358 m, and where all types of skiing like mono-skiing, snowboarding are possible, including the use of snow shoes, on 32 km of Alpine ski runs. Pal has a natural park, 218 snow cannons and 12 ski lifts with a capacity of 13,500 skiers per hour and provides 80 Alpine ski instructors.

la Rabassa, at an altitude of 2,050 m, is a cross-country skiing station with 15 km runs, equipment sale and hire facilities, snow shoe circuits and an area for children where they can toboggan, sledge and build igloos.

Ordino-Arcalís, to the North of Arinsal has 24 km of Alpine runs up to 2,600 m, 12 snow cannons and 12 ski lifts. It can accommodate 13,500 skiers per hour who have the services of 40 Alpine skiing instructors.

Pas de la Casa-Grau Roig has 88 km Alpine runs going up to 2,640 m. With 27 ski lifts, 325 snow cannons and 150 instructors, 40,615 skiers per hour can be accommodated. Monoskiing, snowboarding, sleighing and skiing at night can be practised on the floodlit Font Negre run.

Soldeu-el Tarter, has 68 km Alpine ski slopes going up to 2,560 m. The station has 21 ski lifts, 244 snow cannons and 200 Alpine ski, snowboarding, telemark... instructors. It has a capacity of 21,800 skiers per hour.

SHOPPING IN ADORRA

The Andorran commercial tradition is widely known. The competitive prices are the result of a lower tax level than other countries. Shops have become more specialized in order to offer more professionalism to the customers and this trend has converted Andorra into a universe of exclusive and original mall. Wide range of items and very competitive products may be found in jewelry, opticians, perfumeries, sports shops, antiquarians, shops of electronics, scale models, delicatessen or those dedicated to fashion clothes.

The excellent prices and outstanding quality are the hallmark of Andorra's retail trade. Some 4,000 shops endorse the commercial credit of the country.
The department stores do not close neither at midday nor on holidays, and on Sunday most of the shops do not close in the morning, and some are open in the afternoon. Everything is conceived to accommodate the customer.
Another important aspect is the agreement with the European Union on duty-free allowances that substantially extend the quantities and/or values of the duty-free products that may be purchased in Andorra and taken to the countries belonging to the EU.

The duty-free allowances

Coffee	1,000 g of coffee or 400 g of extracts
Tea	200 g of tea or 80 g of extracts
Alcohol (*)	I 1,5L of spirits over 22 proof or 3 lL of spirits and aperitifs below 22 proof, or sparkling wines 5 lL
Tobacco(*)	300 cigarettes or 150 cigars (less than 3 g a piece) or 75 cigars (more than 3 g a piece) or 400 g of pipe tobacco
Other agricultural products	Up to a value of 175 euros Persons under 15 up to a value of 90 euros without exceeding: 2,5 kg of powdered milk 3 kg of condensed milk 6 kg of fresh milk 1 kg of butter 4 kg of cheese 5 kg of sugar and sweets 5 kg of meat
Perfumes	75 ml of perfumes 375 ml of colognes
Other industrial products	Up to a value of 525 euros Persons under 15, up to a value of 270 euros

Maximum quantities and amounts per person
(*) Persons under 17 are not eligible for any duty-free allowance on these products.

When returning to the European Union from a visit to the Principality of Andorra, each person may take with him or her, without paying any customs duties or taxes, the quantities or values of products purchased in Andorra that are listed in the table above. If the limits given here are not exceeded and the products are intended for personal use, it is not necessary to declare them at the Community Customs.

The permissible quantities and values may vary according to visitor's age.
The permissible quantities of alcoholic beverages, tobacco, coffee, tea, perfumes and colognes are limited but their value is not taken into consideration. On the other hand, the permissible quantities of milk, butter, sugar and sweets and meat are also limited and their value is taken into account. For all other agricultural products (foods, beverages and tobacco) or industrial products (manufactured goods not including food), the limit is based on value alone.

All products that exceed the individual duty-free allowances must be declared at customs. The value of allowances may not be accumulated either between travelers or between agricultural and industrial products for the purpose of taking a product whose value exceeds the respective individual allowance.

Before crossing the border, request information at the Community Customs on the special limitations that may apply, particularly on animal or vegetable products, live animals, species in danger of extinction, pharmaceuticals, weapons and ammunition, work of art and collector's items, foreign currency, gold and means of payment.

MONEY

CURRENCY

Although most currencies are accepted, the main currencies in circulation are Spanish Pesetas and, to a lesser extent, French Francs. Please consult the entries for Spain and France later in this book. Currency exchange: Andorran banks and bureaux de change will exchange foreign currency.

CREDIT CARDS

Diners Club, Visa, American Express and Access/Mastercard are accepted. Check with your credit card company for details of merchant acceptability and other services which may be available.

TRAVELERS CHECKS

To avoid additional exchange rate charges, travelers are advised to take travelers checks in Spanish Pesetas, French Francs or Pounds Sterling.

CURRENCY RESTRICTIONS

There are no frontier formalities when entering the country, but French and Spanish authorities may carry out formalities on departure.

CUISINE

Traditional Andorran cooking is simple but authentic. Pork products are many and various. And then there is she shiskabob of cabbage and potatoes, chopped mushrooms or rabbit, trout fried in a pan or "truites de carreroles" (a type of mushroom omelet) or again, the great variety of "coques" (festival cakes with a whole series of names: "de canal", "masegades", "fluixa", "de vellut") or the cheeses like the ancestral "formatge de tupí". Andorra also has a very complete international cuisine to offer to the visitor.

PUBLIC HOLIDAYS

Jan 1New Year's Day, Jan 6 Epiphany, Apr 10 Good Friday.,Apr 13 Easter Monday, May 1 Labor Day, Aug 15 Assumption Day, Sep 8 National Day, Nov 1 All Saints' Day. Dec 25-26 Christmas

GOVERNMENT & PUBLIC SERVICES

MINISTRIES

Ministry of economy and territories (Ministeri d'Economia I Territori)

Department of economics (Department d'Economia)+376 875 600

Department of industry (Department d'Industria) +376 875 600

Department of territories (Department d'Ordenament Territorial) +376 875 701

Department of agriculture (Department d'Agricultura) +376 875 703

MINISTRY OF FOREIGN AFFAIRS (MINISTERI D'AFERES EXTERIORS)

Department of cooperation (Direccio d'Afers Multilaterals I Cooperacio) +376 875 704

Department of bilateral and consular affairs (Direccio d'Afers Bilaterals I Consulars) +376 875 704

Consultation on juridical questions (Area d'Afers General I Juridics) +376 875 704

MINISTRY OF JUSTICE AND INTERNAL AFFAIRS (MINISTERI DE JUSTICA I INTERIOR)

Department of internal affairs (Departament d'Interior) +376 872 080

Department of protection of citizens and emergencies (Departament de Proteccio Civil I Gestio d'Emergencies) +376 890 905

Department of work (Department de Treball) +376 872 086

PROSECUTORS

Andorra la Vella

ARMENGOL PAL, JOAN, C. de la Vall 1, +376 820 150

ARMENGOL VILA, JOAN, Carrer del Pui 20 2-1, +376 825 314

CUBERES CALL, MARIE FRANCE, C. de l'Alzinaret 2, +376 824 777

DIEZ BURGONS, HELENA, Av. Princep Benlloch 75 2-2, +376 839 039

Escaldes-Engordany

CABEZA CASAJUANA, ESTER, Ctra. dels Vilars Ed. Llenguaderes B 2-2, +376 828 486

Sant Julia

CRISTINA FERNANDEZ LOPEZ, Av. Francesc Cairat 20 1-2, +376 844 536

Les Bons

DE OLIVEA MARQUES, ISABEL MARIA, C. de Sant Roma Cs. Bordeta, +376 831 231

MINISTRY OF CULTURE (MINISTERI DE CULTURA)

Central department (Unitat d'Administracio Central) +376 875 700

Department of promotion of culture and lingustic policy (Department de Promocio Cultural I Politica Lingistica) +376 875 700

Department of culture protection (Department de Patrimoni Cultural) +376 844 141

Administrative sector (Seccio dels fons administratius) +376 868 645

MINISTRY OF FINANCE AND PUBLIC COOPERATION (MINISTERI DE FINANCES I FUNCIO PUBLICA)

Finances +376 875 700

Department of licences (Area de Tramits) 150

Department of statistics (Department d'Estadistica) +376 875 714

State administration for public affairs (Secretaria d'Estat de Funcio Publica) +376 875 700

Department of financial control (Unitat d'Intelligencia Financera) +376 806 730

Department of counteraction of corruption (Unitat de Prevencio Lluita contra la Corrupcio) +376 875 700

MINISTRY OF EDUCATION AND YOUTH (MINISTERI D'EDUCACIO I JOVENTUT)

Department of education (Departament d"Educacio) +376 743 300

Departament of cooperation with schools of Andorra (Departament d'Escola Andorrana)

Department of educational systems and international affairs (Departament de Sistemes Educatius I Relacions Internacionals) +376 743 300

Department of professional units (Departament de Formacio Professional I Serveis Escolars) +376 743 300

Department of education support (Departament de Suport a l'Ensenyament) +376 743 300

Department of higher education (Departament d'Ensenyament Superior I Recerca) +376 743 300

Department of youth (Departament de Joventut I Voluntariat) +376 829 456

MINISTRY OF HEALTH AND SOCIAL SECURITY (MINISTERI DE SALUT I BENESTAR)

Department of health (Departament de Recursos Sanitaris) +376 874 800

Department of social security (Departament de Benestar) +376 874 800

MINISTRY OF TOURISM AND ENVIRONMENT (MINISTERI DE TURISME I MEDI AMBIENT)

Department of tourism (Departament de Turisme) +376 875 702

Department of environment (Departament de Medi Ambient) +376 875 707

Department of culture protection (Departament de Patrimoni Natural) +376 875 712

TOURISM SERVICES (GOVERNMENT)

Andorra la Vella

ANDORRATOURS AGENCIA DE VIATGES, C. Joan Maragall 14, +376 872 250

OFICINA DE TURISME DE LA ROTONDA, Pl. de la Rotinda Infraestr. De servei Caseta turisme, +376 730 003

OFICINA NACIONAL DE TURISME, C. Doctor Vilanova 13 PB local-3, +376 820 214

Escaldes-Engordany

ANDORRA ALTITUDS, Av. Fiter I Rossell 73 4-1, +376 869 181

CALDEA-INUU, Parc de la Mola 10, +376 800 999

TURISME D'ESCALDES-ENGORDANY, Pl. de l'Esglesia Caseta Oficina de Turisme, +376 890 881

Arinsal

MON D'EXPERIENCIES W.W., Ctra. les Feixes 24 A5 3-2, +376 838 515

Aixovall

PATRIMONI ARTISTIC NACIONAL, Ctra. General 6 Ed. ITV, +376 844 141

Sant Julia

INFORMACIO I TURISME DE SANT JULIA, Edif. El Moli, +376 744 045

Ordino

OFICINA DE TURISME D'ORDINO, Travessia d'Ordino 8, +376 878 173

La Massana

OFICINA DE TURISME DE LA MASSANA, Pl. de les Fontetes Caseta Oficina de Turisme, +376 835 693

Canillo

OFICINA DE TURISME VALLS DE CANILLO, Pl. Carlemany Ed. Comu, +376 753 600

Encamp

PROMOCIO I TURISME D'ENCAMP, Pl. de Consell 1, +376 731 000

Pas de la Casa

PROMOCIO I TURISME PAS DE LA CASA, Av. del Consell General Infraestr. De servei Antiga Caseta Pro-turisme, +376 755 100

POLITICAL PARTIES

Andorra la Vella
PARTIT SOCIALDEMOCRATA, C. Verge del Pilar 5 3-1, +376 805 260

Escaldes-Engordany
DEMOCRATES PER ANDORRA, Ptge. Antonia Font Caminal 1 C 4-403, +376 805 777

EMBASSIES

Embassy of Spain +376 800 030

Embassy of France +376 736 700

CONSULATES

General consulate of Spain +376 800 080

Ceneral consulate of France +376 736 730

Consulate of Estonia +376 828 183

Consulate of Germany +376 874 918

Consulate of Belgium +376 386 598

Consulate of Philippines +376 863 363

Consulate of Portugal +376 805 305

Consulate of Great Britain +376 862 080

Consulate of Switzerland +376 871 330

Consulate of Ukraine +376 838 376

Consulate of Chile +376 860 370

Consulate of Russia +376 871 844

Local administrations

Comu de Canillo +376 751 036

Comu d'Encamp +376 873 200

Comu d'Ordino +376 878 100

Comu de La Massana +376 736 900

Comu d'Andorra la Vella +376 730 000

Comu de Sant Julia de Loria +376 871 700

Comu d'Escaldes-Engordany +376 890 890

Andorra Telecom 115

ELECTRIC COMPANIES

FORCES ELECTRIQUES D'ANDORRA +376 739 100

NORD ANDORRA +376 738 445

MUTUA ELECTRICA SANT JULIA DE LORIA +376 741 700

SERCENSA +376 732 103 (Encamp); +376 755 095 (Pas de la Casa)

PUBLIC ORGANIZATIONS

Institute of finances of Andorra (INAF) Institut Nacional Andorra de Finances +376 808 898

Department of patents and trademarks of Andorra +376 875 600

Trade chamber of Andorra (Cambra de Comerc, Industria I Serveis d'Andorra) +376 809 292

Department of lingustic policy (Servei de Politica Linguistica) +376 806 670

Social security agency (Caixa Andorrana de Seguretat Social, CASS) 143

Red cross of Andorra (Creu Roja Andorrana) +376 808 225

Post offices (Correus) +376 820 257 (spanish); +376 820 408 (french)

POLICE

+376 872 000 (Central);

+376 831 123 (Encamp);

+376 851 123 (Canillo);

+376 843 222 (Sant Julia);

+376 755 222 (Pas de la Casa);

+376 838 430 (La Massana)

RADIO I TELEVISIO D'ANDORRA, S.L.

RTVA, S.A., +376 873 777

RADIO NATIONAL D'ANDORRA, +376 873 777

ANDORRA TELEVISIO, +376 873 777

TOURIST OFFICES (OFICINES D'INFORMACIO I TURISME)

OFICINA NATIONAL DE TURISME +376 820 214

OFICINA DE TURISME VALLS DE CANILLO +376 753 600

OFICINA DE TURISME D'ENCAMP +376 731 000

OFICINA DE TURISME D'ENCAMP – FUNICAMP +376 834 011

OFICINA DE TURISME PAS DE LA CASA +376 755 100

OFICINA DE TURISME D'ORDINO +376 878 173

OFICINA DE TURISME DE LA MASSANA +376 835 693

OFICINA DE TURISME D'ANDORRA LA VELLA +376 873 103

SANT JULIA DE LORIA – PLACA DE LA GERMANDAT +376 744 045

SANT JULIA DE LORIA – PLACA LAUREDIA +376 744 045

OFICINA DE TURISME D'ESCALDES-ENGORDANY +376 890 881

MEDICAL SERVICES (SERVEI ANDORRA D'ATENCIO SANITARIA)

SERVEI URGENT MEDIC (SUM) 116

TRANSPORT SANITARI PROGRAMAT +376 871 116

HOSPITAL NOSTRA SENYORA DE MERITXELL +376 871 000

MEDICAL CONSULTATIONS

Anesthesiology and reanimation +376 871 984

Endoscopy +376 871 984

Cardiology +376 826 394

General surgery +376 863 019

Dermatology +376 871 100

Allergy +376 871 984

Neurology +376 871 100

Ophthalmology +376 871 100

Pediatrics +376 871 984

Pneumology +376 871 100

Psychiatry) +376 871 178; +376 826 789; +376 826 789

Psychology +376 871 178

Rheumatology +376 871 100

Traumatology +376 871 983

Urology +376 822 390

Oncology +376 871 221

FIRST MEDICAL AID SERVICES (XARXA CENTRES D'ATENCIO PRIMARIA)

Direccio Centres d'Atencio Primaria +376 871 180

Parroquia de Canillo +376 851 050

Parroquia d'Encamp +376 831 711

Parroquia d'Ordino +376 747 025

Parroquia de la Massana +376 738 400

Parroquia d'Andorra la Vella +376 808 942

Parroquia de Sant Julia de Loria +376 843 243

Parroquia d'Escaldes-Engordany

Centre d'Atencio Primaria del Pas de la Casa +376 755 370

Centre d'Atencio Primaria El Fener +376 821 955

Centre d'Atencio Primaria de Santa Coloma +376 725 636

FEDERATIONS

Federation of handball of Andorra (Federacio Andorrana de Handbol) +376 890 360

Federation of riding of Andorra (Federacio Andorrana d'Hipica) +376 890 359

Federation of judo of Andorra (Federacio Andorrana de Judo) +376 890 368

Federation of karate of Andorra (Federacio Andorrana de Karate) +376 890 369

Federation of motosport of Andorra (Federacio Motociclista d'Andorra) +376 890 370

Federation of skiing of Andorra (Federacio Andorrana de Muntanyisme) +376 890 384

Federation of swimming of Andorra (Federacio Andorrana de Natacio) +376 890 371

Federation of skating of Andorra (Federacio Andorrana de Patinage) +376 890 372

IMPORTANT TRADE AND BUSINESS CONTACTS

ACCOUNTANTS AND AUDITORS

Andorra la Vella

ACTIU 3, C. Prat de la Creu 83 PB local-1, +376 862 300

A.E.S. ASSESSORS, C. de l'Aigueta 22 1-7, +376 866 250

AFICO, S.L., C. Doctor Vilanova 9 2-A, +376 822 300

ALFA CAPITAL ASSESSORS I AUDITORS, C. Bonaventura Armengol 10 1 4-4, +376 800 480

ASSESSORS COMPTABLES N+M, Bda. del Moli 5 D 2-4, +376 818 389

AUGE GRUP, S. A., C. Pere d'Urg 10 5-7, +376 803 636

AUDITAND, C. Ciutat de Consuegra 10 3-4, +376 860 199

CARRAU GESTIO, C. Prat de la Creu 59 B 2-3L, +376 812 712

COMPTABILITAT RANKER, C. de Pau Casals 4 B 6-1, +376 827 505

COMPTA-SEGUR, Bda. del Moli 45 S2-1, +376 813 901

COMPTES CLARS, C. Prat de la Creu 96, +376 869 000

CONSULTORS I TECNICS ASSOCIATS, S.L., C. Mossen Tremosa 4 2-1, +376 862 703

DEA CONSULTORS, Bda. del Moli 45, +376 807 470

DINERPRO SOLUCIONS, C. Roc dels Escolls 8 1 4-A, +376 854 400

ECONOMISTES ASSOCIATS, C. Bonaventura Armengol 15 6-2, +376 808 075

ENLLESTIT, Av. Princep Benlloch 66 5-508, +376 823 923

INNOVA GESTORS, Av. Meritxell 128 4-B, +376 827 072

LAUCO ASSESSORS, C. Bonaventura Armengol 10, +376 860 686

MARTICELLA ASSESSORS, Av. del Fener 15 1-E, +376 814 780

OCPS AUDITORS I CONSULTORS, C. Doctor Vilanova 11 C 3-1, +376 804 111

O.T.C.A., C. Bonaventura Armengol 15 3-5, +376 861 697

SUISSA COMPTABILITAT, SL, Av. Merixell 97 1-1, +376 340 992

SUMAND, C. Pere d'Urg 10 2-8, +376 802 222

TEJERO ARNAL JOSEP MARIA, C. Ciutat de Consuegra 10 3-4, +376 860 199

VALOR AFEGIT, Comptable, Fiscal I Laboral, Bda. del Moli 5 C 1-1, +376 845 008

Escaldes-Engordany

ABC ASSESSORS I CONSULTORS, Ptge. Antonia Font Caminal 1 C 3-303, +376 805 060

ACCIA, Av. Carlemany 68 4-D404, +376 811 880

AFSI, Av. Fiter I Rossell 4 2-9, +376 868 903

ANCEI, Consultoria comptable I d'empresa, Av. Carlemany 115 5 local-9, +376 808 176

ARQUEIG GESTIO I ORGANIZACIO D'EMPRESES, Av. de les Escoles 31 B 6-11, +376 865 253

ASSESSORS ANDORRANS G&G SL, Av. Fiter I Rossell 48 5-1, +376 802 250

CLICK AND COMPTABILITAT, Av. del Pont de la Tosca 11 PB local-1, +376 876 876

DHARMA SERVEIS COMPTABLES, Av. del Fener 22 A 3-3, +376 332 813

GABINET COMPTABLE NOU PLA SL, Av. de les Escoles 9 1-1, +376 822 700

GESTIONS J.R., Av. del Pessebre 15 PB local-1, +376 806 410

ITEMS ASSESSORS, SL, C. Isabelle Sandy, 4, 3r, despatx 302, +376 727 170

PROCOMPTA, SL, C. del Parnal 2 A 6-2, +376 823 184

SERAUDIT, SL, Av. Fiter I Rossell 63, +376 867 851

TOSATTI VITORIO, C. del Parnal 2 A 6-2, +376 823 184

Encamp

ASSESORAMENTS I COMPTABILITATS JOSEP MARIA GIRIBET, Av. de Joan Marti 88 1-4, +376 834 821

Sant Julia

BONAPARTE GESTIO, C. Doctor Palau 46 PB local-2, +376 844 899

EURO COMPTABILITAT I MULTI-SERVEIS, Ctra. de la Rabassa 10 PB local, +376 844 492

RLC, Av. Verge de Canolich 124 PB local, +376 741 060

Pas de la Casa

GESTORIA BEARN, C. de Catalunya 15 1-E, +376 855 642

Ordino

GM CONSULTORS, SA, Av. del Castamanya Ed. Prat de Vilella PB local-1, +376 737 600

S I R SERVEIS INTEGRALS, C. Major 5 PB, +376 847 234

Pal

PAS DE COMPTES, Cs. 6 Urb. L'Espalmera, +376 636 183

ADVERTISMENT

14.08.2014 // By: admin // All news

Advertisment

Andorra la Vella
APOD, Antic Carrer Major 1 1, +376 869 215
BON DIA, C. Maria Pla 28 1, +376 808 888
CATTIE EUROPA, S.L., Av. del Fener 11 4-6, +376 802 050
DUETT&CO, C. Ciutat de Consuegra 10 3-2, +376 816 100
ESTUDI GRAFIC, C. Pere d'Urg 10 4-5, +376 868 720
JECOM DISSENY, C. Bonaventura Armengol 10 1 6-6, +376 806 180
NIVELL 10 PUBLICITAT, Av. del Fener 11 1-3, +376 863 336
NURIA PUBLICITAT, C. Terra Vella 22 PB, +376 860 504
PIXEL CONCERTE GRAFIC, Bda. Del Moli 5 D 2-3, +376 829 740
PUBLI REGAL, C. Bonavista 8, +376 828 575
PUBLIGEL, C. Gil Torres 61 2-2, +376 824 769
PUBLIMEDIA, Cami de la Grau 20 PB local-1, +376 720 020
R CONSULTORS, Av. Meritxell 105 5-5, +376 865 757
REFLEX PUBLICITAT, C. Prat de la Creu 8 1-103, +376 812 100
TOT STOCK, Antic Cami Ral 1 A PB local-1, A PB local-1, +376 866 003
VERONA COMUNICACIO, S.A., Av. de Salou 56 1-3B, +376 720 620
FACTORIA DE LA COMUNICACIO ANDORRA PLATO, Antic Carre Major 26 PB local, +376 869 500
OTEESE, C. Prat de la Creu 8 3-306, +376 805 400

Escaldes-Engordany
FITE + ASSOCIATS, C. dels Escalls 9 2-201, +376 807 280
NOMES 3 DIGITAL, Av. Fiter I Rossell 4, +376 864 904
PROMOCIONS PUBLICITARIES, S.A., Av. del Pont de la Tosca 7 C PB local-4, +376 803 130

La Massana
9 MARKTING, S.L., Av. de Sant Antoni 93 B PB-1, +376 839 965
STYL-AND, S.L., Av. de Sant Antoni 43 2-2, +376 835 757

Arinsal
A.L. SERVEI, Ctra. General 5 Ed. Prat de Verdu PB-B, +376 836 383

Sant Julia
AYMARA, Ctra. de Nagol 32 B PB local, +376 841 320
Encamp
PROMARTS, S.A., Av. Princep Benlloch 24 PB local, +376 732 000

- Share this story:
- Tumblr
- Pinterest
- LinkedIn
- Reddit

- Digg

PUBS

14.08.2014 // By: admin // All news

Pubs

Escaldes-Engordany
PUB CORTINHIA, C. de Sant Antoni 3 PB local-2, +376 824 653
PUB INDIANA, Av. del Pont de la Tosca 3 A PB local-1, +376 828 666
PUB POLARIS, C. de la Unio 11 C PB local, +376 826 281

Canillo
PUB LA RODA, C. Perdut Restaurant Roda, +376 852 670

Ordino
PUB XALOC, C. Major 22 PB local-1, +376 847 070

ARCHITECTS

01.10.2014 // By: admin // All news

Architects

Andorra la Vella
ADSERA GRIFE, JOSEP, C. Prat de la Creu 91 2 1-1, +376 806 365
AEPA – AGRUPACIO D'ARQUITECTES EXPERTS PERICIALS D'ANDORRA, Av. Dr. Mitjavila 3 1, +376 861 202
AIXAS ESPAR, PERE, Antic Cami Ral 1 A PB-1, +376 824 001
ALBOS COLOMBIER, MIQUEL, Bda. del Moli 9 4-4B, +376 862 861
ALBOS, ROBERT-DESPATX D'ARQUITECTURA, Av. del Fener 15 1-D, +376 868 020
BLASI PALACIN, VICTOR, C. Prat de la Creu 8 3-307, +376 865 290
CALL REIG, JULIA, Pl. Guillemo 5 1-1, +376 869 643
CARLES PUIG MONTANYA, Cami del Currubell 1 1-2, +376 800 420
CERVOS CARDONA, PERE, Arquitecte I Urbaniste, Av. Santa Coloma 89 1-2, +376 868 942
COLL CAPO, JOAN, C. de la Sardana 16, +376 819 580
COLLEGI D'ARQUITECTES D'ANDORRA, Av. Dr. Mitjavila 5 1, +376 861 202
D.A.U ARQUITECTURA I URBANISME, C. Prat de la Creu 92, +376 867 777
ESPUGA SORRIBES, PERE, C. Bonaventura Armengol 10 2 3-4, +376 802 000
ESTUDI D'ARQUITECTURA I URBANISME, PERE CERVOS, Av. Santa Coloma 89 1-2, +376 868 942
FAURA PAVIA, ELISABET, C. del Valira 2 1-1, +376 805 205
FELIPO CODINA, JOSEP MARIA, Av. Meritxell 9 5-2, +376 822 630
GRAS FERNANDEZ, CARLES, C. Doctor Molines 2 3 1-3, +376 868 075
INTEGRAL, C. Prat de la Creu 8 3-307, +376 865 290
MARTI PEDESCOLL, ROBERT, Av. del Fener 15 1-D, +376 868 020
MOLSE SAUQUET, ANTONI, Av. Dr. Mitjavila 3 5-B, +376 828 661

OROBITG, ARQUITECTURA I ENGINYERIA, C. Roc dels Escolls 8 1 2-E, +376 808 720
OROBITG JIMENEZ, JOSEP LLUIS, C. Roc dels Escolls 8 1 2-E, +376 808 720
PURROY CHICOT, JOAN ANTONI, Av. Princep Benlloch 79 S1-1, +376 820 504
REBES, FRANCESC, C. les Canals 21, +376 825 188
ROSSELL DURO, MANEL, Antic Carrer Major 10, +376 821 992
VECIANA MEMBRADO, GERARD, C. del Valira 2 1-1, +376 805 205
VICENTE SOLA, FELIX, Arquitecte I Urbaniste, C. Prat de la Creu 92, +376 807 777
VIDAL QUILEZ, JORDI, Av. Meritxell 59 1-1, +376 865 924

Escaldes Engordany
ALVAREZ RIBA, LLUIS, Pl. Creu Blanca 2, +376 862 459
DESPATX ARQUITECTURA V.NAUDI-J.SALA, C. Manuel Cerqueda Escaler 3 3-2, +376 808 345
DILME BEJARANO, ENRIC, Av. Fiter I Rossell 109 B PB-2, +376 869 558
ESTUDI D'ARQUITECTURA, C. del Parnal 4 C 1-2, +376 822 129
GIL ARQUITECTURA, C. del Parnal 10 Atic, +376 820 476
NAUDI ZAMORA, VICTOR, C. Manuel Cerqueda Escaler 3 3-2, +376 808 345
PASCAL RIERA, ESTHER, C. Josep Viladomat 38 A 6-2, +376 860 634
PUBILL ARMENGOL, JOSEP, Av. Carlemany 26 1-2, +376 826 606
SALA MOMPEL, JORDI, C. Manuel Cerqueda Escaler 3 3-2, +376 808 345
SANCHEZ FORES, LAURA, Av. de les Escoles 17 D PB-2, +376 822 664
SORIANDO VIDAL, JOSEP, Av. Carlemany 117 5-A, +376 864 949
TRAVE SIRVENT, JOSEP, C. del Parnal 10 1-3, +376 820 476
VALDES PUIG, ALFONS, C. del Parnal 4 C 1-2, +376 822 129

Anyos
ALEIX PALOU, XAVIER, X. Aleix Urb. Els Oriosos, +376 815 445

Encamp
APUNT D'ARQUITECTURA, Av. de Joan Marti 117 PB local-2, +376 817 666

La Cortinada
ARQUITECTONIA, Cap del Carrer Cs. Adellach 1, +376 850 195

Sant Julia
BATLLE JORDANA, JORDI, Av. de Rocafort 24, +376 842 600
CASAMAJOR ARQUITECTES, Ctra. de la Rabassa Ed. Caborreu Urb. Costes de Nagol 4-B, +376 841 777
GINJAUME GRATACOS, LLUIS, C. de les Escoles 24 B 1-1, +376 741 710
TALLER D'ARQUITECTURA I TECNICA SA, C. de les Escoles 24 B 1-1, +376 741 710

Sispony
LOPEZ-MATEOS MORENO, ARTURO, C. de les Agudes 24, +376 839 831

Ordino
MONTANE TOMAS JOSEP ANTONI, C. de la Grau Cs. Nova Quim, +376 837 279
ORTEU RIBA, XAVIER, Ctra. del Coll d'Ordino Ed. Prat Gran PB, +376 835 200

Canillo
NADAL I BENTADE ZAIRA, Pcta. De Sant Cerni Era Mangautxa, +376 851 095
POL I SOLE, ANTONI, Pcta. De Sant Cerni Era Mandautxa, +376 851 095

La Massana
PERINA MORENO, MOISES, Av. el Traves 28 PB-1, +376 839 183
PROJECTES NOU SOL, SL, Arquitectura I Urbanisme, Av. el Traves 28 PB-1, +376 839 183

Sta. Coloma
VILLAMAYOR ROZADOS ALBERT, C. del Cadre 5 B 2-C, +376 724 577

AUDIO VISUAL PRODUCTION

13.08.2014 // By: admin // All news

Audio visual production

Andorra la Vella
ESPAI DE MUSICA MODERNA-E.M.M., Doctor Nequi 7 1 1-D, +376 861 999
TRIPLE ACCES, S.L., Av. Santa Coloma 65 Atic-2, +376 327 991

AUTOPARTS

Andorra la Vella

AUTO PARTS R, Av. de Tarragona 47 PB local-6, +376 869 933

AUTO RALLYE, S.A., Ctra. de la Comella 41 3-301, +376 803 440

CARS CONCEPT, Cami de la Grau 21 D PB local, +376 727 228

COVIMA, S.L., Av. de Salou 56 PB local-1, +376 724 333

EURO-RECANVIS, S.L., Av. de Salou 51 1, +376 725 448

MOTOR9, Av. Santa Coloma 26 PB local-1, +376 816 999

RECANVIS S.M.A., Av. Princep Benlloch 81 PB local-2, +376 813 377

TECNOMOBIL, Ctra. de la Comella 35, +376 806 280

Sta. Coloma

CENTRAL DE RECANVIS CARROI, S.L., Cami Ral Ed. Pic de Maia Estanyo Residencial Prat Condal PB local-3, +376 722 218

ESTABLIMENTS COLL VALIRA, Av. d'Enclar 61, +376 724 563

BANKS

Andorra la Vella

ANDBANK, Pl. Rebes, 8, +376 881 800

BANCSABADELL D´ANDORRA, S.A., Av. del Fener 7 A, +376 735 600
BANCSABADELL D´ANDORRA, S.A., SERVIES CENTRALS, Av. del Fener 7 A, +376 735 600

BANCSABADELL D´ANDORRA, S.A., BANCA A DISTANCIA, Av. del Fener 7 A, +376 735 666

BANCSABADELL D´ANDORRA, S.A., BANCA PRIVADA, Av. del Fener 7 A, +376 735 610

BANCSABADELL D´ANDORRA, S.A., Av. Meritxell 85 PB local-1, +376 803 600

CREDIT ANDORRA, S.A., Av. Meritxell 80, +376 888 600

CREDIT ANDORRA, S.A., Pl. Rebes 3, +376 888 360

CREDIT ANDORRA, S.A., OFICINA BANCA EMPRESES CORPORATE, Av. Meritxell 80, +376 889 300

CREDIT ANDORRA, S.A., Area Direccio General, Av. Meritxell 80, +376 888 010

CREDIT ANDORRA, S.A., Relacions Humanes, Av. Meritxell 80, +376 888 090

CREDIT ANDORRA, S.A. , Fundacio Credit Andorra, Av. Meritxell 80, +376 888 880

CREDIT ANDORRA, S.A., Serveis Centrals, C. Bonaventura Armengol 6 2, +376 888 888

CREDIT ANDORRA, S.A., Assistencia Tecnica 24 h, C. Bonaventura Armengol 6 2, +376 888 700

MORABANC, Seu Social, Av. Meritxell 96, +376 884 488

MORABANC, TELEBANC, Av. Meritxell 96, +376 884 884

MORABANC, BANCA D'EMPRESES I COOPERATIVA, Av. Meritxell 96, +376 884 235

MORABANC, BANCA INSTUCIONAL, Av. Meritxell 96, +376 884 530

MORABANC, ANDORRA, Av. Meritxell 38, +376 884 705

MORABANC, Banca Personal Andorra la Vella, Av. Meritxell 96, +376 884 255
MORABANC, Privat Banking, Av. Meritxell 96, +376 884 255

Escaldes-Engordany

ANDBANK, SERVIES CENTRALS, C. Manuel Cerqueda Escaler 6, +376 873 333

ANDBANK, SERVIES DIGITAL, C. Manuel Cerqueda Escaler 6, +376 873 300

ANDBANK, INFORMACIO GENERAL, C. Manuel Cerqueda Escaler 6, +376 739 011

ANDBANK, OFICINA PRADA RAMON, C. Maria Pla 35, +376 881 870

CREDIT ANDORRA, S.A., OFICINA PRADA RAMON, C. Maria Pla 30 PB local, +376 888 670

CREDIT ANDORRA, S.A., Av. Carlemany 42 PB local, +376 888 200

CREDIT ANDORRA, S.A., Credit Assegurances, S.A.U., Av. Fiter i Rossell 22, +376 888 900

CREDIT ANDORRA, S.A., Vincles, C. Josep Viladomat 17, +376 888 900

MORABANC, Pl. Coprinceps 2, +376 884 505

MORABANC, Banca Personal Escaldes-Engordany, Pl. Coprinceps 2, +376 884 555

Sant Julia

ANDBANK, Av. Verge de Canolich 53, +376 881 670

BANCSABADELL D´ANDORRA, S.A., Av. Francesc Cairat 22 PB local-1, +376 742 600

CREDIT ANDORRA, S.A., Av. Verge de Canolich 55 PB local, +376 888 340

MORABANC, Ctra. De la Rabassa 2 A PB local, +376 884 835

Encamp

ANDBANK, Av. de Joan Marti 6 PB local, +376 881 820

BANCSABADELL D´ANDORRA, S.A., Av. de Joan Marti 4 PB local, +376 732 600

CREDIT ANDORRA, S.A., Pl. Del Consell 7 PB local, +376 888 400

MORABANC, Pl. Del Consell 14 2, +376 884 605

Canillo

ANDBANK, Av. Sant Joan de Caselles Hotel Font d'Argent, +376 881 940

CREDIT ANDORRA, S.A., C. Peu del Carrer Cs. Agusti PB local, +376 888 460

MORABANC, Av. Sant Joan de Caselles Cs. Sinfreu PB local, +376 884 635

Pas de la Casa

ANDBANK, C. Sant Jordi 12, +376 881 840

BANCSABADELL D´ANDORRA, S.A., C. de les Abelletes 8 1 local, +376 755 600

CREDIT ANDORRA, S.A., Av. d'Encamp 8, +376 888 440

MORABANC, C. de Catalunya 5 PB local, +376 884 655

La Massana

ANDBANK, Av. de Sant Antoni 32, +376 881 900

BANCSABADELL D´ANDORRA, S.A., Av. de Sant Antoni 41 B PB local-2, +376 738 600

CREDIT ANDORRA, S.A., Av. de Sant Antoni 34 PB local, +376 888 500

MORABANC, Av. de Sant Antoni 21 PB local, +376 884 805

Ordino

ANDBANK, Travessia d'Ordino 8 PB local-1, +376 881 920

ANDBANK Banca Privada, Travessia d'Ordino 8 PB local-1, +376 873 308

ANDBANK, Banca Privada International, Travessia d'Ordino 8 PB local-1, +376 873 345

CREDIT ANDORRA, S.A., C. Major 6, +376 888 550

MORABANC, Ctra. Del Coll d'Ordino 1 PB local-1, +376 884 785

Santa Coloma

CREDIT ANDORRA, S.A., Av. d'Enclar 53, +376 888 180

CAR DEALERS

Andorra la Vella

AUTOMOBLIS ASSISTENCIA A.C., Av. Santa Coloma 104 2-D, +376 822 522

CARS CONCEPT, Cami de la Grau 21 D PB local, +376 727 228

GARATGE SPORT, C. Verge del Pilar, 10-12, +376 809 140

HONDA AUTOMOBLIS, Av. Princep Benlloch 89, +376 821 295

JEEP-LANCIA AUTOMOBILS, Av. Princep Benlloch 89, +376 862 420

MOTORAUTO, S.L., Av. Santa Coloma 52, +376 809 100

NISSAN, C. Verge del Pilar 12, +376 809 144

SAAB, C.Verge del Pilar, 12 +376 809 144

Escaldes-Engordany

Europ-Auto, S.A., Carretera d'Engolasters, 1, Comercial +376 825 671, Administracio +376 808 840

TOYOTA, Avinguda Fiter i Rossell Num, 4, +376 828 527

Sta. Coloma

A.MERCAUTO, Av. d'Enclar 74, +376 824 242

BECIER VEHICLES, Av. d'Enclar 144, +376 871 807

SEUWAGEN, Av. Santa Coloma 85 PB local-1, +376 864 449

SCODA, Av. d'Enclar 48, +376 890 000

Andorra la Vella

ANDORRA ASSISTENCIA, Ctra. De la Comella Nau 1 Zona ind. Encorces de Can Nyerro, +376 860 366

AUTO ASSISTENCIA PACO, Nau 4 Zona ind. Terra Vella, +376 827 489

AUTOMOBILS ASSISTENCIA A.C., Av. Santa Coloma 104 2-D, +376 822 522

GEMCONS, Av. Santa Coloma 41 PB local-1, +376 803 030

GRUES ANDORRA ASSISTENCIA, Ctra. De la Comella Nau 1 Zona ind. Enclores de Can Nyerro, +376 860 366

Escaldes-Engordany

GRUALTA, S.L., C. de l'Etang-Sale Ed. Teulades 12 3-1, +376 823 166

Encamp (Les Bons)

EFI GRUES, S.L., C. de Sant Roma Cs. Abat, +376 833 443; +376 362 013

Encamp

GRUES BENJAMI, Av. De Joan Marti 44 PB local-C, +376 831 338

La Margineda

SERGRU, Ctra. De la Marginada 7, +376 722 151

Pas de la Casa

SERVEIS DRD ASSISTENCIA SAI, Av. D'Encamp 15 3-7B, +376 855 308

CLOTHES & FASHION

Andorra la Vella

AQUA-BASIC, C. Bra. Riberaygua 17, +376 869 403

ARMANI JEANS, Av. Meritxell 100, +376 872 640

BKF, C. Maria Pla 12 PB local-2, +376 867 817

BOTONS, C. la Llacuna 1, +376 824 737

CASHMERE SHOP, Av. Meritxell 90 PB local, +376 801 890

CCA-CENTRE COMERCIAL ANDORRA, Av. Meritxell 94, +376 870 310

C.D.C., C. Ciutat de Consuegra 5 PB local-3, +376 824 714

CO2, C. Doctor Nequi 7 1 PB local-3, +376 823 111

COCO BIS, Av. Meritxell 20 3 PB local, +376 804 343

DESIGUAL, Av. Meritxell 94, +376 879 340

DU PAREIL AU MEME, Av. Meritxell 12, +376 879 370

DUBTES BOUTIQUE, C. Doctor Nequi 6 PB local-7, +376 862 462

G DE GUAX, C. Bra. Riberaygua 15 PB local, +376 866 970

GALLERY, Av. Meritxell 61 PB local, +376 810 908

GANDEN, Pl. Guillemo 8, +376 868 222

GUESS, Av. Meritxell 60, +376 879 350

IKKA'S, C. de la Sardana 6, +376 868 617

JAVIER SIMORRA, C. Maria Pla 1 PB local-19, +376 865 302

JEANS CULTE, Av. Meritxell 10, +376 879 365

L B D LITLE BLACK DRESS, C. Sant Salvador 2, +376 727 272

LACOSTE, Av. Meritxell 46 PB local-1, +376 820 261

MARRECS, C. les Canals 7, +376 822 878

NOW, C. Maria Pla 1 PB local-1, +376 804 550

OPTIONS, Av. Meritxell 85, +376 760 240

OPTIONS, Av. Meritxell 87, +376 760 200

OUTLET FACTORY, Av. de Tarragona 51, +376 879 375

OUTLET POLYANNA, C. de Callaueta 4 PB local, +376 803 146

PATXOCA, C. Maria Pla 2 PB local-2, +376 863 260

POLLYANNA GRUP, C. de l'Aigueta 14 PB local-2, +376 803 140

PUNT ROMA, Av. Meritxell 114 PB local, +376 829 147

SEVENTEEN POLLYANNA, C. de Callaueta 2 PB local-1, +376 803 140

SEVENTEEN POLLANNA, Av. Carlemany 97 PB local-1, +376 803 140

SHIBORI, Av. Meritxell 100, +376 872 600

SITA MURT, C. Maria Pla 1 PB local-16, +376 816 700

SOHO, Av. Meritxell 99, +376 808 280

TOGA-BOUTIQUE, Cap del Carrer 2, +376 821 158

TU I JO, C. Doctor Nequi 1 PB local-1, +376 827 262

URBAN, Av. Meritxell 23, +376 879 300

VIA MODA, Av. Meritxell 87, +376 806 515

VIA MODA OFICINES, C. de l'Aigueta 2 4, +376 879 200

WE AR, Av. Meritxell 24, +376 879 360

ZARA, Av. Meritxell, +376 868 676

Escaldes-Engordany

012 BENETTON, Av. Carlemany 70, +376 882 440

ALCOTT, Av. Carlemany 70, +376 882 435

BUICK, Av. Carlemany 91, +376 806 975

CO2, Av. Carlemany 55 PB local-1, +376 868 811

DESIGUAL ILLA, Av. Carlemany 70, +376 882 450

DIESEL, Av. Carlemany 70, +376 882 425

G DE GUAX, Av. Carlemany 44 PB local-1, +376 828 872

G-STAR RAW, Av. Carlemany 70, +376 882 400

HUGO BOSS, Av. Carlemany 70, +376 882 410

JACK&JONES/VERO MODA, Av. Carlemany 70, +376 882 420

LACOSTE, Av. Carlemany 80 1-A7, +376 825 021

LEVI'S, Av. Carlemany 70, +376 882 430

MARINA RINALDI, Av. Carlemany 87, +376 879 380

MILS ALEIX, LLUIS, X. Cau del Sola Urb. Ermengol Serra, +376 827 816

MITGES I MITJONS UNIO, Av. Carlemany 121 PB local-B, +376 865 992

MITICS, Av. Carlemany 101, +376 806 430

NAPAPIJRI, Av. Carlemany 70, +376 882 445

PEPE JEANS, Av. Carlemany 70, +376 882 405

PICCADILLY, Av. Carlemany 46, +376 885 615

POLLYANNA DONA, Av. Carlemany 97 PB local-1, +376 803 140

POLLYANNA HOME&DONA, C. Coprincep Francois Mitterrand 2 PB local-1, +376 803 140

POLLYANNA HOME&DONA, Av. Carlemany 121 PB local-B, +376 803 140

POLLYANNA NENS, Av. Carlemany 83 PB local-2, +376 803 140

TANGO, Av. Carlemany 70, +376 882 415

TENDENCIES, Av. Carlemany 44 PB local-6, +376 827 378

TOTA TALLA, Av. Carlemany 28, +376 865 057

Pas de la Casa

ARPAS, C. Major 22, +376 739 885

D'VOTION, C. Sant Jordi 12, +376 855 065

D'VOTION, Pl. dels Coprinceps 15, +376 855 724

D'VOTION, Av. d'Encamp 23, +376 855 425

ESPRIT, C. Major 15, +376 855 691

G-STAR RAW, C. Major 16, +376 855 999

IT, C. Major 20, +376 739 850

Sant Julia

CONFETTI, Ctra. de Nagol 1 PB local, +376 842 262

MARINA MODES, Av. de Rocafort 7 PB local-12, +376 842 131

MODES KMK, C. Doctor Palau 7 PB local-2, +376 843 677

CONFECTIONERIES

Andorra la Vella

CROISSANTERIA LA CLARIANA, C. Roureda de Sansa 13 PB local, +376 866 256

FLOR I NATA, C. la Llacuna 15 PB local, +376 813 963

GRANJA I PASTISSERIA COMBI, S.L., +376 829 596

GRANJA PASTISSERIA DOLCA, Av. Princep Benlloch 27 PB local-1, +376 821 429

LA GORMANDERIA, Av. Dr. Mitjavila 28, +376 827 736

PASTISSERIA EL TORTELL, C. Ciutat de Valls 42 PB local-2, +376 821 681

PASTISSERIA EL TORTELL 3, C. Bra. Riberaygua 9 PB local-3, +376 821 095

PASTISSERIA GRANJA LA GRANDALLA, C. Doctor Nequi 3, +376 824 525

PASTISSERIA GRANJA LA LIONESA, C. de l'Aigueta 2, +376 863 509

PASTISSERIA I GRANJA REINA, Av. Princep Benlloch 78, +376 865 712

PASTISSERIA L'ESPIGA D'OR, C. Bonavista 33, +376 827 231

PASTISSERIA L'ESPIGA D'OR 2, C. Bra. Riberaygua 24, +376 823 491

PASTISSERIA L'ESPIGA D'OR 3, C. Prat de la Creu 59 PB local-3A, +376 860 336

Escaldes-Engordany

GRANJA DOLC I SALAT, Av. de les Escoles 16 PB local-2, +376 822 202

LA CASETA DE XOCOLATA, Av. Carlemany 38 PB local-1, +376 869 965

LES CALDES PASTISSERIA, Av. de les Escoles 19 PB local-2, +376 865 824

PASTISSERIA CAFETERIA FORN DE LLENYA, Av. Carlemany 45 PB local-2, +376 819 220

PASTISSERIA ENGORDANY, Av. del Pessebre 21 PB local-1, +376 823 863

PASTISSERIA ESTOPINAN, Av. Coprincep de Gaulle 6, +376 821 323

TALLER GORMAND PATRICE BERNARD, Pl. Creu Blanca 8 PB local-1, +376 822 900

La Massana

CUSI CAFÉ, Av. de Sant Antoni 52 1 PB local-2, +376 840 940

GRANJA PASTISSERIA PASQUAL I FILLS, Av. de Sant Antoni 27 PB local, +376 839 220

Ordino

FLECA FONT, C. de l'Anglada 6 S2 local, +376 847 064

Encamp

FLECA PASTIS I GRANJA L'ESPIGA, Av. Princep Benlloch 44 B PB local, +376 731 830

GRANJA PASTISSERIA FLOR DE NEU, Av. de Joan Marti 84 PB local-1, +376 832 933

GRANJA CAFETERIA XOCOLATI, Av. Princep Benlloch 12 PB local-1, +376 832 426

GRANJA SEGLE XXI, Av. de Joan Marti 74 B PB, +376 832 690

PASTISSERIA CASAL, Pl. del Consell 3 1, +376 833 000

Sta. Coloma

GRANJA BAR LA CANTONADA, Av. d'Enclar 34 PB local-1, +376 722 205

Canillo

GRANJA PASTISSERIA CAL FRANCES, Av. Sant Joan de Caselles Cs. Nova Frances PB local, +376 852 422

LES DELICIES DEL JIMMY, Av. Sant Joan de Caselles Ed. Cases PB local-1, +376 852 145

Pas de la Casa

PASTISSERIA CAMARGUESA, Av. d'Encamp 29, +376 855 256

Sant Julia

PASTISSERIA LACASA, C. Doctor Palau 42 PB local-1, +376 842 472

CONSTRUCTING COMPANIES (DEVELOPERS)

Andorra la Vella

A.C.O.D.A., C. Prat de la Creu 59 B 2-3E, +376 824 991

C.A.P.I.C.S.A., C. dels Marginets 7 4-4, +376 862 220

CERVOS I JOVE, PERE, Av. Santa Coloma 89 PB local, +376 820 183

ARDIS JOSEP NAVAS I FUILLS, C. Mossen Lluis Pujol Nau Navas PB local-1, +376 722 302

AUXINI, S.A., C. Prat de la Creu 85, +376 868 055

CONSTRUCCIONS BERGES, Av. Santa Coloma 61 2-2, +376 829 064

CONSTRUCCIONS BUJES, S.A., C. Prat de la Creu 87 1-1, +376 822 969

CONSTRUCCIONS VERDAGUER, Av. Dr. Mitjavila 85, +376 828 811

CONSTRUCCIONS EL CASTELL, Av. Santa Coloma 16 1-1, +376 828 542

CONSTRUCCIONS URCOSA, C. dels Barres 21 PB local-2, +376 720 975

CONSTRUCCIONS ENTRIMO, S.L., Bda. Del Moli 7 4 3B, +376 802 947

CONSTRUCCIONS FLORA, Antic Carrer Major 25 1-1, +376 810 970

CONSTRUCCIONS TECNON, C. Doctor Nequi 7 15-C, +376 825 479

CONSTRUCCIONS MORAIS, S.L., C. del Puial 12 2, +376 824 261

CONSTRUCCIONS PURROY, S.L., Av. Princep Benlloch 79 S1-1, +376 820 504

CONSTRUCCIONS RIO CALDO, Av. Princep Belloch 68 3-313, +376 868 498

CONSTRUCCIONS SANTIAGO ESPINO, C. dee la Closa 8 4-2, +376 866 035

CONSTRUCCIONS SEIC, C. de Callaueta 10 1-3, +376 805 620

DRAGA, S.A., Ctra. de la Comella 11, +376 871 340

EDICOM, S.A. Ctra. de la Comella 41 2-203, +376 868 680

E.M.P.U.B., C. Doctor Vilanova 9 1-D, +376 807 333

ESPAI 9 REHABILITACIO CONSTRUCCIO, Av. d'Enclar 130 PB local, +376 831 610

FIC, C. Prat de la Creu, 96 3-2, +376 805 508

GENERAL DE CONTRUCCIO I SERVEIS, Av. Carlemany 95 D 2-1, +376 808 708

LOCUB, S.A., C. Maria Pla 16 2-3, +376 808 645

MADECSA, C. Doctor Vilanova 9 PB local-B, +376 827 434

NEU I MAR S.A., C. Sant Esteve 5 PB local-1, +376 833 033

PIDASA SERVEIS, S.L., Av. d'Enclar 26 5, +376 721 445

PROMOCIONS I OBRS PIRINENQUES, S.A., Av. Meritxell, 62 5-1, +376 862 244

Escaldes-Engordany

CEVALLS, Av. Consell de la Terra 14, +376 877 900

CONSTRUCCIONS MODERNES, S.A., Av. Carlemany 117 2-B, +376 802 350

CONSTRUCCIONS VILLAVERDE, Av. del Pessebre 26 2-1, +376 806 384

CONSTRUCCIONS CARRACEDO, Av. Fiter I Rossell 70, +376 827 548

CONSTRUCCIONS IMMOBILIARIA CARRACEDO, Av. Fiter I Rossell 70 1-1, +376 822 552

COANSA, Ptge. Antonia Font Caminal 1 C 5-501, +376 811 000

CONSTRUCCIONS A.B.C., Av. de les Escoles 31 B 5-25, +376 823 099

CONSTRUCCIONS ALT MINYO, S.L., Av. del Pessebre 44 PB local-2, +376 869 960

CONSTRUCCIONS DA ROCHA, S.L., Cami d'Ensucaranes 3 PB local, +376 868 834

CONSTRUCCIONS ERNEST, Av. Fiter I Rossell 91 3-1, +376 822 654

CONSTRUCCIONS FERGON, SLU, Ed. Orri Urb. De la Planta Atic-3, +376 324 651

CONSTRUCCIONS MARINE, S.A., Parc de la Mola 8 PB local, +376 821 163

COPSA, Ptge. Antonia Font Caminal, 1 C 6, +376 877 300

GRUP HERACLES, Av. Consell de la Terra 14, +376 805 600

PROGEC, S.A., C. dels Escalls 7 PB-2, +376 805 050

Encamp

AC Construccions, Av. de Joan Marti 39 PB local-B, +376 830 586

CONSTRUCCIONS BAIXENCH, C. de la Mosquera 5 4-2, +376 831 257

COIMA, S.A., Cami de l'Arena 7 1, +376 732 230

CONSTRUCCIONS ENDARI, C. d'Engolasters Ed. Telecabina PB local-5, +376 830 840

CONSTRUCCIONS ESTEVES, C. del Tremat 21 1, +376 832 432

CONSTRUCCIONS ESTRUCTURES CALMA, S.L., Ctra. dels Cortals d'Encamp X. Alis, +376 830 600

CONSTRUCCIONS J. QUIROS, C. Sant Miquel 5 2-1, +376 831 344

CONSTRUCCIONS NUNEZ, C. d'Engolasters 18 PB local-2, +376 832 204

CONSTRUCCIONS PORRAL, C. dels Avellaners 7 1-1, +376 832 613

CONSTRUCCIONS SOLANA, C. dels Ajustants 8 Atic-A, +376 831 356

CONSTRUCCIONS ROCA, Av. de Rouillac 19 PB local, Les Bons, +376 731 215

DARO, S.L.U, Av. Princep Benlloch 20, +376 834 894

DOPPELMAYR, S.A., Av. de Joan Marti 114 PB local-2, +376 732 732

MIVA, S.L., Ctra. d'Engolasters Ed. Molleres 2 PB-D, +376 828 198

NAUDI RICARD, VICTOR, Hortalets del Ribot, 5 3, +376 821 637

La Massana

ARC-ARQUITECTURA/CONSTRUCCIO, Av. de Sant-Antoni 34 PB local, +376 835 255

CONSTRUCCIONS BRINGUERET, S.A., La Massana, +376 737 388

CONSTRUCCIONS FERRADAS-COFE, Ctra. les Feixex 14 PB-1, Arinsal, +376 835 216

CONSTRUCCIONS I SERVEIS L'ENLLAC, Ctra. General 5 41 A 2-B, Arinsal, +376 840 313

CONSTRUCCIONS JOGAR, Av. de Sant Antoni 82 A PB local 3A, +376 737 690

CONSTRUCCIONS LLESUI, S.L., Av. de Sant Antoni 66 1-1, +376 839 440

CONSTRUCCIONS SOUTO, S.L., Av. de Sant Antoni 18 1, +376 738 900

IMMOBILIARIA OCEANIC, Av. de Sant Antoni 12 B PB local-1, +376 738 000

INTRIORS I DECORACIONS FRANCESC, La Massana, +376 838 915

Sant Julia de Loria

CONSTRUCCIONS J.M. NEIRA, Ctra. de la Rabassa 14 PB local-10, +376 843 688

CONSTRUCCIONS LOAN S.A., Ctra. de Fontaneda 12 PB local, +376 841 841

CONSTRUCCIONS MIQUEL GINE-MIGI, Ctra. de la Rabassa 10 3, +376 841 268

CONSTRUCCIONS NEIRA, Ctra. de Fontaneda Ed. Sola A 4-B, +376 842 698

CONSTRUCCIONS PALA I PIC, C. Doctor Palau 4 1-2, +376 844 407

CONSTRUCCIONS PUJAL, S.A., C. de Loria 1, +376 741 000

PROCONSA SERVEIS, Ctra. de Fontaneda 7, +376 844 266

Ordino

CONSTRUCCIONS A. NAUDI, C. de la Clota Verda 7 PB, +376 835 777

CONSTRUCCIONS CATALANES S.L., C. de la Clota Verda 4 1-1, +376 835 987

REFORMES HABITAT RUSTIC, C. de l'Alfals 1 PB-A, Anyos, +376 835 392

Canillo

CALBO ALTA MUNTANYA, Ctra. General 2, +376 870 560

CONSTRUCCIONS I T.P. LA COMA, C. Peu del Carrer Cs. Agusti PB local, +376 801 234

CONSULTING COMPANIES

Andorra la Vella

AEDES TRUST S.A., C. les Canals 7 2-1, +376 807 807

ALFA CAPITAL ASSESSORS I AUDITORS, C.Bonaventura Armengol 10 1 4-4, +376 800 480

ASSESSORS COMPTABLES N+M, Bda. del Moli 5 D 2-4, +376 818 389

AUGE GRUP, S. A., C. Pere d'Urg 10 5-7, +376 803 636

CLIENTING, S.L., C. de la Sardana 26 5-2, +376 865 133

GASSO AUDITORS, S.L., C.Prat de la Creu 59 B 3-3A, +376 866 010

GAUDIT, C. Bonaventura Armengol 15 6-2, +376 808 136

GESTORIA CENTRAL, Av. Meritxell 75 3-17, +376 860 369

DELOITTE ANDORRA AUDITORS I ASSESSORS, S.L., C.Bonaventura Armengol 10 1 1-4, +376 800 380

EASEM, S.L., C. de Callaueta 8 B 1-3, +376 864 468

ECONOMISTES ASSOCIATS, C. Bonaventura Armengol 15 6-2, +808 075

MARTICELLA ASSESSORS, Av. del Fener 15 1-E, +376 814 780

R CONSULTORS, Av. Meritxell 105 5-5, +376 865 757

SEEMA, CENTRE NATURAL, C. de la Unio 2 3-E, +376 722 100

STREATEGOS, S.L., C. Prat de la Creu 59 D 1-4A, +376 805 705

Escaldes-Engordany

ABC ASSESSORS I CONSULTORS, Ptge. Antonia Font Caminal 1 C 3-303, +376 805 060

ANCEI, Av. Carlemany 115 5 local-9, +376 808 176

ARBRE DE LA SALUT, C. dels Escalls 19 2-C, +376 727 070

ASSESSORS ANDORRANS G&G SL, Av. Fiter I Rossell 48 5-1, +376 802 250

CONSULTORS I TECNICS ASSOCIATS, S.L., C. Mossen Tremosa 4 2-1, +376 862 703

CABINET COMPTABLE NOU PLA S.L., Av. de lees Escoles 9 1-1, +376 822 700

ELECTRIC COMPANIES

Encamp

FEDA (FORCES ELECTRIQUES D'ANDORRA), Av. De la Bartra Ed. FEDA, +376 739 100

SERVEI TECNIC, Av. De la Bartra Ed. FEDA, +376 739 173

SERCENSA, Av. De Francois Mitterrand 1 1-1, +376 732 103

Andorra la Vella

SERVEI COMERCIAL, Pl. del Consell General Cs. Comuna, +376 739 191

AVARIES (numero gratuit) 145

Sant Julia

MUTUA ELECTRICA SANT JULIA DE LORIA, Av. Francesc Cairat 28 PB local-1, +376 741 700

La Massana

NORD ANDORRA, S.A., Serveis Generals + Avaries, Av. El Traves 31 1-2, +376 738 445

Pas de la Casa

SERCENSA, C. e Bearn 3 PB local-4, +376 755 095

ELECTRIC EQUIPMENT

Andorra la Vella

CAIRO, Av. De Salou 55 PB local, +376 879 079

ELECTRODOMESTICS MARTINEZ S.L., C. Bra. Riberaygua 42, +376 808 989

GENERAL ELECTRICA ANDORRANA, S.A., C. de les Costes 10, +376 721 212

INDUSTRIAL HOTELERA, C. Gil Torres 5 PB local, +376 824 029

MARFONT, C. Doctor Nequi 8 PB local-5, +376 820 135

MOBI-PLUS, C. Prat de la Creu 94 PB local, +376 869 765

PALMIR ESPINETA, S.A., Av. Santa Coloma 108, +376 804 020

LLUMSA, SUBMINISTRAMENTS ELECTRICS, Ctra. De la Comella 41 5-501A, +376 864 810

Ctra. De la Margineda 23 +376 721 717

Escaldes-Engordany

ANDO-ELECTRONICA, C. del Parnal 12 PB local-1, +376 820 935

SUSSI ELECTRODOMESTICS, Av. Carlemany 73 PB local-3, +376 821 114

CUBIC, Av. Del Fener 15 PB local-1, +376 806 800

Encamp

COMERCIAL EVARSITO, C. Rene Baulard 11 1-1, +376 831 260

SERVEI TECNIC JUANJO, Av. De Joan Marti 88 PB local-3, +376 831 759

Ordino

SIR COMERCIAL, Importador exclusiu iRobot/Roomba; Servei tecnic I guaranties, C. Major 5 PB, +376 847 234

ELECTRIC EQUIPMENT SHOPS

Andorra la Vella

CAIRO, Av. De Salou 55 PB local, +376 879 079

ELECTRODOMESTICS MARTINEZ S.L., C. Bra. Riberaygua 42, +376 808 989

GENERAL ELECTRICA ANDORRANA, S.A., C. de les Costes 10, +376 721 212

INDUSTRIAL HOTELERA, C. Gil Torres 5 PB local, +376 824 029

MARFONT, C. Doctor Nequi 8 PB local-5, +376 820 135

MOBI-PLUS, C. Prat de la Creu 94 PB local, +376 869 765

PALMIR ESPINETA, S.A., Av. Santa Coloma 108, +376 804 020

LLUMSA, SUBMINISTRAMENTS ELECTRICS, Ctra. De la Comella 41 5-501A, +376 864 810

Ctra. De la Margineda 23 +376 721 717

Escaldes-Engordany

ANDO-ELECTRONICA, C. del Parnal 12 PB local-1, +376 820 935

SUSSI ELECTRODOMESTICS, Av. Carlemany 73 PB local-3, +376 821 114

CUBIC, Av. Del Fener 15 PB local-1, +376 806 800

Encamp

COMERCIAL EVARSITO, C. Rene Baulard 11 1-1, +376 831 260

SERVEI TECNIC JUANJO, Av. De Joan Marti 88 PB local-3, +376 831 759

Ordino

SIR COMERCIAL, Importador exclusiu iRobot/Roomba; Servei tecnic I guaranties, C. Major 5 PB, +376 847 234

ELECTRONICS & PHOTO

Andorra la Vella

3 DIMENSIONS, Av. De Salou 53 1, +376 723 007

ALFA ELECTRONICA, Av. Meritxell 72 PB local-1, +376 817 456

ANDORRAFREEMARKET, Av. De Tarragona 50, +376 845 986

ATLANTIC TRADERS, C. de l'Aigueta 19 1-1, +376 808 500

AUDIO LIMIT.COM, C. de Callaueta 18, +376 824 260

COMERC CAPTURA, Av. Meritxell 71 PB local, +376 817 799

COMERCIAL CHAMEN, Av. Princep Benlloch 46, +376 823 898

DIGIT IMPORT-EXPORT, Ctra. De la Comella 31, +376 802 700

ENNLLAC, S.A., C. de les Costes Nau 17 Zona ind. Magatzems Cevos 2, +376 722 769

ESTABLIMENTS TAGORE, Av. Princep Benlloch 13 PB local-1, +376 821 456

EUROVISION, Av. Meritxell 109 1-1, +376 821 625

GALILEU ELECTRONICA, Av. Meritxell 9 PB local-1, +376 828 766

LOTUS, C. Doctor Nequi, +376 826 653

LOTUS IMPORT-EXPORT, C. Doctor Nequi 8 3, +376 827 566

MARCO-2, Av. Meritxell 62, +376 821 071

MENFIS, Av. Princep Benlloch 13 PB-1, +376 821 670

ORLY, Av. Meritxell 30, +376 825 958

QUARTS MEGASTORE, Av. Meritxell 75, +376 874 940

RADIOCOM, C. Terra Vella 7 A 2 PB local, +376 811 235

SONIMAG, Av. Meritxell 97, +376 860 039; +376 861 445

TAGORE, Av. Princep Benlloch 19, +376 823 885

TECNOVIT, C. Terra Vella 7 A 2 PB local, +376 811 235

TEMPUS, Av. Santa Coloma 27 3 PB local-1, +376 820 928

UDISM, Ctra. De la Comella 14 1, +376 810 283

VICOM, Ctra. De la Comella 41 6-603, +376 801 717

Escaldes-Engordany

EXPOVIRTUAL, Av. Fiter I Rossell 70 PB local-1, +376 800 700

JESSICA, Av. Carlemany 77 PB local-2, +376 826 163

J&M ELECTRONICS, Av. Carlemany 68, +376 864 864

NEW PORT, Av. Carlemany 51 PB local-1, +376 867 548

QUARTS ESCALDES 2, Av. Carlemany 62 PB local-9, +376 874 936

SOVITEL ELECTRONICA, C. Josep Viladomat 6, +376 828 036

TRESEL, Av. Fiter I Rossell 107 C PB local, +376 825 095

ZENER ELECTRONICA, Av. del Pessebre 22, +376 824 975

Pas de la Casa

ACTION, C. Comtes de Foix 6 PB local-1, +376 855 302

BOTIGA MASTERS, C. Sant Jordi 3 PB local-6, +376 855 639

EXCEL, Av. d'Encamp 2, +376 755 410

LASER, C. de Catalunya 12 PB local-3, +376 855 824

L'ESCALA, Av. del Consell General 19, +376 855 032

MAGATZEMS B.P. 15, Av. d'Encamp 5, +376 855 783

Encamp

COMUNICACIO I TELEFONIA COMITEL, Av. De Francois Mitterrand 60 PB local, +376 731 500

acer, sony, panasonic, hp, apple, samsung, nokia, canon, nikon, fuji, daewoo, lg, haier, lenovo, olympus, pioneer, philips, sanyo, shivaki, supra, toshiba, volta, motorola, leica, iphone, samsung galaxy, cheap electronics

ENGINEERING

Andorra la Vella

ENGINESA, Av. Meritxell 30 C S1, +376 877 400

ENGINYERIA 321, Bda. del Moli 15 2, +376 824 449

ENGITEC, C. Bonaventura Armengol 10 2 3-4, +376 802 000

GESPRO, Av. Meritxell 30, +376 877 429

OROBITG, ARQUITECTURA I ENGINYERIA, C. Roc dels Escolls 8 1 2-E, +376 808 720

PROTERRA, Av. Princep Benlloch 66 6-602, +376 865 556

R3E, C.de Pau Casals 6 A 3-4, +376 869 777

SEMSA, C. Bonaventura Armengol 10 2 2-2, +376 807 790

SILVAGRINA, S.L., C. Doctor Nequi 5 2, +376 827 688

SINUS ENGINY, C. del Pui 2 PB local, +376 824 178

Sta. Coloma

A.T.E.C.I.S.A. (ASS. TECNICA), C. del Cedre 8 B PB local-1, +376 729 500

ENGINYERIA BERNABE RODRIGUEZ, C. del Cedre 23 C Atic-C, +376 723 962

Sant Julia

AUREA, Av. Francesc Cairat 20 1-2, +376 842 805

PROJECTIA, Av. Verge de Canolich 90 PB local, +376 841 541

Escaldes-Engordany

GEOMA-2-CONSULT, S.L., Av. Fiter I Rossell 50 1 PB, +376 869 976

G.E.T.C.E. XAVIER BEAL S.L., Av. Fiter I Rossell 23, +376 864 720

EUROCONSULT, C. Maria Pla 33 C 3-2, +376 800 250

La Massana

MECA INDUSTRIA, Ctra. General 4 19 PB local-1, +376 737 750

ENGINEERING TECHNICAL

Andorra la Vella

REMOLINS ISANT, NADAL, Av. Meritxell 30 C S1, +376 877 420

RIBERAYGUA SASPLUGAS, BONAVENTURA, Av. Meritxell 30 C S1, +376 877 444

Escaldes-Engordany

CODINA FARRAS, SALVADOR, X. Codina Urb. Can Noguer 1, +376 821 859

ENGINEERING TELECOMMUNICATIONS

Andorra la Vella

JIMENEZ BELTRAN, XAVIER, C. Prada Casadet 2 E 1-3, +376 825 952

PALACIOS ALBACAR, XAVIER, C. Bonavista 23 4-2, +376 861 667

ENGINEERS INDUSTRIAL

Andorra la Vella

ALDOSA CASES, SALVADOR, Av. Meritxell 30 C S1, +376 877 420

LLOVERA MASSANA, JORDI, Av. Meritxell 30 C S1, +376 877 430

OROBITG PEREZ, JOEL, C. Roc dels Escolls 8 1 2-E, +376 808 720

Escaldes-Engordany

CEREZA PEREZ, RAMON, C.de la Devesa 4, +376 820 999

EQUIPMENT COMMERCIAL

Andorra la Vella

PARTY FIESTA, C. Prat de la Creu 29 A PB local-2, +376 820 643

INDUSTRIES FARGA, S.L., C. Esteve Dolsa Pujal 22, +376 820 462

ADA, S.L., Antic Cami Ral 17 PB local, +376 802 802

DECOTEL, S.A., C. Prat de la Creu 94 PB local, +376 825 249

INDUSTRIAL HOTELERA, C. Gil Torres 5, +376 824 029

MOBI-PLUS, C. Prat de la Creu 94 PB local, +376 869 765

TECNOVIT, C. Terra Vella 7 A 2 PB, +376 811 235

GM PROTECCIO LABORAL-LAFONT, C. Ciutat de Valls 4 PB local, +376 868 870

Escaldes-Engordany

COMERCIAL GRAELLS, Av. del Fener 22 C PB local-7, +376 828 077

EXCLUSIVES SERVEIS, Av. Coprincep de Gaulle 8 1-3, +376 820 624

FAMAGUSTA, S.L., Av. Coprincep de Gaulle 9 PB-1, +376 811 829

SAMTEX, Av. del Pessebre 24 PB local-2, +376 863 883

Encamp

COMERCIAL EVARISTO, C. Rene Baulard 11 3-2, +376 831 830

EXHIBITION HALLS

Encamp

SALA D'EXPOSICIONS D'ENCAMP, Centre esp. Encamp, +376 732 700

Pas de la Casa

SALA D'EXPOSICIONS PAS DE LA CASA, Av. Del Consell General Aparc. Comunal, +376 755 111

FASHION DESIGNERS

Andorra la Vella

ELENA MATO MODISTA, C. de la Unio 2 1-E, +376 845 400

FISH TRADING

Andorra la Vella

ANDOMAR, S.A., C. Esteve Dolsa Pujal 48 1, +376 829 231

Escaldes-Engordany

PEIXATERIA EL CANTABRIC 4, C. Santa Anna 14 PB local-1, +376 820 912

PEIXATERIA NAVINA, Av. de les Escoles 22 PB local-2, +376 820 763

Sant Julia

PEIX I CONGELAT MAR BLAU, C. Doctor Palau 27 PB local, +376 842 830

PEIXATERIA EL CANTABRIC 1, Av. Verge de Canolich 41 PB local-2, +376 841 302

FURNITURE

Andorra la Vella

CENT MOBEL, C. Bra. Riberaygua 41, +376 860 934

DIANA DESCANS, C. de l'Aigueta 24 PB local-4, +376 826 778

DUGAR, Av. de Tarragona 71, +376 821 645

KIT DESCANS, Bda. Del Moli 10 PB local, +376 860 024

LA TEVA IDEA DE CASA, C. de Callaueta 20 PB local, +376 864 064

LOSANGE MOBLES I DECORACIO, C. de la Sardana 21, +376 828 249

MOBI-PLUS, C. Prat de la Creu 94 PB local, +376 869 765

MOBLES ANDORRANS, Av. Santa Coloma 12 PB local, +376 722 659

MOBLES DIANA, C. Pere d'Urg 10 PB local-2, +376 862 405

MOBLES LA FABRICA, C. Prat de la Creu 15, +376 808 830

BRICOLAGE, C. Prat de la Creu 56, +376 800 680

REHABILIT, C. Esteve Dolsa Pujal 34, +376 867 055

TRIEDRE, C. de Pau Casals 2 C PB local-1, +376 802 727

Escaldes-Engordany

DELTA MOBLE I DECORACIO, C. Josep Viladomat 10 PB local, +376 807 244

La Massana

ART I FUSTA, Av. el Traves 37 PB local, +376 839 238

FURNITURE FOR OFFICE

Andorra la Vella

LOSANGE MOBLES I DECORACIO, C. de la Sardana 21, +376 828 249

Encamp

COMERCIAL EVARISTO, C. Rene Baulard 11 3-2, +376 831 830

FURS

Andorra la Vella

ARIES PELLETERIA, C. Mossen Cinto Verdaguer 2, +376 827 411

PELLETERIA ORFI, Av. Dr. Mitjavila 1, +376 869 262

Encamp

PELLETERIA PANTHER, C. Balco del Sola 27 A 1-2, +376 831 817

GAS SHOPS

Andorra la Vella

BUTAGAZ, Ctra. de la Comella 11, +376 871 325

GAS CONTROLS, C. de les Costes Nau 12 Zona ind. Magatzems Cervos 2, +376 723 813

PETROLIS PRINCIPATS.A., Ctra. de la Comella 11, +376 871 325

Sta. Coloma

CADESA-GAS (REPSOL BUTA), Av. d'Enclar 142, +376 871 888

VALLGAS, S.A., +376 722 468

FLAMA COMERCIAL S.L., GAS INDUSTRIAL, Ctra. General 1 Nau Magatzems Gas Buta, +376 722 159

La Massana

ENGAS, S.A., C. dels Hortals 8 PB local, +376 738 121

GEOLOGICAL EQUIPMENT

Andorra la Vella

EUROCONSULT, C. Maria 33 C 3-2, +376 800 250

IGEOTEST S.L., Av. Princep Benlloch 66 4-407, +376 820 323

Escaldes-Engordany

GEOMA-2-CONSULT, S.L., Av. Filter I Rossell 50 1 PB, +376 869 976

INACCES, Av. Consell de la Terra 14, +376 877 900

Encamp (Les Bons)

GEICO, Av. de Rouillac 22 PB local, +376 832 570

Sant Julia

GEOTECH, S.A., Av. de Rocafort 38 PB local, +376 732 210

Canillo

TECSOL, S.L., Av. Sant Joan de Caselles Ed. Pirot 1-1, +376 751 275

GIFTS

Andorra la Vella

AROMATIC, Pl. Princep Benlloch 6, +376 820 110

BAUSTORE, LA BAUHAUS CONCEPT STORE, C. Bonaventura Armengol 5, +376 802 236

CASA BELLA, Av. Princep Benlloch 30 PB local-4, +376 813 343

CASA DANESA-REGALS, C. les Canals 3 PB local-2, +376 826 171

D-KORA, C. Bra. Riberaygua 38 PB local-3, +376 854 300

NATURA, C. Babot Camp 15, +376 826 998

PONS I BARTUMEU JOIERS, Pl. Rebes 5, +376 805 075

PONS I BARTUMEU JOIERS, Av. Meritxell 97, +376 820 421

PONS I BARTUMEU JOIERS, Av. Meritxell 33, +376 828 672

PUBLI REGAL, C. Bonavista 8, +376 828 575

TOT STOCK, Antic Cami Ral 1 A PB local-1, +376 866 003

VENUS, Av. Princep Benlloch 42, +376 825 841

Escaldes-Engordany

COMERCIAL PONT, C. Nou 3 PB local-2, +376 821 063

GRANIT, Av. Carlemany 117 PB local, +376 827 625

MIKEI'S, Av. Carlemany 45 PB local-1, +376 820 848

Pas de la Casa

COMERC SONIA NOVA, Av. d'Encamp 23, +376 855 047

HABERDASHERIE

Andorra la Vella

CONFECCIONS LIDIA, C. Ciutat de Valls 32 PB local, +376 825 164

MERCERIA TOTI, C. de Callaueta 19, +376 824 793

Escaldes-Engordany

TOT A PUNT, Av. Carlemany 12 PB local-1, +376 846 611

VIVARA, Av. Carlemany 31 PB local-1, +376 821 103

Sant Julia

MERCERIA BETES I FILS, Av. Verge de Canolich 45 PB local-2, +376 844 008

MERCERIA PANTEBRE, Av. Verge de Canolich 9 S2, +376 843 682

La Massana

MERCERIA MARISOL, Av. de Sant Antoni 22 PB local-1, +376 839 781

Encamp

MES LABORS, C. Major 15 1, +376 831 602

HEAD HUNTERS

Andorra la Vella

ADECCO RECURSOS HUMANS, S.A., C. Pere d'Urg 10 4-1, +376 800 490

CERQUEDA RECURSOS HUMANS, S.L., C. Mossen Tremosa 4 3-1, +376 869 577

GAMMA MANAGEMENT, Av. Meritxell 9 1-3, +376 805 888

LIDERA, S.L., C. Bonaventura Armengol 10 1 6-1, +376 803 680

RANDSTAD RECURSOS HUMANS, C. Sant Salvador 10 3-9, +376 807 890

TREBALL TEMPORAL, S.L., C. Bra. Ribeaygua 39 4-1, +376 805 666

HOSPITALS

Escaldes-Engordany

CLINICA VERGE DE MERITXELL, C. dels Escalls 16, +376 871 100

HOSPITAL NOSTRA SENYORA DE MERITXELL, Av. Fiter I Rossell 5, +376 871 000

HOTELS

Andorra la Vella

ANDORRA CENTER HOTEL, C. Doctor Nequi 10 4, +376 824 999

ANDORRA PARK HOTEL, C. les Canals 24, +376 877 777

APARTHOTEL FONTVERD, C. Cuitat de Consuegra 2, +376 803 525

CENTRIC HOTEL, Av. Meritxell 87, +376 877 500

HOTEL ANDORRA PALACE, Av. Meritxell 58 PB local, +376 873 601

HOTEL BELLPI, Av. Santa Coloma 30 2, +376 804 935

HOTEL CASSANY, Av. Meritxell 28, +376 820 636

HOTEL CERVOL, Av. Santa Coloma 46, +376 803 111

HOTEL DIPLOMATIC, Av. De Tarragona 45, +376 802 780

HOTEL ELS ISARDS, Av. Meritxell 34, +376 876 800

HOTEL FESTA BRAVA, C. la Llacuna 7, +376 820 741

HOTEL FLORIDA, C. la Llacuna 15, +376 820 105

HOTEL GARCIA, Av. Princep Benlloch 51, +376 820 968

HOTEL HOLIDAY INN, C. Prat de la Creu 88, +376 874 444

HOTEL JAUME 1, C. Roureda de Sansa 2, +376 820 061

HOTEL MAGIC ANDORRA, Av. Dr. Mitjavila 3, +376 876 900

HOTEL MERCURE, C. de la Roda 2, +376 873 602

HOTEL NORMANDIA, Av. Princep Benlloch 49 4-1, +376 820 125

HOTEL PITIUSA, C. d'Emprivat 11, +376 861 816

HOTEL PLAZA, C. Maria Pla 19, +376 879 444

HOTEL PRESIDENT, Av. Santa Coloma 42, +376 877 277

HOTEL PYRENEES, Av. Princep Benlloch 20, +376 879 879

HOTEL RESTAURANT CELLER D'EN TONI, C. Verge del Pilar 4, +376 821 252

HOTEL RESTAURANT GARCIA, Av. Princep Benlloch 51, +376 824 591

HOTEL ROC DEL SOLA, Av. Santa Coloma 42, +376 877 377

HOTEL SALVIA, Av. Meritxell 68, +376 827 200

HOTEL SANT JORDI, Av. Princep Benlloch 45, +376 876 200

HOTEL TIVOLI, C. Sant Salvador 3, +376 804 265

NOVOTEL, C. Prat de la Creu 12 PB local, +376 873 603

PRESTIGI HOTELS, S.A., C. de la Roda 2, +376 873 600

SOMRIU HOTELS, C. Ciutat de Consuerga 10 4-4, +376 826 826

UNIO HOTELERA DE LES VALLS D'ANDORRA, Antic. Carrer Major 18 PB-1, +376 809 602

Escaldes-Engordany

A HOTELS PRINCEP, C. de la Unio 5, +376 870 400

A HOTEL PRISMA, Av. Del Fener 14, +376 802 930

ARTHOTEL, C. Prat de la Creu 15, +376 760 303

HOTANSA, Ptge. Antonia Font Caminal 1 C 5-502, +376 875 500

HOTEL BATLLE VELL, C. d'Engordany 14, +376 803 705

HOTEL CAMP DEL SERRAT, Ctra. d'Engolasters Restaurant Camp del Serrat, +376 809 590

HOTEL CARLEMANY, Av. Carlemany 4, +376 870 050

HOTEL CASA CANUT RESTAURANT, Av. Carlemany 107, +376 739 900

HOTEL COMTES D'URGELL, Av. De les Escoles 29, +376 876 000

HOTEL CONTINENTAL, Av. Del Pessebre 1 PB local-2, +376 803 705

HOTEL CONTINENTAL, S.L., Av. Del Pessebre 1, +376 820 515

HOTELS COSMAS, Av. De les Escoles 10, +376 870 750

HOTEL DELFOS, Av. Del Fener 17, +376 877 000

HOTEL ESPEL, Pl. Creu Blanca 1, +376 820 855; +376 820 944

HOTEL EUREKA, Av. Carlemany 36, +376 880 666

HOTEL EUROPA, Av. Del Fener 4, +376 821 354

HOTEL EUROTEL, Av. Fiter I Rossell 51, +376 863 031

HOTEL FENIX, C. del Prat Gran Hotel Fenix, +376 760 760

HOTEL LES 7 CLAUS, Av. Fiter I Rossell 49, +376 803 480

HOTEL LES CLOSES, Av. Carlemany 93, +376 808 393

HOTEL MRFANY, Av. Carlemany 99, +376 825 957

HOTEL METROPOLIS, Av. De les Escoles 25, +376 808 363

HOTEL MOLA PARC, Parc de la Mola 4, +376 882 000

HOTEL MUNTANYA, Av. Carlemany 19, +376 821 409

HOTEL ORIOL, Pl. Coprinceps 4, +376 810 058; +376 821 105

HOTEL PANORAMA, Ctra. de l'Obac Est. de servei Repsol, +376 873 400

HOTEL RIMAG, Av. Coprincep de Gaulle Resid. Rimag, +376 822 985

HOTEL ROC BLANC, Pl. Coprinceps 5 S2, +376 871 400

HOTEL ROC DE CALDES, Ctra. d'Engolasters Hotel Roc de Caldes, +376 874 555

HOTEL SIRACUSA, Av. Carlemany 14, +376 821 125

HOTEL TROPICAL, Av. Del Pont de la Tosca 25 PB local, +376 872 300

HOTEL TUDEL, Pl. Coprinceps 8 PB local-1, +376 820 563

Anyos

ANYOSPARK APARTHOTEL, Ctra. De Sant Cristofol, +376 737 173

HOTEL ANYOSPARK, Ctra. De Sant Cristofol, +376 737 173

Soldeu

A HOTELS, Ctra. General 2, +376 871 760

A HOTEL PIOLETS & SPA, Ctra. General 2, +376 872 787

A HOTELS PIOLETS PARK & SPA, Ctra. General 2 Ed. Casa Aspen PB local-1, +376 871 787

HOTEL BRUXELLES, +376 851 010

HOTEL CONFORT, Bordes d'Envalira Hotel Confort, +376 852 288

HOTEL HIMALAIA-SOLDEU, Ctra. General 2 Ed. Himalaia, +376 878 515

HOTEL MONTANA, Ctra. General 2 Hotel Xalet Montana, +376 739 333

HOTEL NAUDI, Ctra. General 2 Hotel Xalet Montana, +376 739 300

HOTEL ROC DE SANT MIQUEL, +376 851 079

HOTEL SOLDEU-MAISTRE, +376 801 963

HOTEL SPORTHOTEL, Ctra. General 2, +376 870 600

SPORT HOTELS, Ctra. General 2, +376 870 500

Canillo

APARTHOTEL ELS MENERS, Ctra. General 2 Aparthotel Meners, +376 751 454

HOTEL BONAVIDA, C. Peu del Carrer Cs. Agusti PB local, +376 751 300

HOTEL FONT D'ARGENT, Av. Sant Joan de Caselles Hotel Font d'Argent, +376 753 753

HOTEL MAGIC CANILO, Ctra. del Forn Hotel Magic Urb. Ribagrossa, +376 876 700

HOTEL OBAGA BLANCA, Ctra. del Forn Hotel Obaga Blanca, +376 751 200

HOTEL ROC DEL CASTELL, Av. Sant Joan de Caselles Hotel Roc del Castell, +376 851 825

HOTEL SKI PLAZA, Av. Sant Joan de Caselles Cs. Sinfreu PB local, +376 739 444

HOTEL L'ERMITA, Meritxell (Sanctuary de Meritxell), +365 751 050

Encamp

APARTHOTEL L'ORRI, Av. De Joan Marti 9B, +376 832 320

HOTEL CORAY, C. dels Cavallers 38, +376 831 513

HOTEL ENCAMP, Av. De Joan Marti 95, +376 733 999

HOTEL GUILLEM, C. dels Arinsols 10, +376 733 900

HOTEL MILA, Ctra. dels Cortals d'Encamp Hotel Mila, +376 731 313

HOTEL MONTECARLO, Av. De Joan Marti 104, +376 731 116

HOTEL OROS, Pl. del Consell 11, +376 831 222

HOTEL PARIS, Av. De Joan Marti 2, +376 731 525

HOTEL PERE D'URG, C. Pas de la Casa 8, +376 831 515; +376 831 523

HOTEL UNIVERS, C. Rene Baulard 13, +376 731 105

Arinsal

APARTHOTEL PATAGONIA AUSTRAL, Ctra. De Comallempla Aparthotel Patagonia Austral, +376 735 777

HOTEL CREST, +376 737 070

HOTEL MICOLAU, Ctra. Genaral 5 15, +376 737 707

HOTEL MONTANE, C. la Grella 1, +376 737 535

HOTEL PALOME, Ctra. General 5 Hotel Palome, +376 738 500

HOTEL XALET BESOLI, Ctra. l'Escladella 13, +376 836 336

HOTEL XALET VERDU, Ctra. General 5, +376 737 140

Pas de la Casa

APARTHOTEL SOLARIS, C. de la Solana Apmt. Solaris, +376 855 158

HOTEL BAR RESTAURANT MIRTIL, C. de Catalunya 12 PB local-1, +376 855 318

HOTEL CAL RUIZ, Av. Del Consell General 10, +376 800 765

HOTEL CAMELLOT, C. de la Sontana Hotel Camelot, +376 755 435

HOTEL CASADO, C. de Catalunya 23, +376 855 219

HOTEL CENTRAL, C. de les Abelletes 5, +376 855 375; +376 855 379; +376 855 383

HOTEL CONFORT, C. de Catalunya 27, +376 856 664

HOTEL CRISTINA PARK, C. de la Solana Apmt. Solaris, +376 736 800

HOTEL CUBIL, C. de la Solana Resid. Snow Lake PB local, +376 856 156

HOTEL DE LES NEUS, C. Comte de Foix 2, +376 855 085

HOTEL FONT D'ARGENT, C. de Bearn 20, +376 739 739

HOTEL GRAU ROIG, Pleta Moreto, +376 755 556

HOTEL GUINEU, Av. D'Encamp 23, +376 856 661

HOTEL KANDAHAR, C. de Bearn 5, +376 755 700

HOTEL LES TRUITES, C. dels Pareatges 8, +376 755 155

HOTEL LLAC NEGRE, C. Sant Jordi 41, +376 855 198

HOTEL MAGIC PAS, C. Sant Jordi 19, +376 756 900

HOTEL META, Pl. dels Coprinceps 15, +376 755 635

HOTEL PANDA, Pl. dels Coprinceps 16, +376 755 035

HOTEL PARMA, Av. D'Encamp 23, +376 855 323

HOTEL PIC MAIA, Ctra. General 2 Hotel Pic Maia, +376 755 856

HOTEL REIAL PIRINEUS, C. de la Solana 66, +376 855 855

HOTEL RESIDENCIA CATALUNYA, C. de Catalunya 8, +376 755 710

HOTEL SPORTING, C. de Catalunya 1, +376 755 355

PETIT HOTEL, C. Sant Jordi 18, +376 755 240

Ransol

CENTRE DE VACANCES SNOOPY, Ctra. Dels Plans de Ransol Aparthotel Ransol, +376 852 562

HOTEL RANSOL, +376 735 100

HOTEL SEGLE XX, +376 853 003

La Massana

GRAN HOTEL FONT, Av. Del Ravell 2 PB local-1, +376 838 444

HOTEL DEL BISSET, Ctra. de la Creu Blanca 9, +376 837 555

HOTEL DEL PUI, +376 738 300

HOTEL MAGIC ESQUI, Av. Del Ravell 8, +376 734 900

HOTEL MAGIC LA MASSANA, Av. El Traves 7, +376 735 900

HOTEL MARCO POLO, Av. De Sant Antoni 36, +376 738 363

HOTEL PALANQUES, +376 835 007

HOTEL RESIDENCIA ALDOSA, +376 835 086

HOTEL RUTLLAN, +376 738 738

La Cortinada

HOTEL ANTIC, Av. De la Posa Hotel Daina, +376 850 988

HOTEL MU, Av. De la Cortinada Hotel Mu, +376 749 020

HOTEL SUCARA, Av. De la Cortinada Hotel Sucara, +376 850 151

Ordino

HOTEL BABOT, Ctra. Del Coll d'Ordino Hotel Cabana, +376 747 047

HOTEL COMA, C. Mossen Cinto Verdaguer Hotel Coma, +376 736 100

HOTEL LA CABANA, Ctra. del Coll d'Ordino Hotel Cabana, +376 835 767

HOTEL LA PLANADA, C. del Condalet 4 3-1, +376 737 635

HOTEL ORDINO, C. Mossen Cinto Verdaguer 1, +376 747 474

HOTEL QUIM, +376 835 013

HOTEL SANTA BARBARA VALL D'ORDINO, Pl. Major Hotel Santa Barbara, +376 738 100

Aixovall

HOTEL BARCELONA, +376 841 177

HOTEL PERALBA, Ctra. General 6 Hotel Peralba, +376 841 141

El Serrat

HOTEL BRINGUE, Av. De Sant Pere 16, +376 736 999

HOTEL NIUNIT, Cami Vell Hotel Serrat, +376 735 735

Juberri

HOTEL COMA BELLA, Hotel Comabella, +376 742 030

Sant Julia

HOTEL CO-PRINCEPS, C. J. Cavajal de Hue 1, +376 841 002

HOTEL FOLCH, C. de Loria 6, +376 735 200

HOTEL IMPERIAL, Av. De Rocafort 27, +376 843 478

HOTEL PRINCIPAL, Pl. Major 5, +376 841 023

HOTEL SANT ELOI, Ctra. General 1 Hotel Sant Eloi, +376 743 100

HOTEL SOL-PARK, Ctra. de Fontaneda Hotel Sol Parc, +376 843 540; +376 841 043

El Tarter

HOTEL DEL CLOS, +376 753 500

HOTEL DEL TARTER, Ctra. General 2 Hotel Tarter, +376 802 080

HOTEL EL XALET, Pleta Sant Pere PB local-17, +376 851 852

HOTEL LLOP GRIS, Hotel Llop Gris, +376 751 515

HOTEL NORDIC, Hotel Nordic, +376 739 500

MOUNTAIN HOSTEL TARTER, +376 330 412

Incles (between Tarter & Soldeu)

HOTEL EURO SKI, Ctra. General 2 Hotel Euro Ski, +376 736 666

HOTEL GALANTHUS, Hotel Galantus Urb. La Devesa d'Incles, +376 753 300

HOTEL PARADOR CANARO, Ctra. General 2 Hotel Parador Canaro, +376 751 150

HOTEL VALL ESQUI, Ctra. General 2, +376 851 546; +376 851 582

Erts

HOTEL PALARINE, Ctra. General 4 Hotel Palarine, +376 835 440; +376 737 393

HOTEL ST. GOTHARD, Ctra. General 5 Hotel Sant Gothard, +376 738 787

Ansalonga

HOTEL SANT MIQUEL, Av. De Sant Miquel Hotel Sant Miquel, +376 749 000

Sispony

SUITE HOTEL, Ctra. de Sispony 11, +376 737 30

HOUSEHOLD APPLIANCES

Andorra la Vella

ESTABLIMENTS J. MOLLES ISERN, Ctra. General 1 13, +376 720 860

FERRETERIA NOVA 98, S.L., Bda. Del Moli 19 1 PB local-1, +376 807 050

MATERIALS RIBA, Av. De Salou 40, +376 729 800

BRICOLAGE, C. Prat de la Creu 56, +376 800 680

Escaldes-Engordany

FERRETERIA DEL POBLE, C. Josep Viladomat 4 S1 local, +376 865 700

La Massana

FERMASS FERRETERIA, C. el Traves Ed. Traves 2 PB local, +376 840 350

FERRETERIA BONS, Ctra. General 4 9 PB local-1, +376 838 040

FERRETERIA NOVA 98 S.L., Av. De Sant Antoni 58 3 PB local-3, +376 840 910

Sant Julia

FERRETERIA PRINCIPAT, Av. Verge de Canolich 32, +376 742 020

FERRETERIA MAVID, S.A., Ctra. General 6 Ed. Codi, +376 741 010

Encamp

FERRETERIA NOVA 98 S.L., Av. De Joan Marti 28 PB local, +376 833 910

IMPORT

Andorra la Vella

DIGIT IMPORT-EXPORT, Ctra. de la Comella 31, +376 802 700

SERVIT, S.L. (electronics, photo), Ctra. De la Comella 29 1-3, +376 825 808

TOT STOCK, Av. Santa Coloma 37 S1, +376 865 003

Sant Julia

ARMETISA, Av. Verge de Canolich 124 1-3, +376 869 900

La Margineda

ESTABLIMENTS VIDAL, C. dels Emprius Nau Establiments Vidal, +376 720 700

Escaldes-Engordany

RACEL S.A., C. de les Boigues Ed. Racel PB local, +376 810 881

INSURANCE COMPANIES

Andorra la Vella

ASSAP ASSEGURANCES, Av. d'Enclar 26, Sta. Coloma, +376 729 200

ASSEGA AGENCIA D' ASSEGURANCES, Bda. De Moli 1 local-2, +376 868 622

ASSEGUR, Oficina Central, C. de Pau Casals 10 2, +376 876 555

ASSEGURANCES BERCIA, S.A., C. de la Sardana 14 1, +376 827 967

ASSEGURANCES DOVAL, C. Roureda de Sansa 36 PB-E, +376 807 550

ASSEGURANCES FIATC DELEGACIO AND, Av. d'Enclar 26, Sta. Coloma, +376 729 200

ASSEGURANCES GENERALS, S.A., C. Sant Salvador 7 B PB local-1, +376 877 677

ASSEGURANCES IVORI – ASSIVORI, C. Prat de la Creu 96 2-3, +376 801 683

ASSEGURANCES PATRIMOINE, Pl. Guillemo 6, +376 805 020

ASSEGURANCES PUENTE, C. Sant Esteve 5 PB local-1, +376 863 621

ASSEGURANCES SANTAMARIA COSAN, Av. Meritxell 88, +376 804 490

ASSEGURANCES ZURICH DELEGACIO AND., Av. d'Enclar 26, Sta. Coloma, +376 729 200

BECIER ASSEGURANCES, Av. d'Enclar 142, Sta. Coloma, +376 871 830

BPA ASSEGURANCES, S.A., C. Prat de la Creu 59 PB local-3B, +376 812 111

COMPANYIA ANDORRANA D'ASSEGURANCES, Av. Meritxell 88, +376 806 806

CONSELL ASSEGURADOR, S.A., C. Prat de la Creu 8 4-401, +376 803 903

DKV SEGUROS Y REASEGUROS S.A.E., C. Prat de la Creu 91 2 PB local-2, +376 806 240

FINANCERA D'ASSEGURANCES, S.A., C. Babot Camp 11, +376 890 300

LLORENC MIQUEL ASSEGURANCES, C. de l'Alzinaret 9 PB local-1, +376 826 355

MB CORREDORS D'ASSEGURANCES, C. de la Sardana 14 1 PB local-1, +376 827 967

MB CORREDORS D'ASSEGURANCES, C. Prat de la Creu 59 PB local-3B, +376 812 111

MULTISEGUR ASSEGURANCES, S.A., Bda. Del Moli 14 PB local-1, +376 808 808

POVEDANO ASSEGURANCES, C. de la Sardana 14 1, +376 861 902

SANTAMARIA COSAN ASSEGURANCES, Av. Meritxell, 88, +376 804 490

TM ASSEGURANCES, Av. Princep Benlloch 38 PB local, +376 800 900

ASSEGURANCES RC, Av. Dr. Mitjavila 3 6, +376 807 373

Escaldes-Engordany

AP CORREDORIA D'ASSEGURANCES, Pl. Coprinceps 2, +376 864 440

ASSEGURANCES CATALANA OCCIDENT, Av. Carlemany 65 2, +376 808 444

ASSEGURANCES, Av. Coprincep de Gaulle 1 PB local-1, +376 865 631

ASSEGURANCES PONT, Av. de les Escoles 18 PB local-4, +376 801 201

CENTRE D'ASSEGURANCES, Av. Carlemany 115 4 local-8, +376 807 160

CREDIT ASSEGURANCES, S.A.U., Av. Filter I Rossell 22, +376 888 900

MORA ASSEGURANCES, S.A.U., Pl. Coprinceps 2, +376 884 874

PATRIMOINE ASSEGURANCES, Av. Coprincep de Gaulle 1 PB local-1, +376 865 631

VILELLA & JORGE ASSOCIATS ASSEGURANCES, Av. Carlemany 117 4-A, +376 821 717

Sant Julia de Loria

ASSEGURANCES PATRIMOINE, Av. Verge de Canolich 34, +376 842 202

BONAPARTE ASSEGURANCES, C. Doctor Palau 46 PB local-2, +376 844 898

ASSEGURANCES CATALANA OCCIDENT, Av. Verge de Canolich 80, +376 741 574

Encamp

ASSEGURANCES PATRIMOINE, Av. de Francois Mitterrand 7 PB local-9, +376 832 520

ASSEGURA'T D.G., Av. de Joan Marti 105 PB local-2, +376 731 777

Pas de la Casa

ASSEGURANCES PATRIMOINE, C. Estret 1 1, Pas, +376 855 835

La Massana

ASSEGURANCES PATRIMOINE, Av. de Sant Antoni 14, +376 840 440

ASSIDU, Av. de Sant Antoni 79 PB local-2, +376 838 494

BETA ASSEGURANCES, Av. de Sant Antoni 25 PB local-3, +376 737 666

JEWELER WORKSHOPS

Andorra la Vella

GAUDIA, C. Maria Pla 19, +376 827 001

MAZAL, C. Doctor Nequi 8 3, +376 865 875

QUIRATS TALLER DE JOIERIA, C. Roc dels Escolls 7 3 4-C, +376 808 160

TALLER DE JOIERIA FUS, C. Roc dels Escolls 10 2 1-A, +376 825 200; +376 825 203

TALLER DE JOIERIA L'AGUILA D'OR, C. la Llacuna 11, +376 827 537

TALLER DE JOIERIA SAFIR BLAU, C. Roc dels Escolls 10 2, +376 826 110

TALLER JOIERIA – 3 OR, C. de Callaueta 15, +376 862 422

JEWELRY TRADERS

Andorra la Vella

ANA BUSQUETS, C. Maria Pla 1 PB local-7, +376 861 848

BOUTIQUE CELLINI, Av. Meritxell 22, +376 824 908

DANIEL, Av. Meritxell 106, +376 828 224

FASCINI, Av. Meritxell 47 PB local-2, +376 868 998

JOIERIA BERNA, Av. Meritxell 53, +376 803 180

JOIERIA CELLINI, Av. Meritxell 22, +376 803 585

JOIERIA GENEVE, Av. Meritxell 124 3, +376 800 500

JOIERIA LA GRANDALLA D'OR, C. de l'Aiguete 16, +376 820 140

JOIERIA L'AGUILA D'OR, C. la Llacuna 11, +376 827 537

JOIERIA LLAURADO, Av. Meritxell 108, +376 803 426

JOIERIA OBIOLS, Av. Meritxell 88 PB local-1, +376 828 576

JOIERIA RELLOGERIA TRAVESSET, Av. Meritxell 44, +376 824 682

JOIERIA RELLOGERIA CARME, C. Roc dels Escolls 2 1, +376 823 706

JOIERIA RELLOGERIA FORTIOR, Av. Princep Benlloch 2 PB local-2, +376 820 279

JOIERIA RELLOGERIA GERMANS, C. Doctor Nequi 8 PB local-1, +376 825 345

JOIERIA RELLOTGERIA SUISSA, Av. Meritxell 37, +376 806 350

JOIERIA RELLOTGERIA SUISSA, Av. Meritxell 101, +376 861 220

JOIERIA SAFIR BLAU, C. Roc dels Escolls 10 2, +376 826 110

JOIERIA SANSA, Av. Santa Coloma 6 PB local-2, +376 822 336

JOIERIA VALL D'INCLES, Av. Meritxell 86, +376 821 142

JOIERIA VASARI, Av. Meritxell 16, +376 807 475

LES TEVES PERLES, C. de la Sardana 1 D, +376 867 086

MERCAT DE L'OR, Av. Meritxell 52 1, +376 806 470

MERCAT DEL DIAMANT, Av. Meritxell 18, +376 800 630

NOVA JOIA, C. Bra. Riberaygua 6 PB local-1, +376 869 080

OBIOLS JOIERS 2, Av. Meritxell 66 PB local-1, +376 861 720

ORGEM, Av. Dr. Mitjavila 36 PB local-2, +376 825 980

PERLERIA DE TAHITI, C. Roc dels Escolls 2, +376 865 822

PONS I BARTUMEU JOIERS, Pl. Rebes 5, +376 805 075

PONS I BARTUMEU JOIERS, Av. Meritxell 97, +376 820 421

PONS I BARTUMEU JOIERS, Av. Meritxell 33, +376 828 672

QUARS MEGASTORE CARTIER, Av. Meritxell 75, +376 874 939

WATCH GALLERY, Av. Meritxell 101, +376 861 220

Escaldes-Engordany

ANDOR-GEMS, Pl. Coprinceps 6, +376 824 724

CONRAD MARINA, Av. Carlemany 38 PB local-9, +376 820 937

DI MILANO, Av. Carlemany 80 PB-B5, +376 824 717

DIAMANT DIFUSIO, Av. Carlemany 54 PB local-1, +376 806 790

GEMMES GALERIA, C. Santa Anna 14 PB local-9, +376 824 339

JOIERIA CELLINI, Av. Carlemany 97, +376 803 988

JOIERIA HVNGARI, Av. Carlemany 117 PB local, +376 803 080

JOIERIA LA MINA, Av. Carlemany 38 PB local-9, +376 820 937

JOIERIA RELLOTGERIA SOLANS, Av. Carlemany 65 PB local-15, +376 821 463

JOIERIA RELLOTGERIA SUISSA, Av. Carlemany 52, +376 806 355

JOIERIA TOUS, Av. Carlemany 103, +376 865 767

QUARS ESCALDES CARTIER, Av. Carlemany 58 PB local-2, +376 874 934

Pas de la Casa

GRESOL 2, C. Sant Jordi 8 PB local-2, +376 855 702

JOIERIA BAGUE, Av. d'Encamp 3 PB local-7, +376 855 518

JOIERIA CRISTI, Av. d'Encamp 6 PB local-1, +376 856 223

JOIERIA ELS BENVINGUTS, C. dels Pareatges 6 5, +376 855 150

JOIERIA ELS BENVINGUTS, C. Major 23 1 local, +376 855 177

JOIERIA JAIS, Av. del Consell General Centre educ. Escoles, +376 855 104

JOIERIA RICHARD, Av. d'Encamp 6 PB local-1, +376 855 373

JOIERIA ALFONS BORRA, C. Major 1, +376 856 032

QUARS CARTIER PAS DE LA CASA, C. Major 2 PB local-5, +376 874 938

La Massana

JOIERIA GRESOL, Av. de Sant Antoni 11 PB local, +376 838 221

RECORDS DE LA MASSANA, +376 835 336

Sant Julia

JOIERIA RELLOTGERIA OPAL, C. de Loria 2, +376 842 518

cartier, tiffani, korloff, bulgari, van cleef & arpels, harry winston, mikimoto, piaget, chopard, buccellati

LAWYERS

Andorra la Vella

DAS CHEVALERDAUD CAROLE-ADVOCAT, C. la Llacuna-2 1-B, +376 866 014

ADVOCATS FORNE, C. les Canals 12 PB, +376 800 888

ALEIX CHAULET NATALIA, Av. Meritxell 75 1-10, +376 820 020

ALEIX TUGAS NADIA, C. Doctor Nequi 6 2 5-6, +376 820 233

ARQUES I TOMAS DANIEL, ARQUES RIBERT JUNYER ADVOCATS, C. Bonaventura Armengol 6 4, +376 809 000

AUGE GRUP, S. A., C. Pere d'Urg 10 5-7, +376 803 636

BADIA ADVOCATS, BADIA GOMIS FRANCESC I MONTSERRAT, C. les Canals 7 2-2, +376 810 800

BAIXENCH MARCO SONIA, C. Bonaventura Armengol 10 1 3-4, +376 806 050

BALLESTER ECHENIQUE LLORENC, Legalis advocats, C. Prat de la Creu 93-1, +376 808 111

BARO SOLA LADISLAU, C. les Canals 5, +376 804 040

BARTUMEU CASSANY JAUME, C. Prat de la Creu 59, +376 809 777

BELLERA GRACIA MIQUEL, C. Bonaventura Armengol 10 1 3-2, +376 830 003

BELLOCO ANNEY SOPHIE, C. Doctor Vilanova 13 C 2-1, +376 812 200

BETRIU&BOURGEAUD ADVOCATS, C. de la Vinyeta 2 PB, +376 807 555

BORRELL GALLEGO ANTON, C. Bonaventura Armengol, 10 1 1-1, +376 810 010

BOURGEAUD IZA MAITE, C. de la Vinyeta 2 PB, +376 807 555

BUFET PUJADAS, Av. Dr. Mitjavila 5 2, +376 802 047

CAMPOS ARAUZ EMILI, C. Prat de la Creu 8 3-301, +376 860 850

CANTURRI ORTIZ MIREA, C. la Llacuna 2 1-A, +376 822 229

CAPDEVILA PALLARES SALVADOR, Av. Meritxell 75 3, +376 800 850

CASADEVALL/ADVOCATS, C. Prat de la Creu 32, +376 809 090

CASADO GARCIA LAËTITA, C. les Canals, +376 864 153

CASAL RUIZ MANEL, Legalis advocats, C. Prat de la Creu 93 1, +376 808 111

COLLEGI D'ADVOCATS D'ANDORRA, C. Doctor Nequi 7 1 2-G, +376 806 930

CRIADO I FERNANDES CONCEPCIO, C. Bonaventura Armengol 6 4, +376 809 000

CRISTINA BIFET GARCIA, C. Prat de la Creu 93 1 1-4, +376 808 111

DOLSA PALLE ESTEVE, C. Esteve Dolsa Pujal 36, +376 820 240

DONAIRE MENA ALFONSA, C. Prat de la Creu 83 PB local-2, +376 809 992

GIMENEZ DIAZ ENRIC, C. Prat de la Creu, 59, +376 809 777

JETHANI ASWANI ARJAN, C. Prat de la Creu 32 1-1, +376 805 450

JIMENEZ NAUDI JESUS, C. de l'Alzinaret 22 1, +376 803 567

JORDANA MADERO CARLES, Cami de la Creu 22 1 local-3, +376 803 700

JORDANA ROSSELL JORDI, C. Ciutat de Consuegra 10 4-1, +376 801 900

JORDANA ROSSELL XAVIER, Pl. Rebes 8 2, +376 807 030

JUNYER RICART JORDI, C. Bonaventura Armengol 6 4, +376 809 000

KINDER ESPINOSA, LLUIS ALFONS, Av. Meritxell 75 3, +376 800 850

LEGALIS ADVOCATS, C. Prat de la Creu 93 1, +376 808 111

LOPEZ AMBATLLE LAURA, C. Bonaventura Armengol 10 1 3-2, +376 804 280

LOPEZ HERRERO EVA, C. les Canals 5, +376 804 040

LOPEZ HORISCHNIK XAVIER, C. Doctor Vilanova 13 C 2-1, +376 812 200

LOPEZ MONTANYA ANTONI, C. de l'Alzinaret 22 1, +376 803 567

MANCIET FOUCHIER MAITENA, C. Ciutat de Consuegra 16 A 3-1, +376 809 809

MARSOL RIART CONXITA, C. Prat de la Creu 93 1 PB local-2, +376 821 081

MARTINEZ PIFARRE JOAQUIM, C. Doctor Vilanova 9 4-B, +376 868 286

MAS SANTURE ANNA, C. Bonaventura Armengol 10 1 4-1, +376 807 480

MERITXELL VERDU MARQUILLO ADVOCATS, Av. Princep Benlloch 32 PB local-2, +376 814 757

MINO ROSER ADVOCAT, C. Maria Pla 33 C 3-1, +376 808 686

MOLES PEREZ CARME, C. Maria Pla 33 C 2-1, +376 806 848

MOLNE SOLDEVILA ESTER I OLGA, C. de Callaueta 7 1-2, +376 826 199

MONEGAL BLASI JOAN, C. les Canals 7, +376 801 420

MONTEL MONTERET OLIVER, C. Ciutat de Consuegra 16 A 3-1, +376 809 809

MORA I ORTEGA ADVOCATS, Pg. d'Europa 2 1-2, +376 807 040

MORELL MORA ANTONI, C. de l'Alzinaret 9, +376 824 400

MORERA PORTA, MARIA TERESA, C. Doctor Nequi 8 3 1-3, +376 868 151

ORTEGA MONTSERAT ELOISA, Pg. d'Europa 2 1-2, +376 807 040

PONCE CASAL ESTEVE, C. de l'Alzinaret 22 1, +376 803 567

PUIGCERNAL SOLE JUDITH, C. Prat de la Creu 8 4-404, +376 821 182

PUJAL TORRES LAURA, C. Bonaventura Armengol 10 1 4-1, +376 807 480

RAMENTOL PUJOL BORRELL & VILAMAJO SL, C. Bonaventura Armengol 10 1 1-1, +376 810 810

RAMOS REBOREDO, JOAN CARLES, C. Bonaventura Armengol 6 4, +376 809 000

RASCAGNERES LLAGOSTERA, JOAN MIQUEL, C. les Canals 7, +376 801 420

RIBEIROGONCALVES MARISA, C. Prat de la Creu 59 A 3-2A, +376 809 777

RIBERA BAZTAN JOSEP, C. de la Unio 13 2-2, +376 828 405

RIBERAYGUA MARME FRANCA, C. Doctor Nequi 8 3 1-3, +376 868 151

RIBERT LLOVET JAUME, C. Bonaventura Armengol 6 4, +376 809 000

RIESTRA GONZALEZ DE UBIETA ANTONI, C. Doctor Nequi 7 1 3-B, +376 821 518

RIPOLL DAZA MARC, Av. de Tarragona 57, +376 863 867

ROSSA TORRES BIBIANA, C. Prat de la Creu 59 D 1-4D, +376 808 850

SANCHEZ MURIEL, ANA, C. de Pau Casals 10, +376 820 006

SANSA MATAMOROS GEMMA, C. Doctor Nequi 7 1 5-A, +376 821 547

SANSA RENE JAUME, C. Doctor Nequi 7 1 5-A, +376 824 780

SANSA SANTAMARIA ALBERT, Av. Princep Benlloch 8 4-1, +376 808 090

SANSA TORRES JOSEP, C. Prat de la Creu 83 1-2, +376 802 464

SEGURA COBO JORDI, C. de Pau Casals Ed. Cornella 2 5-2, +376 807 830

SILVESTRE ADVOCATS, C. Prat de la Creu 8 2-201, +376 803 344

SOLA RUIZ IOLANDA, C. dels Pareatges 6 1-2, +376 855 569

SOLE AGUSTI, ANNA MARIA, C. Doctor Vilanova 13 C 2-1, +376 812 200

VALENTI MARTI ADVOCAT, Pl. Guillemo 3 1-2, +376 885 050

VILA AMIGO MARC, C. les Canals 5, +376 804 040

VINYES DABAD THAIS, C. Doctor Vilanova 11 C 6-1, +376 802 380

VIVES ARMENGOL, MARIA NEUS, C. Prat de la Creu 83 1-2, +376 802 464

Escaldes-Engordany

ABC ASSESSORS I CONSULTORS, Ptge. Antonia Font Caminal 1 C 3-303, +376 805 060

AL-LEGA, Patricia Braganca (Advocada), C. de la Unio 9 A 1-1, +376 839 222

ALONSO MARTINEZ LOURDES, C. de les Boigues Ed. Pic Blanc 6-601, +376 828 118

BRAGANCA VARELA PATRICIA, C. de la Unio 9 A 1-1, +376 839 222

BUFET RUIZ/MONTANYA-ADVOCATS, Av. Carlemany 80 5 D503, +376 868 999

CASAJUANA GARRIGOS JOAN MIQUEL, Ptge. Antonia Font Caminal 1 C 4-404, +376 810 044

CLAVERA ARIZTI ALFONS, Av. Fiter I Rossell 4 2-6, +376 820 019

CODINA ROQUET OLGA, Ptge. Antonia Font Caminal 1 C 3-303, +805 060

CONSULT – GABINET D'ADVOCATS, Ptge. Antonia Font Caminal 1 C 2-202, +376 823 990

FINANA PIFARRE ANTONI, Ptge. Antonia Font Caminal 1 C 2-202, +376 823 990

FORNE MOLNE FRANCESC, C. les Canals 12 PB, +376 800 888

GARCIA BADIA JOSEP, C. les Canals 7 2-2, +376 810 800

GARCIA GARCIA STEPHANIE, C. Doctor Vilanova 13 C 2-1, +376 812 200

GARRALLA TOMAS SOFIA, C.Prat de la Creu 36 3-1, +376 809 080

OLIVE SAURET GUILLEM, C. dels Escalls 9 1-101, +376 827 846

RUIZ I VALLS LLUIS, Av. Carlemany 80 5-D503, +376 868 999

SOPENA GONZALEZ XAVIER, Ptge. Antonia Font Caminal 1 C 2-202, +376 823 990

VALS TORRALLARDONA MERITXELL, Av. Carlemany 38 4-1, +376 807 977

LUBRICANTS

Sant Julia

CARBURANTS SANT ELOI – LUBRICANTS TOTAL, Ctra. General 1 Est. de servei Sant Eloi, +376 743 120

Encamp

GARATGE OROS, Av. de Francois Mitterrand 7 PB local-8, +376 833 823

MEDIA (NEWSPAPERS, STATE RADIO AND TV)

Andorra la Vella

ART DE VIURE, C. Terra Vella 22 C 13 PB local-1, +376 860 504

BON DIA, C. Maria Pla 28 1, +376 808 888

DIARI D'ANDORRA, C. Bra. Riberaygua 39 5, +376 877 477

MES ANDORRA, C. Maria Pla 28 1, +376 808 888

PREMSA ANDORRANA, S.A., C. Bra. Riberaygua 39 5, +376 877 477

RADIO i TELEVISIO d'ANDORRA, SA, RTVA, State Radio & TV company (ANDORRA DIFUSIÓ), c/Baixada del Molí 24, +376 873 777

SET DIES, C. Bra. Riberaygua 39 5, +376 877 477

VISUALTEC, C. de la Vall 22 PB, +376 866 044

Escaldes-Engordany

ALL-ANDORRA.COM, Carrer L'Etang Salle, Edif. Les Teulades, Bl. VIII 3R 2A, +376 332 674

EL PERIODIC D'ANDORRA, Av. Fiter I Rossell 4 2-2, +376 736 200

MEDICAL EQUIPMENT

Andorra la Vella

SUBMINISTRES DENTAL EDELWEISS, C. Prada Motxilla 16, +376 825 258

SUBMINISTRES PODOLOGICS I MEDIC TEJERO, C. Bra. Riberaygua 9, +376 860 516

Escaldes-Engordany

BIOMEDICS MORENO, Av. Fiter I Rossell 62 PB local, +376 862 770

EXPO MEDICA, Av. Carlemany 105 PB local-1, +376 801 873

METALWORKS

Andorra la Vella

ESTRUCTURES METAL.LIQUES ANTONI, Av. de Salou 52 1, +376 722 972

INDUSTRIES FARGA S.L., C. Esteve Dolsa Pujal 22, +376 820 462

SERRALLERIA INDUSTRIAL JOAN, C. Camp Bastida 6, +376 807 770

SERRALLERIA INDUSTRIAL MAFIDA S.A., C. Camp Pauet 10, +376 722 210

SERRALLERIA LOPEZ & LOPEZ, C. de les Costes Nau 2 Zona ind.Magatzems Cervos 2, +376 723 872

SERRALLERIA RARDO, Av. de Salou Camping Valira, +376 772 209

SERRALLERIA VICTORIA, Ctra. de la Comella 41 3-305, +376 827 061

Escaldes-Engordany

SERRALLERIA JC, Av. Fiter I Rossell 45 B PB local, +376 867 012

TALLER LLADOS, Hortalets de Guem X. Pons, +376 807 380

Canillo

HOYO, Ctra. de Montaup Ed. Cirici-Estanyo PB-1, +376 852 952

Aixovall

INDUSTRIAL SERRALLERA MOLES, Ctra. General 6 Ed. Serralleria Moles, +376 841 212

SERRALLERIA ELS CORTALS S.L., Ctra. General 6 Nau 2 Zona ind. Camp de l'Avancader 4, +376 800 065

La Massana

SERRALLERIA BONS, Ctra. General 4 9 PB local-1, +376 738 964

SERRALLERIA CERETANA, Ctra. General 4 9 PB local-1, +376 738 964

SERRALLERIA EL MARTINET, Ctra. General 3 Ed. Prat de les Moles 1 local-4, +376 840 600

Encamp

SERRALLERIA INDUSTRIAL EL PORTUGUES, Av. de Joan Marti 127, +376 731 590

SERRALLERIA INDUSTRIAL JJ, C. de la Palanca Nau Coma PB local-2, +376 726 177

Sta. Coloma

SERRALLERIA LANAO, C. de la Plana 13, +376 720 992

SERRALLERIA TECNO-METALL S.L.U., Ctra. General 1 37 PB local-2, +376 742 350

TALLER DE SERRALLERIA LANAO, C. de la Plana 13, +376 720 992

Sant Julia

SERRALLERIA PUY, Nau 27 Zona ind. Borda del Germa, +376 842 105

SERRALLERIA SERGE, Nau 36 Zona ind. Borda del Germa, +376 843 999

MOTORCYCLES & SCOOTER

Andorra la Vella

AUTO MOTO RACING, Av. Santa Coloma 77, +376 800 010; +376 822 009

MARTI MOTOS, Av. Santa Coloma 22, +376 824 114

MOTO CARISMA ENDURO, C. Prada Motxilla 6 PB local-3, +376 860 082

MOTORAUTO, S.L., Av. Santa Coloma 52, +376 809 100

TOP MOTO, Bda. Del Moli 52, +376 869 200

Escaldes-Engordany

AUTO MOTO RACING, Av. Carlemany 44, +376 826 011

Sta. Coloma

A.MERCUATO, Av. d'Enclar 74, +376 824 242

MOTO SPRINT, Av. d'Enclar 120, +376 720 420

Pas de la Casa

AUTO MOTO RACING, C. del Maia 25, +376 855 221

NOTARIES

1. Bartumeu Martinez, Isidre

C. Prat de la Creu, 36, Andorra la Vella. Tel.: +376 801 000

2. Notaria Estañol

Av. del Consell d´Europa, 13, Andorra la Vella. Tel.: +376 801 280

3. Notaria Roza Ferrandiz

Bda del Moli, 9, 1-5a, Andorra la Vella. Tel.: +376 802 660

4. Rodriguez Miñana, Joan Carles

Av. Carlemany, 105, 5-3, Escaldes-Engordany. Tel.: +376 890 030

OFFICE MATERIALS

Andorra la Vella

CANON-SERVEI-C, C. de les Lloses 3 1, +376 821 648

CARLIN HIPERPAPERERA/OFIMARKET, C. Maria Pla 29, +376 809 050

OFI 3, Av. Santa Coloma 47 PB local-2, +376 808 990

OFIJET, C. Riger Bernat III 20 PB local-1, +376 802 580

Sant Julia

NATUR PAPER, Av. Verge de Canolich 86 PB local, +376 844 640

Sta. Coloma

UNIPAPER ANDORRA, S.A., Av. d'Enclar 26 PB local, +376 724 413

OPTICS CENTRES

Andorra la Vella

CENTRE OPTIC, C. Bra. Riberaygua 19, +376 824 299

DURO OPTIC, Pl. Rebes 4, +376 823 459

EURO OPTICA, Av. Princep Benlloch 18, +376 828 505

LOPTI-K, C. Bonaventura Armengol 10 PB local-1, +376 807 277

OPTICA OFTALMICA PASTEUR, Av. Meritxell 95, +376 760 600

OPTICA PASTEUR 2, C. Bonaventura Armengol 15 1-1, +376 864 111

OPTICA PASTEUR 3, Av. Meritxell 22, +376 865 741

OPTICA PASTEUR 6, Av. Meritxell 77 PB local-2, +376 807 600

Escaldes-Engordany

OPTICA ALAIN AFFLELOU, Av. Carlemany 70, +376 846 667

OPTICA PASTEUR 4, Av. Carlemany 81 PB local-1, +376 866 520

OPTICA PASTEUR 7, Av. Carlemany 62 PB local-9, +376 866 420

OPTICA SORTENY, Pl. Coprinceps 1 PB local-1, +376 824 072

OPTICA VISUAL ESCALDES, Av. Carlemany 73 PB local-3, +376 874 933

Sant Julia

OPTICA CREU VERDA, Av. Francesc Cairat 2, +376 841 294

OPTICA CREU VERDA, Av. Verge de Canolich 1 PB local, +376 843 141

OPTICA DE LORIA, Av. Verge de Canolich 58 A, +376 844 375

La Massana

OPTICA PASTEUR 5 (FARMACIA), Av. de Sant Antoni 22 PB local-1, +376 836 183

sunglasses, alexander mcqueen, anna-karin karlsson, armani, babiators, bvlgari, balenciaga, bottega veneta, carrera, cazal, celine, chopard, christian dior, dolce&gabbana, dsquared, fendi, gf ferre, givenchy, gucchi, hugo boss, max mara, polaroid, ray ban, roberto cavalli, saint laurent, silhouette, tiffany & Co, tom ford, tommy hilfiger, versace, vogue, marc jacobs, john galliano, cesare paciotti

PAINTINGS

Andorra la Vella

CAL COLORS, Av. Dr. Mitjavila 36 Entl. 2, +376 818 010

FEBRA, S.L., C. Roger Bernat III 16, +376 872 400

PINTURES BLANCOLOR, C. de la Borda 5 A 5-1, +376 820 694

PINTURES ESTIL XXI, Bda. Del Moli 30 3, +376 866 342

PINTURES LA FONT, Ctra. de la Comella 132 PB local-3, +376 821 464

PINTURES MILLAS, S.L., C. de Tobira 17 PB local, +376 861 361

Escaldes-Engordany

DECORACIO LUXE, C. dels Escalls 19 1-C, +376 622 335

PINTURES BLANCOLOR, Av. Carlemany 17 2-3, +376 826 902

PIINTURES NOVA GENERACIO, Av. Sant Jaume 28 PB local, +376 866 730

Encamp

PINTURA ART I DECORACIO, C. del Tremat 4, +376 834 428

PINTURES PI, Av. de Joan Marti 39 PB local-A, +376 833 145

Sta. Coloma

PINTUREKA, S.L., Av. d'Enclar 28 PB local-1, +376 727 117

PINTURES RUPESTRES, S.L., Cami Ral Ed. Pic d'Enclar Residencial Prat Condal PB local-2, +376 862 354

Sant Julia

PINTURES BENET, C. J. Carvajal de Hue 2 3-1, +376 842 743

PINTURES ESTUCOLOR, Av. Verge de Canolich 126 5-1, +376 841 428

PINTURES GALERA, C. Doctor Palau 46 PB local-2, +376 843 121

PNTURES NOVA LINIA, S.L., Av. Francesc Cairat 34 PB local, +376 842 155

La Massana

POLINET, S.L., Av. del Ravell 30 PB local, +376 838 792

PERFUMERY, COSMETICS

Andorra la Vella

FLORMAR MAKE UP, Av. Meritxell 105, +376 846 739

GLOB, C. Maria Pla 10 A PB local-2, +376 846 668

LUXURY, Av. Meritxell 93, +376 822 377

PERFUMERIA LA PERLA, Av. Meritxell 51, +376 820 302

PERFUMERIA ORQUIDIA, Av. Meritxell 106, +376 820 517

PERFUMERIA TINA, Av. Princep Benlloch 26, +376 864 054

PERFUMERIA EL TRIANON, Av. Meritxell 69, +376 820 703

PERFUMERIA EL TRIANON, Av. Meritxell 9, +376 820 706

Escaldes-Engordany

BODY SHOP, Av. Carlemany 40 PB local-1, +376 867 297

GALA PERFUMERIES, Av. Carlemany 99, +376 813 431

GALA PERFUMERIES, C. de Sant Antoni 1, +376 802 655

GALA PERFUMERIES, Av. Carlemany 44 PB local-9, +376 802 915

GALA PERFUMERIES, Pl. Coprinceps 1, +376 802 670

PERFUMERIA JULIA, (museum), Av. Carlemany 115, +376 892 200

Sant Julia

GALA PERFUMERIES, Av. Francesc Cairat 6 2, +376 842 711

PERFUMERIA MARIA LLUISA, Av. Francesc Cairat 6 2 A PB local-1, +376 842 051

La Massana

GALA PERFUMERIES, Av. de Sant Antoni 22 PB local-3, +376 737 105

Pas de la Casa

GALA PERFUMERIES, C. Sant Jordi 23, +376 855 712

GALA PERFUMERIES, C. de Catalunya 8, +376 855 909

GALA PERFUMERIES, Av. d'Encamp 5 PB local-2, +376 855 897

GALA PERFUMERIES, C. Sant Jordi 3 PB local-8, +376 855 894

GALA PERFUMERIES, C. de l'Abeurador 1 PB local-1, +376 855 229

GALA PERFUMERIES, C. de les Abelletes 3, +376 855 539

GALA PERFUMERIES, Av. del Consell General 15, +376 855 508

GALA PERFUMERIES, Pl. dels Coprinceps 10, +376 856 449

GALA PERFUMERIES, C. de les Abelletes 9 PB local-1, +376 856 490

GALA PERFUMERIES, Av. d'Encamp 33, +376 855 867

GALA PERFUMERIES, C. Major 27, +376 855 960

GALA PERFUMERIES, C. Major 11, +376 855 552

GALA PERFUMERIES, Av. del Consell General 9 PB local-2, +376 855 397

PERFUMERIA ARIANE, C. Bernat III 6, +376 855 960

narciso rodriguez, valentino, versace, escada, naomi campbell, rochas, max factor, clinique, michael Kors, nina ricci, paco rabanne, lancome, lanvin, trussardi, natural cosmetics

PHARMACEUTICALS

Andorra la Vella

Farmacia Edelweiss, C. Bra. Riberaygua, 31 PB local-2, +376 831 227

Farmacia Central, C. Bra. Riberaygua 20, +376 805 380

Farmacia del fener, C. Bra Riberaygua 2, +376 861 761

Farmacia Pasteur, Avda. Meritxell, 84, +376 800 970

Farmacia Nova, Avda. Sta. Coloma 25, +376 823 621

Farmacia Sant Ermengol, C. Bonaventura Armengol 7 PB local-2, +376 818 323

Farmacia Rocamora, Avda. Meritxell, 130, +376 804 777

Farmacia Galeno, Avda. Meritxell, 91 4-405, +376 828 717

Farmacia font de la Call, Avda. Princep Benlloch, 30, +376 862 672

Farmacia Guerrero 2, Avda. Meritxell 39 PB local-1, +376 801 856

Farmacia Guitart, C. Prat de la Creu 59 PB local-1A, +376 825 003

Farmacia International, Avda. Meritxell, 16, +376 820 162

Farmacia del Pont, Avda. Meritxell, 68, +376 801 111

Farmacia les Anelletes, Av. Dr. Mitjavilla 30 PB local, +376 863 313

Farmacia Rosella, Avda. Meritxell, 65, +376 821 954

Farmacia Roser Miro, C. Maria Pla 14 PB local-1, +376 867 344

Farmacia les Tres Creus, C. les Canals 5, +376 820 212

Farmacia El Cedre, Av. d'Encar 32 PB local-2, Sta. Coloma, +376 723 383

Farmacia Enclar, Av. Princep Benlloch, 87, +376 804 333

Farmacia Meritxell, C. Dr. Nequi, 7, +376 826 060

Farmacia Mitjavila, Pl. Princep Benlloch 3, +376 820 224

Farmacia Gonzalez-Adrio, Avda. Meritxell, 30, +376 864 946

Farmacia Gran, Avda. Meritxell, 83, +376 828 009

Farmacia Valira, C. Prat de la Creu 17, +376 829 160

Farmacia Santa Coloma, Av. d'Enclar 72 1-1, +376 722 613

Escaldes-Engordany

Farmacia Aristot, C.de la Constititucio Ed. Salita Parc D, +376 821 116

Farmacia Carlemany, Av. Carlemany 83, +376 805 444

Farmacia de les Escoles, Av. De les Escoles 17 D, +376 820 768

Farmacia de les Valls, C. Mossen Guillem Adellach 1 PB local, +376 820 824

Farmacia Europea, Av. Carlemany 105 PB local-1, +376 801 868

Farmacia Guerrero, Av. Carlemany t61 PB local-2, +376 801 859

Farmacia Margalef, Av. del Pessebre 24 PB local-1, +376 821 512

Farmacia Morets, Av. Filter I Rossel 4, +376 829 400

Farmacia Tristana, C. dels Escalls 7 PB local-3, +376 847 900

Sant Julia de Loria

Farmacia Creu Verda, Av. Francesc Cairat 2, +376 841 294

Farmacia de Loria, Av. Verge de Canolich 58 A, +376 741 221

Farmacia Pasteur, Ctra. d'Espanya, Centre Comercial River, +376 741 565

Farmacia Mallor-Sunyer, Ctra. General 1 Centre com. Punt de Trobada, +376 800 666

Farmacia Sant Eloi, Ctra. General, 1 Est. de servei Total PB local, +376 842 053

Canillo

Farmacia Abarset, Av. Sant Joan de Caselles Cs. Nova Som 1 PB local-2, +376 851 540

Farmacia Piolets, Ctra. General 2 Hotel Piolets PB local, Soldeu, +376 852 296

Encamp

Farmacia Baixench, C. Major 3 PB local, +376 832 732

Farmacia Manresa, Pl. del Consell 10 PB local, +376 834 997

Farmacia Torrent, Av. de Francois Mitterand 5, +376 832 660

Pas de la Casa

Farmacia de les Pistes, Av. d'Encamp 9 PB local-2, +376 856 580

La Massana

Farmacia Carolina Garralla, Av. De Sant Antoni 7 PB local, +376 838 126

Farmacia d'Arinsal, Ctra. General 5 14 PB local-4, Arinsal

Farmacia Pasteur 5, Avda. St. Antony s/n, Aparthotel Rossell, Baixos, +376 836 183

Farmacia Pasteur 5 (optica), Avda. St. Antony 22 PB local-1, +376 836 183

Farmacia d'Arinsal, Ed. Joan Torne, Ctra. General, +376 839 903

Farmacia Genciana, Av. de Sant Antoni 12 B PB local-2, +376 838 166

Sant Julia de Loria

Farmacia Creu Verda, Av. Francesc Cairat 2, +376 841 294

Farmacia de Loria, Av. Verge de Canolich 58 A, +376 741 221

Farmacia Pasteur, Ctra. d'Espanya, Centre Comercial River, +376 741 565

Farmacia Mallor-Sunyer, Ctra. General 1 Centre com. Punt de Trobada, +376 800 666

Farmacia Sant Eloi, Ctra. General, 1 Est. de servei Total PB local, +376 842 053

Ordino

Farmacia Font Freda, Travessia d'Ordino 8 PB local-2, +376 837 000

pharmacy in Andorra, drugstore, buy medicine

PHILATELY SHOPS

Andorra la Vella

FILATELIA ANDORRANA, Antic Carrer Major 23 PB local, +376 825 829;

PORCELAIN & TABLEWARE

Andorra la Vella

CUINA 2000, S.A., C. Ciutat de Valls 30 PB local, +376 805 455

MAGATZEMS GALICIA, C. Maria Pla 28 6, +376 821 663

PANIBERCIA, S.L., C. Ciutat de Valls 30 PB local, +376 805 455

Escaldes-Engordany

CASA CANUT, Av. Carlemany 107, +376 827 867

RADIOSTATIONS

Andorra la Vella

AD RADIO, C. Bra. Riberaygua 39 5, +376 877 477

AM-ANDORRA MUSICA, Bda. Del Moli 24, +376 873 777

ANDORRA 1, Av. Meritxell 75 2-1, 1802 0304

FLAIX FM, Av. Meritxell 75 2-1, 1802 0304

RADIO SER PRINCIPAT D'ANDORRA, C. Prat de la Creu 32 PB local, +376 808 300

RNA-RADIO NACIONAL D'ANDORRA, Bda. Del Moli 24, +376 873 777

Escaldes-Engordany

UNIO DE RADIOAFICIONATS ANDORRANS, Av. Fiter I Rossell 71 2-1, +376 825 380

Encamp

CADENA PIRENACIA DE RADIO I TELEVISIO, Av. Princep Benlloch 24 PB local, +376 732 000

PROXIMA FM, Av. Princep Benlloch 24 PB local, +376 731 515

R7P RADIO, Av. Princep Benlloch 24 PB local, +376 731 414

RADIO VALIRA, Av. Princep Benlloch 24 PB local, +376 732 000

REAL ESTATE COMPANY (AGENCIES)

Andorra la Vella

7 CLAUS IMMOBILIARIA, C. de l'Aigueta 14 Entl. A1, +376 868 066

AGENCIA IMMOB. ATTIC, Av. Meritxell 75 1-15, +376 828 878

AGENCIA IMMOB. PUBLI-ANDORRA (P.A.), C. Prat de la Creu 22 C 2-1, +376 820 505

AGIA-COLLEGI PROFESSIONAL, Av. del Fener 11 3-6, +376 801 115

ATMOSFERA IMMOBILIARIA, S.L., C. de Pau Casals Ed. Cornella 2 3-1, +376 866 262

AUGE REAL ESTATE Carrer de l'Aigüeta, num. 14 Entresol Despatx num. 1, +376 724 888

CRISTINA FONT IMMOBILIARIA, C. Babot Camp 13 4-1, +376 809 040

EIX IMMOBILIARIA, S.A., Pl. Rebes 8, +376 874 050

EURO FINQUES, C. Bra. Riberaygua 39 4-2, +376 801 065

FIABCI ANDORRA, Av. del Fener 11 3-6, +376 801 115

FINQUES DEL PIRINEU, C. Ciutat de Consuegra 10 2-3, +376 860 606; +376 820 554

FINQUES VISENT, C. Bonaventura Armengol 10 1 2-4, +376 821 801; +376 821 829

FONT CASA IMMOBILIARIA, C. Babot Camp 13 4-1, +376 809 040

GESTIM, C. Bra. Riberaygua 27, +376 807 888

GESTIO D'HABITATGE 76, C. Doctor Nequi 6 1 local-11, +376 821 644

GESTORIA IMMOBILIARIA, S.A., C. de la Borda 5 A 2-1, +376 801 999

GESTSERVEIS, Av. del Fener 11 5-4B, +376 862 800

G.I.S.A., C. de la Borda 5 A 2-1, +376 801 999

GRUP IMMOBILIARI CIERCO, S.A., Ctra. de la Comella 11, +376 871 350

HABITAREA GRUP PROMOTOR, S.L., C. de l'Alzinaret 2 PB local, +376 822 282

IMMO GESTIO, C. Doctor Vilanova 13 C 4-1, +376 869 540

IMMOBILIARIA ALPINA, C. de l'Aigueta 12 1-119, +376 825 428

IMMOBILIARIA CALVET, S.L., Av. Meritxell 91 4-401, +376 862 540

IMMOBILIARIA CEL, S.A., Ctra. de la Comella 11, +376 871 375

IMMOBILIARIA D'ENCAMP, Pl. Guillemo 3 2-1, +376 806 300

IMMOBILIARIA FLODOR, Av. Meritxell 97 1-2, +376 800 300

IMMOBILIARIA GAUDI, Av. Dr. Mitjavila 33 A 5-1, +376 861 014

IMMOBILIARIA GESTORIA LA VALL, C. Doctor Vilanova 11 PB local-1, +376 802 234

IMMOBILIARIA IMMOJET, Av. Princep Benlloch 89 PB local-1, +376 826 201

IMMOBILIARIA IMTERSA, C. Sant Salvador 7 B, +376 861 000

IMMOBILIARIA LA VALL, C. Doctor Vilanova 11 PB local-1, +376 802 232

IMMOBILIARIA LES SOLANES, C. Gil Torres 38 5-2, +376 862 551

IMMOBILIARIA L'ESTALL S.A., C. Prat de la Creu 8 3-303, +376 860 997

IMMOBILIARIA MULTIFINQUES, S.L., C. de l'Alzinaret 24 PB local, +376 807 077

IMMOBILIARIA OFESIM, C. Mossen Tremosa 4 PB local-1, +376 820 344

IMMOBILIARIA PREMIUM, Bda. Del Moli 39 PB local, +376 862 009

IMMOBILIARIA PUBLI-ANDORRA (P.A.), C. Prat de la Creu 22 C 2-1, +376 820 505

IMMOBILIARIA REIG, Av. Meritxell 106, +376 808 380

IMMOBILIARIA SICORIS, C. Prat de la Creu 93 1 PB local-2, +376 864 081

IMMOBILIARIA SOLANA DE RANSOL, C. Doctor Nequi 6 1 local-34, +376 861 100

IMMOBILIARIA SOL-IXENT, Av. Dr. Mitjavila 2 PB local-4, +376 825 545

IMMOBILIARIA SUPERIOR, S.A., C. de la Sardana 5 PB local-2, +376 808 080

IMMOBILITZA'T, C. Esteve Dolsa Pujal 39, +376 824 582

IMMOSER DEL PIRINEU, S.L., C. Bra. Riberaygua 8 1-1, +376 805 355

JEN INTERNACIONAL, S.L., C. de Tobira 22 6-703, +376 827 026

LAND, S.A., C. Bra. Riberaygua 2, +376 800 000

LINIA IMMOBILIARIA, C. Verge del Pilar 5 PB local-28, +376 885 588

MARCOR, Av. Princep Benlloch 87 9-1, +376 826 508

MULTIFINQUES, S.L., C. de l'Alzinaret 24 PB local, +376 807 077

NOU AIRE IMMOBILIARIA, Av. Meritxell 75 4, +376 801 601

OBRA VISTA PROMOCIONS, S.L., C. de l'Alzinaret 13 PB local-4, +376 867 222

O.C.C.E.S.A., Av. de Tarragona 58 1-17, +376 820 280

OFICINA D'ESTUDIS IMMOBILIARIS, C. Mossen Tremosa 4 PB local-1, +376 820 344

ON VIURE, C. Prat de la Creu 59 B 3-3K, +376 805 959

PROMESCA, C. Maria Pla 33 C 2-3, +376 821 015

PROMOCIONS C.M.S., S.L., Av. de Tarragona 99 B PB local, +376 810 018

PROMOCIONS NORMA, S.L., C. Doctor Nequi 5 PB local-2, +376 808 680

ROC ESCOLLS, S.A., C. Roc dels Escolls 7 3 4-A, +376 811 016

SIRESA, Ctra. de la Comella Cs. 2 Residencial Kaph, +376 828 928

VALUA, C. Bra. Riberaygua 18 1-1, +376 822 556

Escaldes-Engordany

ATPA, S.L., C. de la Unio 11 A 1-B, +376 809 444

BECA-INTERNACIONAL, C. Santa Anna 12 1, +376 821 544

CASA MUNTANYA, Av. Carlemany 68 5-D501, +376 892 023

CASA NOVA IMMOBILIARIA, C. Manuel Cerqueda Escale 6 2-2, +376 885 300

CONSTRUCTORA IMMOBILIARIA CARRACEDO, Av. Fiter I Rossell 70 1-1, +376 822 552

GESTIO DE SERVEIS A EMPRESES I PROPIETATS-GESAP, Av. del Fener 22, +376 808 450

GESTPROCON, S.L., Av. Carlemany 117 4-B, +376 801 313

GRUP GUEM, Av. del Pessebre 52 A PB-1, +376 812 115

IMMOBILIARIA BESOLI, C. Santa Anna 12 1, +376 821 544

IMMOBILIARIA CARRACEDO, Av. Fiter I Rossell 70, +376 827 548

IMMOBILIARIA ZONA HABITABLE, Av. de les Escoles 18 PB local-2, +376 801 200

IMMOBILIARIA-AGENCIA SANCHEZ – IMMOAS, Av. de les Escoles 17 D PB-2, +376 333 340

IMMOBILIARIA DEL PIRINEU, S.L., C. Bra. Riberaygua 8 1-1, +376 805 355

INVERSIONS F. ESPORT, Ptge. Antonia Font Caminal 1 C 3-301, +376 810 700

METRES QUADRATS-M2, C. Isabelle Sandy 6 1-5, +376 722 244

ORADA IMMOBILIARIA, Ptge. Antonia Font Caminal 1 C 5-502, +376 875 551

PICART IMMOBILIARIA, C. de la Unio 11 A 1-B, +376 809 444

ROLS IMMOBILIARIA, Av. Carlemany 55 PB local-1, +376 805 300

SERIANN, S.L., Av. Carlemany 80 4-D403, +376 829 804

SERIMA, Av. Carlemany 31 PB local-1, +376 820 852

SIM IMMOBILIARIA, S.L., Av. Carlemany 68 4-8, +376 864 848

La Cortinada

AC IMMOBILIARIA S.A., Av. de la Cortinada Ed. Prat de les Mates B PB-A, +376 850 700

Pas de la Casa

AGENCIA IMMOBILIARIA GRIFO, S.A., Av. Encamp 29, +376 855 250

AGENCIA PEDROUS, Av. d'Encamp 35 PB local-1, +376 855 669

AGENCIA SHERPA, Pl. dels Vaquers 15 PB local, +376 855 299; +376 856 179

IMMOBILIARIA ALTISSIM, Av. d'Encamp 37 PB-4, +376 855 044

IMMOBILIARIA DEL PAS, Av. d'Encamp 23, +376 755 450

IMMOBILIARIA PIC BLANC, S.L., Av. d'Encamp 1 1-4, +376 855 475

Sant Julia

ANDORGEST, Av. Verge de Canolich 62 PB local, +376 741 486

GLOBAL HABITAT MANEJAMENT, Av. Verge de Canolich 51 Entl., +376 742 123

GREC IMMOBILIARIS, S.L., Pl. de la Germandat 9, +376 800 516

ORBENTIS, Pl. Major 7 PB local, +376 844 777

La Massana

API. AD, Av. de Sant Antoni 82 A PB local-1A, +376 738 838

ARIES-BELIER, S.L., Av. del Ravell 28 PB local-1, +376 738 700

CISA, Av. de Sant Antoni 32 PB local-1, +376 737 373

CISA SERVEI, S.L., Av. de Sant Antoni 91 A PB local, +376 737 773

F.I. A.S.A. IMMOBILIARIA, Av. de Sant Antoni 49 PB local-1, +376 738 073

GESTORIA DE VIVENDES DE LES VALLS, S.A., C. el Traves Ed. Traves, +376 855 980

IMMOBILIARIA D'ORDINO, Av. de Sant Antoni 82 A PB local-2A, +376 739 690

IMMOBILIARIA MASSANDOR, Av. de Sant Antoni 25 PB local-1, +376 737 222

IMMOBILIARIA OCEANIC, Av. de Sant Antoni 12 B PB local-1, +376 738 000

INVICO, S.L., Av. de Sant Antoni 47 PB local-3, +376 807 970

ROC PROPIETATS, Av. el Traves 5 PB local-1, +376 835 346

SERVISSIM, Av. de Sant Antoni 26 PB local-1, +376 737 900

Sta. Coloma

BECIER IMMOBILIARIA, Av. d'Enclar 140, +376 871 871

Encamp

BUSCAT, S.A., Av. de Francois Mitterrand 92 2-1, +376 833 960

FINQUES MARCA, Av. de Joan Marti 82 PB local-2, +376 732 020

FINQUES TRES CASES, Av. de Joan Marti 102 PB local-1, +376 872 222

GESICO, Av. Princep Benlloch 26 PB local, +376 731 431

GESTORIA IMMOBILIARIA EDUARD, C. Balco del Sola 5 B PB local-2, +376 868 666

HANSON PROMOTORIA IMMOBILIARIA, Av. de Joan Marti 106 PB local-1, +376 832 088

IMMOBILIARIA BENET II, Av. de Francois Mitterrand 120 PB local, +376 833 121

IMMOBILIARIA CIUTAT PUBILLA, Av. de Joan Marti 42 PB local-D, +376 834 134

IMMOBILIARIA ESTEL BLAU, C. Balco del Sola 3 A PB local-1, +376 831 700

IMMOBILIARIA MASSUET, Av. de Francois Mitterrand 55 PB local-1, +376 834 646

IMMOBILIARIA SOLANA DUCH, Av. de Joan Marti 78 PB local-2, +376 833 543

IMMO-DECO, Av. de Joan Marti 73 PB local-1, +376 832 552

PROMOCIONS FIMAR, Av. de Joan Marti 75 A 1-3, +376 831 497

Soldeu

CALBO ALTA MUNTANYA, Ctra. General 2, +376 870 560

SOLDEU-PARADIS, S.L., Ctra. General 2 Ed. Himalaia PB local-6, +376 851 485

TAL, Ctra. General 2 Ed. Palinquero Pleta de Soldeu 2 PB-1, +376 853 028

VIVA SOL VACANCES, Bordes d'Envalira Resid. Supervalira, +376 851 082

Arinsal

FERCAMP, S.A., +376 738 721

SCAN, S.A., Ctra. General 5 Urb. Bordes d'Arinsal, +376 836 626

VALORS CARLES CORAL, Ctra. General 5 39 PB local-2, +376 815 777

Ordino

GEISER, S.A., C. Major 15 PB, +376 837 879

IMMOBILIARIA LA PORTELLA, Travessia d'Ordino 10 PB, +376 747 747

MANTENIMENT I SERVEIS, S.L., Pleta Terra Major PB local, +376 836 903; +376 835 800

Canillo

ORIOL IMMOBLES, Ed. Carles Armany PB local-1, +376 853 864

Les Bons

PROMOCIONS MARAND, C. 14 de Marc 1 1 PB-2, +376 832 717

Anyos

TANDEM IMMOBILIARIA, Ctra. de Sant Cristofol, +376 839 900

RECYCLING

Escaldes-Engordany

PIRINENCA DE SERVEIS, Av. Consell de la Terra 14, +376 810 510

REVANOSA, Av. Consell de la Terra 14, +376 801 020

Sta. Coloma

L'HOME DEL SAC, Av. d'Enclar 25 PB local, +376 722 292

REFESA, Ctra. General 1 21, +376 722 607

Aixovall

LOGISTICA I SERVEIS DEL RECICLATGE, Nau 7 Urb. Prat de Jaia, +376 844 133

Encamp

REVANOSA, Av. de la Bartra, +376 801 020

RESTAURANTS

Andorra la Vella

120, Av. Meritxell 120 PB local, +376 865 345

1940, Av. Princep Benlloch 20, +376 860 006

ANDBURGER ZERO, Cap del Carrer 9 PB local, +376 817 771

ANDORRA PARK HOTEL, C. les Canals 24, +376 877 777

BAR RESTAURANT ESTELA, Bda. Del Moli 15 2, +376 869 077

BAR RESTAURANT LA NOGREDA, Ctra. de la Comella 35 PB local-1, +376 822 181

BAR RESTAURANT VILARRASA, Pl. Guillemo 4, +376 861 517

BAR RESTAURANT ARMADA, C. Ciutat de Valls 63 PB local, +376 822 729

BODEGA POBLET, C. de l'Alzinaret 6, +376 862 722

BUDA ESPAI ANDORRA, Av. de Salou 32, +376 720 777

BURGER KING, Av. de Tarragona 1, +376 863 344

CAFETERIA RESTAURANT CENTRAL GERMANS FERREIRA, Parc Central Restaurant Parc Central, +376 818 910

CAL JULIA, Av. Santa Coloma 110 PB local-1, +376 823 118

CCA-CENTRE COMERCIAL ANDORRA, Av. Meritxell 94, +376 870 310

EL REBOST DEL PADRI, C. de la Sardana 10 A S1-1, +376 868 221

EL REBOST DEL PADRI, C. de la Vall 18, +376 821 212

GRANJA RESTAURANT CAL TEO, C. Pere d'Urg 7 PB local-5, +376 864 215

HENRY RESTAURANT CLUB, C. Prat de la Creu 29 A PB local-1, +376 845 444

HOTEL RESTAURANT EL JAPONES, Av. Meritxell 65, +376 860 400

KILOMBO, Av. Princep Benlloch 11 PB local-2, +376 727 372

LA ADELITA, Pl. Princep Benlloch 44 PB local, +376 863 323

LA BORDA PAIRAL 1630, C. Doctor Vilanova 7, +376 869 999

RESTAURANT BORDA XICA, Cap del Carrer 10, +376 837 190

LA CAVA RONALDO, C. Mossen Cinto Verdaguer 7, +376 820 175

LA FONTANA, C. de l'Aigueta 4 PB local-3, +376 868 600

LA PIAZZA, C. Sant Salvador 2 PB local-2, +376 808 055

LA TAVERNA D'ALI, C. de Callaueta 11, +376 819 000

LA TAVERNA D'EN MALLOR, C. Verge del Pilar 6, +376 867 837

L'ABADIA, Ptge: Isabelle Sandy 2 PB local-2, +376 820 825

L'EESCENARI DE PIZZES, Av. Dr. Mitjavila 19 PB local-3, +376 818 899

LORENZO'S, C. Prat de la Creu 96 PB local-2, +376 862 111

MAMA MARIA, Av. Meritxell 25, +376 869 996

MINIM'S, Antic Carrer Major 5 PB local, +376 867 511

PIZZA VITTO, Av. Princep Benlloch 43 PB local-2, +376 846 222

PIZZERIA CAL CUBA F, C. Ciutat de Valls 3 1 PB local, +376 825 165

PIZZERIA MAGNA, C. Joan Maragall 2 C, +376 824 171

PIZZERIA PRIMAVERA, C. de Callaueta 8, +376 800 530

PLATIN, C. Bra. Riberaygua 8 PB local-1, +376 861 001

POLLASTRE RAPID, Av. Santa Coloma 8, +376 868 068

RESTAURANT ARMES DE FAMILIA, Pl. Rebes 6 PB local, +376 819 681

RESTAURANT BORDA ESTEVET, Ctra. de la Comella 2, +376 874 920

RESTAURANT CA LA CONXITA, C. la Llacuna 12 PB local-4, +376 829 948

RESTAURANT CAFETERIA FONTVERD, C. Ciutat de Consuegra 2, +376 861 193

RESTAURANT CAMPING VALIRA, Av. de Salou Nau Garatge Sola, +376 724 254

RESTAURANT CAN BENET, Antic Carrer Major 9, +376 828 922

RESTAURANT CAN MANEL, C. Mestre Xavier Plana 4 1 2-3, +376 822 397

RESTAURANT CASA TERESA, C. Bonaventura Armengol 11 PB local-1, +376 826 476

RESTAURANT CELLER D'EN TONI, C. Verge del Pilar 4, +376 821 252

RESTAURANT COMA, Pcta. Monjo 3 PB local, +376 854 713

RESTAURANT EL BON RACO, Av. de Salou 86, +376 721 616

RESTAURANT EL CAP BO, C. Babot Camp 11, +376 821 638

RESTAURANT EL CROSTO, Cap del Carrer 7 PB local, +376 862 931

RESTAURANT EL FAISA, Cap del Carrer 4 PB local, +376 823 283

RESTAURANT EL REFUGI ALPI, Av. Meritxell 73 PB local-3, +376 808 100

RESTAURANT EXIMI, C. la Llacuna 5 PB local, +376 827 829

RESTAURANT FONT DEL PUIAL, C. Font del Puial 5 PB local, +376 864 322

RESTAURANT FRESCCO, Av. Dr. Mitjavila 3, +376 863 740

RESTAURANT LA MOSSEGADA, Av. Meritxell 73, +376 823 131

RESTAURANT L'AIGUETA, Av. de Tarragona 58, +376 825 311

RESTAURANT L'ERA DEL ROSSELL, Meritxell, +376 852 800

RESTAURANT ERMITA, Meritxell, +376 751 050

RESTAURANT L'OLIVE, C. Sant Salvador 3, +376 804 265

RESTAURANT L'ORRI, C. Prat de la Creu 55, +376 827 844

RESTAURANT MACARY, C. Mossen Tremosa 6 PB local-2, +376 818 918

RESTAURANT MC DONALD'S, Av. Meritxell 32, +376 885 885

RESTAURANT MC DONALD'S, Av. de Tarragona 49, +376 845 491

RESTAURANT MEXICAN CAFÉ, Av. Princep Benlloch 49 4-1, +376 820 125

RESTAURANT NOU, Av. Dr. Mitjavila 10, +376 863 117

RESTAURANT PAPANICO, Av. Princep Benlloch 4 PB local, +376 867 333

RESTAURANT PIZZERIA CASA TEVA, C. Prada de Moles 3, +376 864 254

RESTAURANT PIZZERIA EATALIAN REPUBLIC, C. Prat de la Creu 29 B PB local-5, +376 821 888

RESTAURANT PIZZERIA EL MENAIRO, Av. Dr. Mitjavila 36, +376 860 611

RESTAURANT PIZZERIA LA CANTINA, Pl. Guillemo 4, +376 823 065

RESTAURANT PLATO, C. Prat de la Creu 15, +376 760 308

RESTAURANT RACO D'EN JOSEP, C. Prat de la Creu 93 1, +376 828 703

RESTAURANT ROMA, Av. Meritxell 70, +376 863 190

RESTAURANT TARRAGONA, Av. de Tarragona 65, +376 824 847

RESTAURANT TATU, Av. de Tarragona 58, +376 824 184

RESTAURANT TRES EIXOS, C. Prat de la Creu 8 PB local-4, +376 846 484

RESTAURANT TREVOL VERD, Av. Santa Coloma 89 PB local, +376 828 497

RESTAURANT VERSAILLES, Cap del Carrer 1, +376 821 331

SUSHI AND GONG, C. Doctor Nequi 6 PB local-2, +376 861 800

TAVERNA ANGEL BELMONTE, C. Ciutat de Consuegra 3, +376 822 460

VIETNAM GOURMET, C. Joan Maragall 22 PB local-1, +376 851 888

Escaldes-Engordany

ANDBURGER ZERO, C. Coprincep Fransois Mitterrand 2 PB local-3, +376 846 046

BAR RESTAURANT CESAR II, C. Santa Anna 8 PB local, +376 824 933

BAR RESTAURANT ELS JARDINS, Parc de la Mola 6, +376 823 308

CAFE CAL PERO, Av. Fiter I Rossell 33 PB local, +376 845 760

CASA DEL BISTEC, Av. Carlemany 105 PB local-4, +376 826 921

CHINA BOOM, Av. Carlemany 80-02, +376 861 613

DEIMONS, CALDEA, Parc de la Mola 10, +376 800 984

DELICIES TURQUES, Av. del Fener 16 PB local-2, +376 864 964

FOREST, Av. Carlemany 44 PB local-4, +376 822 292

HOTEL ROC DE CALDES, Ctra. d'Engolasters Hotel Roc de Caldes, +376 874 555

IO, INUU, Parc de la Mola 10, +376 800 984

L'ENOTECA, C. del Parnal 4 C PB local, +376 813 545

LA DAMA DEL LLAC, Ctra. d'Engolasters Restaurant Llac d'Engolasters, +376 828 206

LA NOVA FORQUILLA, Av. del Fener 24 A, +376 861 810

LA PLACETA DE LES CLOSES, Av. Carlemany 95 D PB local-2, +376 826 667

MANXURIA IMPERIAL RESTAURANT, Av. del Fener 3, +376 826 260

PIZZERIA ANGELO, C. de la Unio 9 PB local-1, +376 805 810

PRAT DEL ROURE, C. Esteve Albert Ed. Prat del Roure, +376 845 777

RESTAURANT BIG-BEN, C. de Sant Antoni 5 PB local-1, +376 824 075

RESTAURANT CAMP DEL SERRAT, Ctra. d'Engolasters Restaurant Camp del Serrat, +376 809 590

RESTAURANT DON DENIS, C. Isabelle Sandy 3 PB local-1, +376 820 692

RESTAURANT DON FELIX LOUNGE, C. Nou 3 PB local-1, +376 846 847

RESTAURANT EL ROURE, Parc de la Mola 9 PB local-2, +376 861 099

RESTAURANT HONG-KONG, Av. Carlemany 56 PB local-1, +376 829 029

RESTAURANT ITALIA FONTANELLA – ESCALDES, Av. del Fener 14, +376 802 930

RESTAURANT LA PINOSA, C. de la Unio 11 A PB local-2, +376 869 113

RESTAURANT LES BARQUES, Av. del Fener 24 A PB local-3, +376 813 200

RESTAURANT LLAC CEL, Ctra. d'Engolasters Restaurant Llac I Cel, +376 822 322

RESTAURANT PIZZEERIA LA TAGLIATELLA, Av. Carlemany 91 PB local-2, +376 866 177

RESTAURANT RUSTIC XIC, C. de la Unio 9 PB local-2, +376 861 636

RESTAURANT VERMELL – ESCALDES, C. de la Unio 5, +376 870 400

RESTAURANT XUP-XUP, Av. del Fener 11 PB local-3, +376 827 900

TERRASSES CAN MARGARIT (обслуживание групп), Av. del Pessebre 1 PB local-2, +376 803 705

TIC TAPA, Av. del Fener 24 A PB local-5, +376 813 969

RESTAURANT CASA CANUT, Av. Carlemany 107, +376 739 900

RESTAURANT EL GRECO, C. de Sant Antoni 5 PB local-1, +376 824 552

RESTAURANT EL MUSSOL, Av. de les Escoles 16 PB local-1, +376 816 675

RESTAURANT EL PASSADIS, Av. Fiter I Rossell 4, +376 865 567

RESTAURANT LA GONDOLA, Av. Fiter I Rossell 2 PB local-1, +376 866 528

Erts

BAMBU RESTAURANT ORIENTAL, Ctra. General 4 Infraestr. De servei Camara de Mobilitat, +376 737 393

BORDA D'ERTS, Ctra. General 5 Restaurant Borda d'Erts, +376 840 820

RESTAURANT L'HORT DE CASA, +376 835 068

Ordino

BAR RESTAURANT BABI, C. Major 24, +376 835 343

EL RACONET DEL NOU VERTICAL, C. Major 19 PB local, +376 854 454

NOU VERTICAL, C. Major 22 PB local-2, +376 817 989

RESTAURANT PIZZERIA COLL D'ORDINO, Ctra. del Coll d'Ordino Ed. Prat Gran PB local-1, +376 839 203

RESTAURANT TOPIC, C. Mossen Cinto Verdaguer Hotel Coma, +376 736 102

Encamp

BAR RESTAURANT BENITO, Av. de Joan Marti 51 PB local, +376 834 525

BAR RESTAURANT CAN FONTCUBERTA, C. del Tremat 12 PB, +376 834 393

BAR RESTAURANT LA BORDA DEL TREMAT, C. Sant Miquel 23, +376 831 615

CAVA LA MORENETA, Av. de Joan Marti 6 PB local, +376 834 045

EL CRESPER, C. Pas de la Casa 4 PB local, +376 854 833

EL PARCO DEL GARRI, Av. de Joan Marti 35 PB local-B, +376 849 136

RESTAURANT BORDA VELLA, Av. Princep Benlloch 22, +376 831 308

RESTAURANT CALIU D'EN JOSEP, Av. de Joan Marti 4 4-1, +376 831 210

RESTAURANT CYRANO DE BERGERAC, Av. de Joan Marti 32, +376 831 913

RESTAURANT LA CIRERA, Av. de Francois Mitterrand 79 PB local, +376 815 919

RESTAURANT LA TAPA D'EN PERE, Av. de Joan Marti 46 PB local-H, +376 815 840

SNACK BAR LA MOSQUERA, Travessera del Jardi 4 PB local, +376 834 384

Incles

BAR RESTAURANT CAN PEP, Ctra. General 2 Ed. Tres B PB local, +376 851 450

RESTAURANT BORDA DEL RECTOR, Ctra. General 2 Borda Rector, +376 852 606

RESTAURANT CAFETERIA VALL-ESQUI, Ctra. General 2 Hotel Vall Esqui, +376 851 546

La Massana

BAR RESTAURANT CASINO, Av. de Sant Antoni 68 PB local-1, +376 840 601

BAR RESTAURANT CONDE, Av. el Traves 27 PB local-2, +376 837 463

BAR RESTAURANT LA BONA TAULA, Av. del Ravell 28 PB local-1, +376 838 508

BAR RESTAURANT PLA DE L'ESTANY, C. Major 2 PB local, +376 835 028

BORDA CASA VELLA PALES, Ctra. de la Creu Blanca Cs. No-no, +376 854 844

EL POLLASTRE VOLADOR, S.L., Av. de Sant Antoni 51, +376 835 999

EL PARCO DE LA FINA, Av. el Traves 3 PB local, +376 815 393

LA CAPRICIOSA, Av. de Sant Antoni 38 A PB local-A, +376 838 386

PIZZA VITTO, Av. de Sant Antoni 79 PB local-1, +376 817 907

RESTAURANT PARC GIBERGA, C. de les Costes de Giberga Urb. Giberga, +376 840 172

RESTAURANT BORDA DE L'AVI, Av. del Ravell 38, +376 835 154

RESTAURANT BORDA RAUBERT, +376 835 420

RESTAURANT CAL SILVINO, Av. el Traves 21 PB local-2, +376 840 720

RESTAURANT EL RUSC, Ctra. General 4 35, +376 838 384

RESTAURANT EL VESUVI, Av. de Sant Antoni 45 PB local, +376 815 227

RESTAURANT LA CUINA D'EN JOAN, Av. de Sant Antoni 3, +376 840 030

RESTAURANT PRAT GRAND DEL PRAT DEL COLAT, Av. del Ravell 11, +376 836 222

VERSIO ORIGINAL V.O., C. de Josep Rossell 12 PB local, +376 839 309

Arinsal

BAR RESTAURANT EL BOSC, Ctra. General 5 39 PB local-3, +376 835 519

DÉJÀ VU RESTAURANT PIZZERIA, Ctra. General 5 15, +376 818 979

EMO, Ctra. General 5 Hotel Palome, +376 738 500

LA LLUM D'OLI – BAR DE TAPES, Ctra. General 5 43 PB local-2, +376 836 701

PAMPA, Ctra. General 5 Ed. Amadeus A PB local-1, +376 839 630

PANORAMIC, Ctra. de Comallempla Ed. Telecabina Estacio d'esqui Pal-Arinsal, +376 835 803

REFUGI D'ARINSAL, Ctra. de Comallempla Ed. Snack Bar Estacio d'esqui Pal-Arinsal, +376 836 767

RESTAURANT PIZZERIA EL MOLI DE LA PLACA, Ctra. General 5 9 Caixer, +376 835 281

RESTAURANT PUB CISCO'S, +376 836 398

RESTAURANT QUO-VADIS, Ctra. General 5 8, +376 837 600

SUPER PIZZA, Borda Giraut, +376 838 069

Pas de la Casa

BAR RESTAURANT LA BORRUFA, Pl. dels Coprinceps 24, +376 856 200

BAR RESTAURANT LA BRASA, Av. d'Encamp 23, +376 855 367

BO & GOLA, C. de Bearn 6 PB local-1, +376 856 777

BURGER KING, C. de Bearn 12, +376 856 844

EL CARLIT DE NEU, Av. d'Encamp 25 1-14, +376 855 211

EL TASTAOLLETES, Av. d'Encamp 27 PB-1, +376 817 927

L'EULARI DE PAL, C. de l'Eulari Restaurant Eulari de Pal, +376 836 400

PISTA NEGRA, C. Sant Jordi 3, +376 855 448

PIZZERIA DE ROMA, Av. d'Encamp 23 PB local-3, +376 855 516

RAPID PASTA-BAR RESTAURANT, Av. d'Encamp 39 PB local-29B, +376 855 436

REFUGI FRA-MIQUEL, Ctra. General 2 Refugi Fray Miquel, +376 817 550

RESTAURANT CAL PADRI, C. de Catalunya 19, +376 856 180

RESTAURANT CAVA CAMPI, C. Major 24, +376 856 556

RESTAURANT CHEZ ANDRE, C. Major 15, +376 855 751

RESTAURANT CHEZ PAULO EL PAS, C. Major 18 PB local-1, +376 855 322

RESTAURANT COLL BLANC-SAETDE, Av. d'Encamp 23, +376 759 195

RESTAURANT COSTA RODONA-SAETDE, Av. d'Encamp 23, +376 885 175

RESTAURANT CUBIL-SAETDE, Pleta Moreto, +376 872 930

RESTAURANT EL FILL D'ASTERIX, C. Sant Jordi 29 PB local-1, +376 855 637

RESTAURANT EL PROVENCAL, Av. d'Encamp 39 PB local-29B, +376 856 006

RESTAURANT ELS FLOCS, Av. d'Encamp 39, +376 856 390

RESTAURANT JUDITA, Av. del Consell General 17 PB local-2, +376 855 833

RESTAURANT LA GRATINADA, Av. d'Encamp 23 PB local-3, +376 855 374

RESTAURANT LA RACLETA, C. de Bearn 16, +376 855 529

RESTAURANT L'HUSKY, Pl. dels Vaquers 15, +376 855 248

RESTAURANT MC DONALD'S, Pl. dels Coprinceps 25, +376 880 512

RESTAURANT PESSOS-SAETDE, Pleta Moreto, +376 759 015

RESTAURANT PIOLETS-SAETDE, Pleta Moreto, +376 759 190

RESTAURANT SOLANELLES-SAETDE, Pleta Moreto, +376 759 008

RESTAURANT-GRILL KSB, Pl. dels Vaquers 13 PB local-1, +376 856 453

SNACK BO BAR, C. Sant Jordi 2 PB local-6, +376 855 378

SNACK BORDE, Av. d'Encamp 25 PB local-1, +376 855 079

Soldeu

BAR RESTAURANT LA CABANETA, Ctra. General 2 Hotel Piolets, +376 851 676

BAR RESTAURANT LA ROSA, Bordes d'Envalira Hotel Austria, +376 851 149

RESTAURANT ITALIA FONTANELLA – SOLDEU, Ctra. General 2, +376 872 787

RESTAURANT LA LLAR DE L'ARTESA, Bordes d'Envalira Aparthotel Residencial Part d'Envalira D, +376 851 078

RESTAURANT SOL I NEU, +376 851 325

Sant Julia

BAR RESTAURANT LA CAULLA, Av. Francesc Cairat 26 PB local-2, +376 844 827

PIZZERIA URUGUAYA, Pl. Major 4, +376 842 903

PIZZERIA VENECIA, C. la Callissa 2 PB local-1, +376 841 796

RESTAURANT CENT PER HORA, Av. Verge de Canolich 10, +376 841 249

RESTAURANT FILL DE TAPA, Av. Verge de Canolich 97, +376 842 890

RESTAURANT MC DONALD'S, Ctra. General 1 Ed. Mc Donald's, +376 742 400

RESTAURANT XENIUS, Av. de Rocafort 32 PB local, +376 842 454

SNACK-BAR FILL DE TAPA, Av. Verge de Canolich 97, +376 842 890

Pal

BAR RESTAURANT LYDIA, Av. Fontanella Restaurant Lydia 1, +376 835 377

BAR RESTAURANT BONET, Av. Fontanella Apmt. Bonet, +376 836 063

Sta. Coloma

BAR RESTAURANT PONTONES, C. de la Plana Camping Nuria, +376 725 511

LA BRASA D'EN JOSEP, C. Verge del Remei 11, +376 845 964

RESTAURANT DON PERNIL, Av. d'Enclar 84, +376 725 255

RESTAURANT JAMAICA, Av. d'Enclar 63 PB local-2, +376 723 836

RESTAURANT PARADOR, Av. d'Enclar 100, +376 722 804

RESTAURANT POBLADO, Ctra. General 1 21, +376 722 350

SNACK-BAR VALOR, Av. d'Enclar 78 PB local-1, +376 722 728

Aixirivall

BORDA DE LES PUBILLES, BAR RESTAURANT, Placa Major s/n, +376 841 201

RESTAURANT BORDA DE L'ARENA, +37 842 574

Anyos

CAN PERE RESTAURANT, Ctra. de Sant Crisofol, +376 835 415

DELIZIOSO, Ctra. de Sant Cristofol, +376 737 573

PIZZERIA DELIZIOSO, Ctra. de Sant Cristofol, +376 737 573

RESTAURANT CAN TONI, Borda Marti, +376 835 923

Canillo

CANTINA DELS RACONS, Ctra. General 2 Restaurants Cantina de Racons, +376 852 877

LA TAULA DELS AMICS, Av. Sant Joan de Caselles Cs. Nova Ros PB local, +376 852 117

PIZZERIA CHEZ LULU, +376 851 427

PIZZERIA L'ARLEQUI, Av. Sant Joan de Caselles Cs. Puigcernal PB local, +376 851 885

RESTAURANT BORDA PATXETA, Ctra. de Montaup Cs. Patxeta, +376 852 244

RESTAURANT CAL BONAVIDA, C. Peu del Carrer Hotel Bonavida, +376 751 302

RESTAURANT EL SOLA DEL LLEMPO, Av. Sant Joan de Caselles Aparthotel Llempo, +376 853 350

RESTAURANT ELS PESSONS, Ctra. General 2 Cs. Traba, +376 852 862

RESTAURANT LA RODA, C. Perdut Restaurant Roda, +376 852 670

RESTAURANT MOLI DEL PEANO, Ctra. General 2 Restaurant Moli del Peano, +376 851 258

Llorts

L'ERA DEL JAUME, Av. de l'Angonella Infraestr. De servei Cabina, +376 850 667

RESTAURANT EL RACO DEL PRAT DE LES MINES, Av. de Ferrers Ed. Prat de les Mines, +376 849 400

RESTAURANT LA NEU, Av. de l'Angonella 14 PB local, +376 850 650

Canolich

PARADOR DE CANOLICH, Ed. Parador – Canolich, +376 842 382

Ransol

RESTAURANT BORDA DE L'HORTO, +376 851 622

La Cortinada

RESTAURANT CAL TONET, C. de les Massanelles Ed. Massanelles E PB local, +376 849 179

RESTAURANT FONT BLANCA, Av. de Sant Marti Ed. Font Blanca PB local, +376 850 068

Xixerella

RESTAURANT CAMPING XIXERELLA, Ctra. General 4 Camping Xixerella, +376 837 452

Arans

RESTAURANT LA FONT D'ARANS, +376 850 830

Mollers

RESTAURANT LA SANGRIA, Ctra. General 2 Restaurant Sangria, +376 851 327

Sispony

RESTAURANT MOLI DELS FANALS, +376 835 380

SECURITY SYSTEMS

Andorra la Vella

ELIT SISTEMES, Av. Pincep Benlloch 66 4-401, +376 826 433

GRUP SERVIFOC, Ctra. de la Comella 33, +376 822 211

INTECOM, Ctra. de la Comella 23, +376 870 100

MAFER SEGURETAT, Ctra. de la Comella 140, +376 810 815

SEGURTEC, Ctra. de la Comella 33, +376 822 211

SEPIR SEGURETAT S.L., Av. Princep Benlloch 6 1-3, +376 825 328

SISTEMES DE SEGURETAT MANEL, Av. Princep Benlloch 66 3-301, +376 828 402

VALIRA SEGURETAT S.L., Ctra. de la Comella 140, +376 810 810

VALLSEGUR, Ctra. de la Comella 33, +376 803 300

Escaldes-Engordany

PROTECVALL, C. de les Boigues Ed. Pic Blanc PB local-1, +376 826 765

VIGILANCIA I PROTECCIO S.A., C. de Sant Antoni 4, +376 803 090

Sant Julia

MASTER CONSULTANTS S.L., Ctra. de Nagol 30 1-1, +376 844 270

SEGURETAT 3 VALLS S.L., Av. Verge de Canolich 124 1-3, +376 844 733

Pas de la Casa

VIGILANCIA I PROTECCIO S.A., C. Sant Jordi 1, +376 755 622

SHOES TRADERS

Andorra la Vella

ALBERT EXTREM, Av. Princep Benlloch 5 PB local-1, +376 863 808

ALBERT JOVE, C. Verge del Pilar 2, +376 821 035

ALEX BOUTIQUE, Av. Meritxell 92, +376 822 115

ALEX BOUTIQUE, Av. Meritxell 91, +376 805 570

ALEX BOUTIQUE, Av. Meritxell 43 PB local, +376 805 573

ANNA SABATERIA, C. de Callaueta 10 PB local-2, +376 861 860

CALCATS ALBERT, C. Doctor Nequi 9 2, +376 811 411

CALCATS GALY, C. Bonaventura Armengol 6, +376 860 490

CALCATS JAMAICA, C. de la Sardana 28, +376 829 796

CALCATS TOSCA, C. Joan Maragall 6, +376 869 337

GUESS, Av. Meritxell 60, +376 879 350

LA BOUTIQUE DEL TACON, C. Bra. Riberaygua 26 PB local-1, +376 854 914

MEPHISTO SHOP, C. Maria Pla 1, +376 862 740

MOLO, C. de Callaueta 13 PB local-1, +376 810 905

MOLO, Av. Princep Benlloch 7, +376 810 907

NOW, C. Maria Pla 1 PB local-1, +376 804 550

OPTIONS, Av. Meritxell 85, +376 760 240

OPTIONS+, Av. Meritxell 87, +376 760 200

OUTLET SEMPRE MODA, C. Bra. Riberaygua 47, +376 818 256

PETIT ALBERT, Av. Princep Benlloch 8 PB local-2, +376 821 450

SABATERIA ANDARAX, C. Prat de la Creu 85 PB local-3, +376 824 250

SABATERIA ANDARAX 2, C. de Callaueta 3, +376 828 250

SHIBORI, Av. Meritxell 100, +376 872 600

SOHO, Av. Meritxell 99, +376 808 280

URBAN, Av. Meritxell 23, +376 879 300

VA I VE, C. Bra. Riberaygua 12 PB local-1, +376 860 595

VA I VE 2, C. Doctor Nequi 9 2 PB local-1, +376 865 860

VERBA & DPEUS, Av. Dr. Mitjavila 7 PB local-4, +376 813 976

VIA MODA, Av. Meritxell 87, +376 806 515

WE AR, Av. Meritxell 24, +376 879 360

ZA-PATITOS, C. Maria Pla 12 PB local-2, +376 869 817

Escaldes-Engordany

ALBERT CALCATS, C. Coprincep Francois Mitterrand 2 PB local-5, +376 869 992

ALEX BOUTIQUE, Av. Carlemany 80, +376 805 685

BUICK, Av. Carlemany 91, +376 806 975

CALCATS GALY, C. Isabelle Sandy 2 PB local-1, +376 822 362

CALCATS PAVI, Pl. Santa Anna 1 2, +376 866 449

DESIGUAL ILLA, Av. Carlemany 70, +376 882 450

LEVI'S, Av. Carlemany 70, +376 882 430

MARINA RINALDI, Av. Carlemany 87, +376 879 380

MITICS, Av. Carlemany 101, +376 806 430

MOLO, Av. Carlemany 44, +376 810 906

SABATERIA LA FORCA, C. Isabelle Sandy 6 Asc., +376 824 372

SABATERIA SPORT, Av. Carlemany 26, +376 820 986

TANGO, Av. Carlemany 70, +376 882 415

VA I VE 3, Av. Carlemany 50 PB local-2, +376 822 075

Pas de la Casa

BOTIGA LAURA, Pl. dels Coprinceps 15 PB local-4, +376 855 090

MARROQUINERIA SAFARI, C. Major 5 1, +376 856 004

Sant Julia

CALCATS MARTA, C. de les Escoles 28 B PB local-2, +376 843 779

SPORTS (CLOTHES AND EQUIPMENT)

Andorra la Vella

ESPORTS BENLLOCH, Av. Princep Benlloch 66 PB local-8, +376 819 840

ESPORTS MONREAL, Av. Princep Benlloch 13 PB-1, +376 826 176

ESPORTS YETI, Av. Meritxell 130 PB local-2, +376 823 375

ESPORTS YETI II, Av. Meritxell 77, +376 861 105

MAGATZEM OLYMPIA ESPORTS, Av. Santa Coloma 124, +376 723 583

MONT-NAUTIC, S.L., Av. de Salou 52 1, +376 723 329

OLYMPIA ESPORTS, Av. Dr. Mitjavila 33 A 1, +376 803 870

OLYMPIA ESPORTS, Av. Meritxell 74, +376 743 210

OLYMPIA ESPORTS, Av. Meritxell 99, +376 743 213

SAFARI MASTERS, C. Bonaventura Armengol 13, +376 824 262

VILADOMAT ESPORTS, C. Esteve Dolsa Pujal 30 A, +376 800 600

INTERSPORT OUTDOOR, Av. Santa Coloma 118, +376 800 916

VILADOMAT ANDORRA, Av. Meritxell 110, +376 800 805

Escaldes-Engordany

ALPESPORT, Av. del Pont de la Tosca 9 D PB local-6, +376 804 108; +376 861 552

DANDY ESPORTS, Av. Carlemany 17 PB local-2, +376 821 308

ESPORTS ALBERT, Av. Carlemany 58 PB local-2, +376 810 355

ETERNAL, C. de les Boigues Ed. Pic Blanc 6-605, +376 843 901

GOLF MASTER, Av. Carlemany 105 PB local-1, +376 801 874

KILVIL, Av. Carlemany 64, +376 800 918

PAUL & SHARK, C. dels Paraires Galeries Monsa, +376 800 807

VILADOMAT NENS, Av. Carlemany 46, +376 800 913

VILADOMAT BOUTIQUE, Av. Carlemany, 63, +376 800 912

VILADOMAT ESCALDES, Av. Carlemany 61 PB local-1, +376 800 911

ALTITUD ESPORT, C. Maria Pla 8 B PB local-3, +376 862 632

ESPORTS PIROT 8, Nou 15 Zona ind. Terra Vella, +376 862 010

GOLFPRO, C. Maria Pla 1 PB local-11, +376 862 947

INOUT, Av. Carlemany 93 PB local, +376 860 440

Sant Julia

ESPORTS JORMA, Av. Francesc Cairat 6 2, +376 741 777

JORMA MOUNTAIN BIKE, Av. Francesc Cairat 4 1, +376 741 777

OLYMPIA ESPORTS, Ctra. General 1 Centre com. Prat de la Teresa PB local-1, +376 743 215

INTERSPORT VILADOMAT, Ctra. General 1 Centre com. River, +376 800 914

Anyos

ANYOSPARC, EL CLUB, Ctra. De Sant Cristofol, +376 737 573

La Massana

BIGFOOT ESPORTS, Av. de Sant Antoni 80 B PB local-3, +376 839 080

ESPORTS BAUSELI, C. del Pui 1 PB local, +376 840 080

ESPORTS PIC NEGRE 1, Av. de Sant Antoni 43 PB local-1, +376 737 780

ESPORTS PIC NEGRE 11, Av. de Sant Antoni 5 PB local, +376 737 350

ESPORTS PIC NEGRE 12, Av. de Sant Antoni 10 PB local-5, +376 737 745

ESPORTS PIROT 9, Av. de Sant Antoni 109 PB local, +376 839 374

ESPORTS ROSSEL, Av. del Ravell 34, +376 837 056; +376 836 028

ESPORTS SENSACIO, Av. de Sant Antoni 30 2 PB local, +376 836 978

VILADOMAT LLOGUER, Av. el Traves 2 PB local, +376 800 818

Arinsal

ESPORTS PIC NEGRE 2, Ctra. General 5 9 PB local, +376 737 8354, +376 837 056

ESPORTS PIC NEGRE 3, Arribada Telecabina, +376 835 751

ESPORTS PIC NEGRE 7, Ctra. General 5 Infraestr. De servei Telecabina, +376 836 427

ESPORT PIC NEGRE 10, Ctra. General 5 Ed. Xalet Moli Urb. Borda Domingo, +376 737 355

ESPORTS SANT MORITZ, Ctra. General 5 14 PB local-1, +376 738 373

Pal

ESPORTS BONET, Av. Fontanella Cs. Francesc PB local, +376 835 617

ESPORTS PAL, Av. Coll de la Botella Ed. Tirader PB local, +376 835 282

ESPORTS ROSSELL, Ed. Caubella Estacio d'esqui Pal-Arinsal PB local-1B, +376 836 846

Soldeu

ESPORTS CALBO, Ctra. General 2 Apmt. Calbo PB-2, +376 851 763, +376 852 763 (rent)

ESPORTS PIC NEGRE 8, Ctra. General 2 Ed. Casa Aspen PB local-1, +376 851 580

ESTABLIMENTS BONELL ESPORTS, Ctra. General 2 Apmt. Bonell PB, +376 851 575

SKI CALBO, Ctra. General 2 Hotel Sporthotel, +376 870 540 (administration)

El Tarter

ESPORTS PIC NEGRE 4, Hotel Llop Gris, +376 851 441; +376 852 441; +376 852 251

ESPORTS PIROT 1, Pleta Sant Pere, +376 852 701

SKI CALBO/EL TARTER, Ctra. General 2 X. Josep Arney, +376 851 040

VILADOMAT EL TARTER, Ed. Pistes el Tarter Estacio d'esqui Soldeu-El Tarter, +376 800 806

Pas de la Casa

EL REFUGI DE L'ARTURO, Av. d'Encamp 6 PB local-1, +376 855 146

ESPORTS 2104, Pl. dels Vaquers 15, +376 855 953

ESPORTS K-2, C. de la Solana 55, +376 856 999

ESPORTS PIROT 5, C. de la Solana 69 PB local-1, +376 855 580

ESPORTS PIC NEGRE 13, Hotel Grau Roig Estacio d'esqui Pas de la Casa – Grau Roig PB local, +376 855 684

ESPORTS PIC NEGRE 15, C. de Bearn 5, +376 855 483

ESPORTS PIROT 2, Pl. dels Vaquers 9, +376 856 000

ESPORTS PIROT 3, Av. d'Encamp 25 PB local-4, +376 855 549

L&D ESPORTS, C. Sant Jordi 13 PB local-1, +376 855 101

OLYMPIA ESPORTS, C. de Bearn Ed. Olympia Centre, +376 743 235

OLYMPIA ESPORTS, Av. d'Encamp 5, +376 743 230

RENTASKI, Av. d'Encamp 39, +376 755 850

SPORTMAN, Av. d'Encamp 27 PB local-2, +376 855 489

URBANS ZONES, C. de Catalunya 4 PB local-1, +376 855 728

VILADOMAT RIBULS, Ed. Comunal-Cubil Estacio d'esqui Pas de la Casa-Grau Roig PB local-1, +376 800 603

VILADOMAT GRAU, Ed. Cubil 2 Estacio d'esqui Pas de la Casa-Grau Roig, +376 800 602

Ordino

CARVING ESPORTS, C. Mossen Cinto Verdaguer 1, +376 850 900

La Cortinada

CARVING ESPORTS, Av. de Sant Marti Ed. Solanet PB local, +376 850 901

Canillo

ESPORTS ELIT, Ctra. General 2 Ed. Forn del calc PB local, +376 852 720

ESPORTS PIC NEGRE 9, Pl. Carlemany Ed. Telecabina 1 local-2, +376 853 005

ESPORTS PIROT, Pl. Carlemany Ed. Telecabina, +376 801 234

ESPORTS PIROT 10, Pl. Carlemany Ed. Telecabina, +376 852 949

ESPORTS ROC VERTICAL, Av. Sant Joan de Caselles Cs. Nova Som 2 PB local-1, +376 851 610

OLYMPIA ESPORTS, Av. Sant Joan de Caselles Ed. Novell 1 B PB local, +376 743 221

Incles

OLYMPIA ESPORTS, Ctra. General 2 Ed. Novell 2, +376 743 225

Ransol

ESPORTS ESPUNYES, Ctra. General 2 Ed. Espunyes PB local, +376 851 207

Encamp

ESPORTS EVEREST, Av. de Francois Mitterrand 85 PB local-1, +376 833 132

ESPORTS PIC NEGRE 14, Av. de Francois Mitterrand 106, +376 833 874

TECNIC ESPORTS, Av. de Francois Mitterrand 96 PB local, +376 832 774

Sornas

ESPORTS LES PLANES, Av. de l'Horto Ed. Jordi Bringue A PB-2, +376 850 334

ESPORTS PIROT 11, Av. de l'Horto Ed. Terra de la Bassa PB local, +376 850 508

nike, adidas, puma, converse, columbia, reebok, esprit

SOLAR ENERGY

Andorra la Vella

SERVEI TERMIC STREICH, Ctra. De la Comella 23, +365 870 130

TECNISA, Ctra. de la Comella 23, +376 800 075

TERMAL INSTAL.LACIONS, SAU, C. de les Costes Nau 15 Zona ind. Magatzems Cervos 1, +376 722 234

Escaldes-Engordany

CALEFACCIONS CALDA, S.L., C. dels Escalls 7 1-1, +376 864 657

Encamp

TECNIQUES DE SOL I AIGUA-TECSAI, Av. de Joan Marti 35 PB local-A, +376 831 645

SURGICAL EQUIPMENT

Andorra la Vella

ESPECIALITATS MEDIQUES, C. de la Unio 4, +376 826 259

INTER-MEDIC, Av. Princep Benlloch 87, +376 804 334

SUBMINISTRES PODOLOGICS I MEDICS TEJERO, C. Bra. Riberaygua 9, +376 860 516

Escaldes-Engordany

BIOMEDICS MORENO, Av. Fiter I Rossell 62 PB local, +376 862 770

TEA

Andorra la Vella

42 TU I TE D'ALERGIA, C. Bra. Riberaygua 42 PB local-4, +376 861 111

TRAMUNTANA, Av. Princep Benlloch 5 PB local-3, +376 868 010

Scaldes-Engordany

GRANJA PACIFIC, Av. del Pessebre 36 PB local-2, +376 820 840

Sant Julia

PA AMB XOCOLATA, Av. Verge de Canolich 25 PB local-1, +376 843 419

La Massana

T DE TE, Av. de Sant Antoni 14 PB local-1, +376 846 040

TELECOMMUNICATION SERVICES

Andorra la Vella

ANDORRA TELECOM, Av. Meritxell 112, +376 875 000

INTECOM, Ctra. de la Comella 23, +376 870 100

RADIOCOM, C. Terra Vella 7 A 2 PB local, +376 811 235

SETI, C. de les Costes Nau 17 Zona ind. Magatzems Cervos 1, +376 722 769

SI O NO COMUNICACIONS, C. Doctor Molines 6 PB local-1, +376 741 550

SIELEC, C. Terra Vella 21 E 9 PB local-1, +376 824 432

SUPER ALTA FREQUENCIA, C. Esteve Dolsa Pujal 15 PB local-1, +376 813 565

TECNOVIT, C. Terra Vella 7 A 2 PB local, +376 811 235

TELESISTEMES S.A., C. Gil Torres 7 PB local-1, +376 800 780

TELEVALLS S.A., Ctra. de la Comella 23, +376 800 070

VICOM, Ctra. de la Comella 41 6-603, +376 801 717

Escaldes-Engordany

TELE-XARXES T.J., C. de les Boigues Ed. Pic Blanc 6-603, +376 828 466

Les Bons

INSTAL.LACIONS SATURN-INSTALSAT, Av. de Rouillac 21 1-7, +376 332 148

Sant Julia

LOAN MINO S.L., C. de Loria 12, +376 801 740

TIRES AND WHEELS

Andorra la Vella

AUTO MOTOR, Av. Santa Coloma 122, +376 724 753

AUTO RALLYE, S.A., Ctra. de la Comella 41 3-301, +376 803 440

CENTRAL DE PNEUMATICS SAM, S.A., Av. Santa Coloma 124, +376 722 229

ES L'OBAC, Av. de Salou, 68, +376 760 023

ES OROS ANRORRA, Av. de Tarragona 83, +376 760 033

ESTACIO I PNEUMATICS PIRINEU, S.A., Av. de Salou 95, +376 723 778

GARATGE BOU, Av. Santa Coloma 28, +376 823 870

LA CASA DEL PNEUMATIC, Av. Santa Coloma 34, +376 820 146

PNEUMATICS SAM, Av. Santa Coloma 104, +376 811 118

PNEUMATICS SAM 3, Av. Santa Coloma 32, +376 820 345

PNEUMATICS UNIO, Av. de Tarragona 97, +376 829 220

Escaldes-Engordany

RODAND.COM, C. Esteve Albert 9 B PB local-2, +376 867 000

TALLERS MATEU, Av. del Pont de la Tosca Cs. Marquet, +376 823 970

La Margineda

ABJ PNEUMATICS, S.L., Ctra. de la Margineda 18 PB, +376 722 701

Pas de la Casa

AUTO ACCESSORIS L'OS BLANC-2, Pl. dels Coprinceps 5 PB local-1, +376 855 593

Sta. Coloma

ESTACIO ENCLAR CARBURANTS ANDORRANS, Av. d'Enclar 64, +376 760 000

PNEUMATICS F1, Av. d'Enclar 22 PB local, +376 723 923

Encamp

ES VIAL – ENCAMP CEPSA, Ctra. General 2 Infraestr. De servei Camara de Mobilitat, +376 760 035

La Massana

ES LA MASSANA, Av. del Ravell Infraestr. De servei Camara de Mobilitat, +376 760 029

RILEI PNEUMATICS, Av. de Sant Antoni 66 PB local, +376 815 222

Sant Julia

PNEUMATICS SAM 2, Av. de Rocafort 7 PB local 1, +376 842 142

Michelin, Continental, Goodyear, Pirelli, Nokian, Brigestone, Yokohama

TOBACCO FACTORIES

Andorra la Vella

INDUSTRIES MONTANYA S.A., Ctra. de la Comella 11, +376 871 300

TABACS ELABORATS S.A., Ctra. de la Comella 41, +376 802 975

Sant Julia

FILLS DE JULIA REIG S.L., Pl. de la Germandat 9, +376 800 515

TABACS REIG S.A., Pl. de la Germandat 9, +376 800 515

TABANDOR S.A., C. de les Escoles Nau Tabandor, +376 876 500

Les Bons

MIT S.A., Nau Fabrica de Tabac Zona ind. Prat de la Coma, +376 833 680

TOBACCO TRADERS

Andorra la Vella

COMERCIAL J.A., C. Bra Riberaygua 8 PB local-1, +376 866 398

LA CASA DEL FUMADOR, Av. Princep Benlloch 44 PB local, +376 820 115

TABACS EL TAMARRO, Av. Dr. Mitjavila 41 PB local-5, +376 854 841

TABACS LES 1000 PIPES, Av. Meritxell 108, +376 821 006

THE CIGAR SHOP, Av. Meritxell 40, +376 826 515

TROTOM S.A., C. Prada de Moles 10, +376 823 303

Escaldes-Engordany

COMERCIAL PONT, C. Nou 3 PB local-2, +376 821 063

COMERCIAL SALLENT, Av. de les Escoles 21 PB local-1, +376 816 450

DAVIDOFF ANDORRA, Av. Carlemany 57, +376 861 150

FRANC-PORT S.A., Av. del Pont de la Tosca 15, +376 803 907

LA CASA DEL HABANO, Pl. Coprinceps 3, +376 869 255

LA CASA DELS TABACS, Av. Carlemany 46 PB local-2, +376 823 421

LA CASA DELS TABACS, Av. Carlemany 65 PB local-15, +376 861 421

LA MINA, Av. Carlemany 40, +376 867 186

Pas de la Casa

ELS 4 MOSQUETERS III, C. Sant Jordi 12 PB local-1, +376 854 763

ROYAL CIGAR PAS, Av. del Consell General 21 PB local-3, +376 856 716

Sant Julia

MARFANY CANTURRI, MARCEL.LI, Ctra. General 1 Ed. Toll de Joves 2-A, +376 841 105

TABACS MARFANY S.A., Ctra. General 1 Ed. Toll de Joves 2-A, +376 741 106

Encamp

ROYAL CIGAR, Pl. del Consell 16 1, +376 834 008

TOYS

Andorra la Vella

IMAGINARIUM, C. Bra. Riberaygua 31 PB local-1, +376 825 381

TIC TOC JOGUETS, Av. Meritxell 62, +376 827 070

TOT STOCK, Av. Santa Coloma 37 S1 local, +376 865 003

Escaldes-Engordany

BASAR VALIRA, Av. de les Escoles 7 2, +376 821 314

BASAR VALIRA, C. del Pico 1 PB local, +376 800 675

TRADING COMPANIES SUPERMARKETS (COMMERCIAL CENTERS)

Andorra la Vella

ANDORRA 2000, Av. Tarragona, 26, +376 880 400

ARMERIA ANDORRANA, C. Bra. Riberaygua 33 PB local-1, +376 860 222

CCA-CENTRE COMERCIAL ANDORRA, Av. Meritxell 94, +376 870 310

E.LECLERC, Av. Meritxell, 93, +376 822 377

SUPER CONTINENT II, C. Prat de la Creu 92 PB local-2, +376 862 472

PYRENEES, Av. Meritxell, 11, Andorra La Vella, + 376 880 000

Escaldes-Engordany

CAPRABO ILLA CARLEMANY, Av. Carlemany 80, +376 802 470

COMERC J.R., Av. Coprincep de Gaulle 8 PB local-1, +376 829 978

SUPER VALLS, C. de Sant Antoni 5 Entl. 1, +376 861 588

Sta. Coloma

ANTAR SUPERMERCAT, Av. d'Enclar 62, +376 814 100

Canillo

CAPRABO CANILLO, Av. Sant Joan de Caselles Ed. Cases PB local-1, +376 851 293

SUPERPAS I, Pl. Montaup Cs. Nova Aleix 1, +376 851 401

La Massana

CAPRABO LA MASSANA, Av. el Traves 1 PB local-2, +376 816 888

COMPRA BE, Ctra. General 3 Nau Giberga, +376 840 180

Sant Julia

CENTRE COMERCIAL SANT ELOI, Ctra. General 1 Hotel Sant Eloi, +376 743 140

SUPERMERCAT CASAL, Av. Verge de Canolich 60 PB local-1, +376 841 054

Encamp

COMERC LA CLEMENTINA, Av. de Joan Marti 46 PB local-C, +376 830 880

SUPERMERCAT ECLER, Av. de Francois Mitterrand 120 PB local, +376 832 788

SUPERMERCAT ECO, Pl. del Consell 15 PB local, +376 832 700

SUPERMERCAT RECORD II, Av. de Francois Mitterrand 7 PB local-3, +376 832 673

SUPERMERCAT RECORD III, C. Major 10, +376 855 124

U EXPRESS ENCAMP, Av. de Joan Marti 66 PB local, +376 731`035

Pas de la Casa

COMERC NOVA RUKI, Pl. dels Coprinceps 22 PB local-1, +376 855 729

HIPER MERCAT DEL PAS IV, C. Major 26, +376 856 538

HIPER MERCAT DEL PAS I, Av. del Consell General 27, +376 855 267

HIPER MERCAT DEL PAS II, C. Sant Jordi 45, +376 855 740

HIPER MERCAT DEL PAS III, Pl. dels Coprinceps 32, +376 855 290

MAGANDOR, Av. del Consell General 33 S2 local, +376 855 431

MAGATZEMS AVINGUDA, Pl. dels Coprinceps 18 PB local-2, +376 855 382

MAGATZEMS PARADIS, C. Sant Jordi 14, +376 855 195

MAXI-MERCAT, Av. del Consell General 23 PB local-1, +376 855 338

SUPER CONTINENT, Av. del Consell General 17 PB local-2, +376 855 833

SUPER PUY PAS DE LA CASA, Pl. dels Coprinceps 38 PB local, +376 855 944

SUPERMERCAT MEGA, C. Sant Jordi 18, +376 856 066

SUPERMERCAT CAMPI I, C. Major 24 PB local, +376 856 056

SUPERMERCAT DEL SUD, C. Sant Jordi 19, +376 855 230

SUPERMERCAT LA CAVA, C. Comte de Foix 4, +376 855 316

SUPERMERCAT LA SOLANA, C. de Catalunya 15, +376 855 303

SUPERMERCAT MATI-MAR, C. Sant Jordi 17 PB local, +376 855 241

SUPERMERCAT META, C. Sant Jordi 18, +376 856 039

SUPERMERCAT PARMA, Pl. dels Coprinceps 20, +376 855 582

SUPERMERCAT RECORD, C. Sant Jordi 4 PB local, +376 855 509

SUPERMERCAT RECORD GEGANT, C. Sant Jordi 6, +376 855 585

SUPERMERCAT TIMY, C. de Bearn 16, +376 755 644

SUPERPAS II, C. Comtes de Foix 8 PB local-2, +376 855 575

Soldeu

SUPERMERCAT DE LA POSTA, +376 851 019

SUPERMERCAT FONT, Cs. Vella Popaire, +376 851 193

Aixovall

SUPERMERCAT MARGINEDA, Ctra. General 1 Est. de servei Total Margineda, +376 841 427

El Tarter

SUPERMERCAT PIROT, Ed. Querol Urb. Sant Pere PB local, +376 851 374

Arinsal

SUPERMERCAT SANT MORITZ, Ctra. General 5 14 PB local-3, +376 737 899

TRANSLATORS

Andorra la Vella

BARTUMEU CASSANY, ROSAURA, Av. Meritxell 48 4-1, +376 860 324

BORNAL, SLU, C. Doctor Vilanova 9 3-A, +376 804 320

CONTEXT TRADUCCIONS, Av. Meritxell 9 4-5, +376 814 840

SEMENTE PUIGDELLIVOL, MARTA, C. Doctor Vilanova 9 3-A, +376 804 320

Escaldes-Engordany

BLASI PALACIN, ESTHER, C. de la Constitucio Ed. Salita Parc D 2-1, +376 825 395

Erts

VINCENT, BRUNO, Ctra. General 5 Ed. Salze 2-6, +376 839 447

TRANSPORT CARGO

Andorra la Vella

A.ALSINA GRAELLS D'AUTOTRANSPORTS, C. Bra. Riberaygua 52, +376 827 379

CADIM, S.L., Ctra. de la Comella 29, +376 801 414

G.T.T. GESTIO, TRANSPORT I TRANSIT, C. de la Closa 15 1, +376 807 255

N.A. GRUP FRANCA, Ctra. de la Comella 29, +376 801 400

TRANS-OXEA, C. dels Marginets 7 1-3, +376 866 747

TRANSPORTS A. ESTRADA, Av. Santa Coloma 41 A 3-2, +376 825 073

TRANSPORT ARENY, Av. de Salou 98, +376 723 779

TRANSPORT ARIZA, C. Doctor Vilanova 5, +376 862 084

TRANSPORT CODISA, Ctra. de la Comella 29, +376 801 400

TRANSPORTS NORD ANDORRA, S.A., Ctra. de la Comella 29, +376 801 400

TRANSPORTS TOMAS, Av. Meritxell 99, +376 822 516

Escaldes-Engordany

CAMINO-BUS, S.L., C. dels Escalls 7 PB-2, +376 965 500

IDALUX, S.L., Av. de les Escoles 31 6-5, +376 860 785

TRANSPORT TOT, S.A., Av. de les Escoles 31 A 5-24, +376 861 876

TRANSPORT BRINGUE, C. Santa Anna 14 D 5-1, +376 820 111

TRANSPORTS MATIES S.L., Ctra. dels Vilars 51, +376 860 628

Sant Julia

CATRANS S.A., Nau 26 Zona ind. Borda del Germa, +376 738 888

FABREGA FUSTA, RAMON, Ctra. de la Rabassa 10, +376 841 085

SEUR, Nau 16 Zona ind. Borda del Germa, +376 741 927

TRALDISPORTA, Nau 16 Zona ind. Borda del Germa, +376 741 200

TRANSPORTS CAPDELIVA, C. Camp de Perot Residencial Camp de Perot D 2-2, +376 841 480

TRANSPORTS JOSEP PUIG (PEPET), Av. Francesc Cairat 6 2, +376 842 711

TRANSPORTS PILAR LOPEZ, C. de les Escoles 22 3-3, +376 842 525

Encamp

DISTRIBUCIO DE PAQUETERIA, Av. de la Barta Ed. Nova Barta D PB local-3, +376 741 230

GELESA, Av. de la Barta Ed. Bomar, +376 736 300

Aixovall

TRANSPORTS INTER-TRANS, Ctra. General 6 Nau Inter-trans, +376 741 100

Sta. Coloma

TRANSPORTS VINYAL, C. dels Barres 33 4-1, +376 723 193

TRANSPORT PASSENGER

Andorra la Vella

COOPERATIVA INTERURBANA ANDORRANA, Av. Princep Benlloch 30 PB local-7, +376 806 555

HISPANO ANDORRANA (LA), Av. Santa Coloma 85, +376 807 000

NOVATEL, S.A., Av. de Tarragona 42, +376 803 789

VIATGES MONTMANTELL, C. Prat de la Creu 85 PB local-1, +376 866 444

Sant Julia

AUTOCARS ESPANYA, Av. de Rocafort 15 PB local-9, +376 841 456

TRAVEL AGENCIES

Andorra la Vella

ANDORRA TOURS AGENCIA DE VIATGES, C. Joan Maragall 14, +376 872 250

BUS SKI, Av. Princep Benlloch 30 PB local-9, +376 817 766

VIATGES NADAL, Av. de Tarragona 44, +376 805 151

VIATGES PYRENEES, Av. Miretxell 11, +376 880 193

A MIDA VIATGES, C. de l'Aigueta 22 1-2, +376 817 676

AGENCIA DE VIATGES PANTOURS, C. Doctor Nequi 6 1 local-3, +376 804 010

AGENCIA DE VIATGES RELAX, C. Mossen Tremosa 2, +376 812 244

AGENCIA DE VIATGES VILANOVA, C. de la Sardana 6, +376 879 978

ANDORRA EVASIONS S.A., Av. Princep Benlloch 43 2-1, +376 870 975

PANTOURS AGENCIA DE VIATGES, C. Doctor Nequi 6 1 local-3, +376 804 010

PLANETA AGENCIA DE VIATGES, Av. Meritxell 105 1-3, +376 810 610

RELAX AGENCIA DE VIATGES, C. Mossen Tremosa 2, +376 812 244

SKIART, C. Doctor Molines 10 C PB local, +376 890 290

SOL I MUNTANYA, C. Prat de la Creu 8 PB local-5, +376 809 010

VIATGES ARAN, C. Prat de la Creu 15, +376 863 536

VIATGES EMOCIONS 3, C. Maria Pla 31 PB local-4, +376 807 900

VIATGES EMOCIONS ANDORRA, Pl. Guillemo 5 PB local, +376 806 006

VIATGES PANTOURS, C. Doctor Nequi 6 1 local-3, +376 804 010

Escaldes-Engordany

GRIVA SERVEIS, Av. Carlemany 35, +376 823 653

TOP VIATGES, C. Isabelle Sandy 6 1-2, +376 822 040

AGENCIA DE VIATGES KEOPS, Av. Carlemany 38 PB local-8, +376 807 730

GIRA MON, Av. del Fener 21 A PB local, +376 810 400

INTERNOVA, S.L., Ctra. d'Engolasters Ed. Santa Maria A 1-1, +376 810 604

VIATGES EMOCIONS ESCALDES, Pl. Coprinceps 4 PB local-3, +376 829 044

Sant Julia

VIATGES ESPANYA, Av. de Rocafort 7 PB local-9, +376 841 569

VIATGES SANT JULIA, Ctra. General 1 Ed. Planella PB local-1, +376 741 400

AGENCIA DE VIATGES I GESTORIA ADMINISTRATIVA ESPANYA, Av. de Rocafort 15 PB local-9, +376 843 166

Encamp

VIATGES ESQUI TOTAL, C. Hort de Godi 5 2-1, +376 833 193

ASTUR TURISME, Ctra. dels Cortals d'Encamp Aparthotel Solana, +376 875 888

SKI SERVEIS, Av. de Francois Mitterrand 92 PB local, +376 739 999

TOT PIRINEU, Ctra. dels Cortals d'Encamp Cs. C2 Residencial el Molla, +376 830 035

Sta. Coloma

BECIER VIATGES, Av. d'Enclar 142, +376 871 890

Ordino

NAB, S.A., C. de la Clota Verda 1 1 1-4, +376 838 165

TV ANTENNAS, SATELLITE EQUIPMENT

Andorra la Vella

SIELEC, C. Terra Vella 21 E 9 PB local-1, +376 824 432

TECNOVIT, C. Terra Vella 7 A 2 PB local, +376 811 235

MOBI-PLUS, TELEVISIO APARELLS, C. Prat de la Creu 94 PB local, +376 869 765

ATV-ANDORRA-TELEVISIO EMISSORES, Bda. Del Moli 24, +376 873 777

Sant Julia

MUNTATGES ELECTRICS TAC S.L., Ctra. de la Rabassa 14 PB local-7, +376 843 321

Encamp

TELE ANDREU, TELEVISIO REPARACIONS, Av. de Francois Mitterrand 51 PB local, +376 832 674

UNDERWEAR

Andorra la Vella

HELIOS HOME, Av. Princep Benlloch 6 PB local-3, +376 823 257

INTIMITATS, Pl. Princep Benlloch 6, +376 818 384

LLENCERIA SOLER-SOLCA, C. Maria Pla 1 PB local-3, +376 816 986

XAPO, Av. Meritxell 42, +376 827 045

Escaldes-Engordany

INTIMISSIMI, Av. Carlemany 44 PB local-16, +376 829 999

MERCERIA FANNY, Av. Carlemany, 18 PB local-2, +376 820 832

UNIVERSITIES

Andorra la Vella

FACULTAT DE CIENCIES ODONTOLOGIQUES DE LES VALLS, C. de Pau Casals 11 PB local-1, +376 813 781

Sant Julia

UNIVERSITAT D'ANDORRA, Pl. de la Germandat Centre educ. Universitat d'Andorra, +376 743 000

La Massana

UNIVERSITAT OBERTA LA SALLE UOLS, Av. el Traves 31 PB local-3, +376 815 388

WATCHES

Andorra la Vella

MAZAL, C. Doctor Nequi 8 3, +376 865 875

MERCAT DE L'OR, Av. Meritxell 52 1, +376 806 470

MERCAT DEL DIAMANT, Av. Meritxell 18, +376 800 630

PATEK PHILIPPE-JOIERIA GENEVE, Av. Meritxell 124 3, +376 800 500

QUARS CENTRE, Av. Meritxell 86, +376 874 932

RELLOGERIA JOIERIA GERMANS, C. Doctor Nequi 8 PB local-1, +376 825 345

Escaldes-Engordany

QUARS ESCALDES 2, Av. Carlemany 60, +376 874 935

QUARS ILLA, Av. Carlemany 80, +376 874 931

QUARS RADIO CLUB, Av. Carlemany 79 PB local-2, +376 874 937

Pas de la Casa

QUARS PAS DE LA CASA, C. Major 2 PB local-5, +376 874 941

Patek Philippe, Vacheron Constantin, Jaeger-LeCoultre, Blancpain, Cartier, Ulysse Nardin, Chopard, Hublot, Piaget, Girard-Perregaux, Rolex, Omega, TAG Heuer, Swatch, Breitling

WINDOWS PRODUCTION

Andorra la Vella

ART I VIDRE MIRETXELL, Ctra. De la Comella 41, +376 864 201

CAMPI JORDANA, ANDREU, Av. Princep Benlloch 75 Atic-1, +376 823 440

Encamp

FINESTRAL, Av. De Joan Marti 63, +376 333 534

SERRALLERIA INDUSTRIAL EL PORTUGUES, Av. De Joan Marti 127, +376 731 590

WINES TRADERS

Andorra la Vella

CELLER DE PIRINEU, C. Doctor Nequi 5, +376 863 066

EUROAND, S.L., C. de l'Alzinaret 16 PB local-A, +376 820 666

L'EXCELLENCE LES SENS DU VIN, Av. Meritxell 9 PB local-2, +376 860 804

SISPONY DISTRIBUCIO, S.A., Ctra. de la Comella 41 2-202, +376 865 586

Escaldes-Engordany

MARQUET, Av. Carlemany 44 PB local-16, +376 820 722

Encamp

BOMAR, S.A., Av. de la Barta Ed. Bomar, +376 736 300

Sant Julia

CENTRAL DE REPRESENTACIONS, Nau 4 Zona ind. Borda del Germa, +376 741 030

La Margineda

ESTABLIMENTS VIDAL, C. dels Emprius Nau Establiments Vidal, +376 720 700

WHOLESALE TRADE

Andorra la Vella

BIFRONT, C. Bonavista 27 PB local, +376 860 950

CAVES ANDORRANES, C. Prat de la Creu 55, +376 806 080

CIMAR, S.A., Ctra. de la Comella 13, +376 806 080

COFISA, C. Esteve Dolsa Pujal 28 A, +376 870 000

COMERCIAL SOLA, Ctra. de la Comella Nau 5 Zona ind. Encores de Can Nyerro, +376 822 408

DIGIT IMPORT-EXPORT, Ctra. de la Comella 31, +376 802 700

DISTRIBUCIONS RESOL, C. Bonavista 10, +376 860 642

MARBA S.L., C. Esteve Dolsa Pujal 32, +376 823 865

MARCH-SEGARRA, S.A., Ctra. de la Comella 45, +376 806 900

PRIMAR, S.A., Ctra. de la Comella 13, +376 806 080

PODISNET, Ctra. de la Comella 41 2-206, +376 868 677

SERCOMAND, C. Bonavista 4 PB local-1, +376 822 637

TOT STOCK, Antic. Cami Ral 1 A PB local-1, +376 865 003

FARMACO, S.A., Cami del Currubell 2, +376 803 000

LABORATORIS ANDOPHARM, S.A., C. de Pau Casals 6 A 2-2, +376 809 829

Escaldes-Engordany

CTC IMPORT-EXPORT, Av. Fiter I Rossell 6, +376 820 331

MOLI NOU, Av. del Pont de la Tosca Cs. Marquet 1-1 Linia 2, +376 830 766

PRACTICSAC, S.A., Av. Fiter I Rossell 90, +376 805 700

PROTECVALL, C. de les Boigues Ed. Pic Blanc PB local-1, +376 826 765

Sant Julia

ARMETISA, Av. Verge de Canolich 124 1-3, +376 869 900

BECIER DISTRIBUCIONS, Nau 4 Zona ind. Borda del Germa, +376 741 030

CAIRAT RIBOT ESTABLIMENTS, Av. Verge de Canolich 23, +376 841 112

COMERCIAL RELLOTGERIA I SERVEIS, Ctra. de Fontaneda 36 3-2, +376 843 607

Sta. Coloma

MAGATZEMS PEDRAFITA, Av. d'Enclar 28, +376 722 497

TROTA GARRABE, JOSEP MARIA, C. del Cedre 9 6-A, +376 722 688

Encamp

BOMAR, S.A., Av. de la Barta Ed. Bomar, +376 736 300

CASABELLA & SIN, S.L., Av. de Francois Mitterrand 96, +376 834 824

COMERCIAL EVARISTO, C. Rene Baulard 11 1-1, +376 831 128; +376 831 830

COMERCIAL QUINOX, Ctra. dels Cortals d'Encamp Ed. Velazquez PB, +376 834 133

DISTRIBUCIONS APA-POUX, Av. Princep Benlloch 32 PB local, +376 831 188

Aixovall

DISAND, S.A., Nau Comercial Mino Urb. Prat de Jaia, +376 841 183

La Massana

DOLCOS U-DOS, Ctra. General 4 8, +376 837 804

La Margineda

ESTABLIMENTS VIDAL, C. dels Emprius Nau Establiments Vidal, +376 720 700

HOTELCO, +376 720 710

SUMALISA, +376 720 720

SUPPLEMENTS

STRATEGIC CONTACTS

GOVERNMENT MINISTRIES

Department Services open to the public : (http://www.tràmits.ad)

MINISTERI D'AFERS EXTERIORS (Ministry of Foreign Affairs)
C/ Prat de la Creu 62-64
Andorra la Vella
Tel : (00 376) 875 700
Fax : (00 376) 869 559
E-Mail: epalacios.gov@andorra.ad
Open from 9.00 to 17.30
Minister : Mr Juli MINOVES

MINISTERI D'EDUCACIÓ JOVENTUT I ESPORT (Ministry of Education, Youth and Sport)
Avinguda Meritxell, 80, Edif. Crédit Center
Andorra la Vella
Tel : (00 376) 861 229
Fax Minister of Sport: (00 376) 868 308
Open from 9.00 to 17.30
Minister : Mr Pere CERVÓS

MINISTERI DE TURISME I CULTURA- (Ministry of Tourism and Culture)
(http://www.turisme.ad)
C/ Prat de la Creu 62-64
Andorra la Vella
Tel : (00 376) 875700
Fax : (00 376) 860184/826707
Open from 9.00 to 17.30
Minister : Mr Enric PUJAL

MINISTERI D'AGRICULTURA I MEDI AMBIENT (Ministry of Agriculture and the Environment)
C/ Prat de la Creu 62-64
Andorra la Vella
Tel : (00 376) 875 700
Fax : (00 376) 828906/860184
Open from 9.00 to 17.30
Minister : Mrs Olga ADELLACH

MINISTERI DE FINANCES (Ministry of Finance) (http://finances.andorra.ad)
C/ Prat de la Creu 62-64
Andorra la Vella

Tel : (00 376) 875 705
Fax : (00 376) 860 962
Open from 9.00 to 17.30
Minister : Mrs Mireia MAESTRE

DUANA ANDORRANA (Andorran customs) (http://www.duana.ad)
C/ Prat de la Creu 6
Andorra la Vella
Tel : (00 376) 879 900
Fax : (00 376) 860360
E-Mail : duana.gov@andorra.ad
Central Office

MINISTERI DE SALUT I BENESTAR- (Ministry of Health and Welfare)
http://www.salutibenestar.ad
Av. Princep Benlloch, 30, 4rt,Edif. Clara Rabassa
Andorra la Vella
Tel : (00 376) 860345
Fax of Ministry Health : (00 376) 861 933
Fax of Ministry Welfare: (00 376) 829 347
Open from 9.00 to 17.30
Minister : Mrs Mónica CODINA

MINISTERI DE JUSTÍCIA I D'INTERIOR (Ministry of Justice and Internal Affairs)
Edifici Serveis de l'Obac
Carretera de l'Obac
Escaldes-engordany
Tel : (00 376) 875700/872080
Fax : (00 376) 822882/869250
Open from 9.00 to 17.30
Minister : Mr Jordi VISENT

MINISTERI D'ORDENAMENT TERRITORIAL - (Ministry of Planning)
C/ Prat de la Creu 62-64
Andorra la Vella
Tel : (00 376) 875 700
Fax : (00 376) 861313
Open from 9.00 to 17.30
Minister : Mr Jordi SERRA

MINISTERI D'ECONOMIA, INDUSTRIA I COMERC (Ministry of Economy, Industry and Commerce)
C/ Prat de la Creu 62-64
Andorra la Vella
Tel : (00 376) 875 700
Fax : (00 376) 828906
Open from 9.00 to 17.30
Minister : Mr Miquel ALVAREZ

Sports and Tourist Council:
c/Prat de la Creu, 62-64, Andorra la Vella
ph: (376) 829 345 / (376) 821 234
fax: (376) 860 184

Tourist Offices of the Principality of Andorra:
In Barcelona: Carrer Mariano Cubi, 159, 08021, Barcelona
ph: (34) 200 0655 / (34) 200 0787
fax: (34)414 1863

In Paris: Av. de L'opéra, 26, 75001, Paris
ph: (33) 42 61 50 55
fax: (33) 42 61 41 91

In New York
ph:(212) 688 8681
fax: (212) 688 8683

In Brussels: 10, rue de la Montagne, 1000.
ph: (15) 502 12 11
fax: (15) 513 39 34

In London: 63, Westover Road, London SW 2rf.
ph: 874 48 06

In Berlin: Finsterwalder Str., 28, d-13435 Berlin.
ph: 030/ 415 49 14

Representatives of the Principality of Andorra:
Mr. Roger Jusforgues - Monte Carlo
ph:(3) 50 71 47

Herr Hans Erik Lofvenmark, Stockholm
ph:(08) 31 26 82

Andorran Permanent Mission to the United Nations:
Two United Nations Plaza, 25th floor, New York, NY 10017
ph:(212) 750 8064
fax: (212) 750 6630

Tourist offices:
Canillo
ph: (376) 851 002

Encamp
ph: (376) 831 878

Pas de la Casa
ph: (376) 855 292

Ordino
ph: (376) 836 963

La Massana
ph: (376) 835 693

Andorra la Vella
ph: (376) 827 117

Sant Julià
ph: (376) 841 352

Escaldes-Engordany
ph: (376) 820 963

Cruïlla D'engolasters
ph: (376) 860 464

Andorra Ski Club
ph: (376) 820 010

Hotel Association of Andorra
ph: (376) 820 625

Caldea Water Baths and Resort
ph: (376) 865 777

POLITICAL PARTIES

ANDORRAN LIBERAL PARTY -PLA
Av. del Fener,11, 1r 4arta
Andorra la vella
Tél : (00 376) 869 708/ 869 718
Fax : (00 376) 869 728

SOCIAL-DEMOCRAT PARTY -PS
C/ Verge del Pilar no.5 3er 1era
E-mail: ps@andorra.ad
Andorra la Vella
Tel: 00 376 820320 Fax: 00 376 867979

DEMOCRAT PARTY - PD
Av. Meritxell, 105, 1er porta 3, edif. Virginia
Andorra la Vella
Tel : (00 376) 821 930
Fax : (00 376) 864 368

USEFUL TELEPHONE NUMBERS

Police office : (00 376) 821 222 emergency :110
Fire brigade office : (00 376) 800 020 emergency :118
Hospital (00 376) 871 000
Ambulances office (00 376) 820 020 emergency :118
Mountain rescue 112
Andorran Red Cross (00 376) 825 225
Andorran Telecommunications Service (00 376) 821 021
Information over the telephone 111
Government of Andorra (00 376) 875 700
Spanish Post Office (00 376) 820 257
French Post Office (00 376) 820 408
Emergency medical services 116

U.S. AMBASSADOR TO ANDORRA

EDWARD L. ROMERO

The President today announced his intent to nominate Edward L. Romero to be U.S. Ambassador to Andorra.

Mr. Edward L. Romero, of Albuquerque, New Mexico, is currently the nominee to be U.S. Ambassador to Spain and would serve as Ambassador to Andorra concurrently and without compensation. Mr. Romero is a Korean War Veteran and the Founder, Chairman and Chief Executive Officer of Advanced Sciences, Inc., an international environmental engineering and waste management corporation that recently merged with Commodore Applied Technologies, Inc., a publicly traded technology company. Fluent in Spanish, Mr. Romero has been a member of the U.S. Trade Representative's Services Policy Advisory Committee and has led a number of U.S. delegations to Mexico. During the Carter Administration, Mr. Romero served on the President's Advisory Committee for Trade Negotiations. He was a member of the U.S. delegation to the Helsinki Accords.

He has served on the President's Hispanic Advisory Committee, was a founding member of the Albuquerque Hispanic Chamber of Commerce, and serves on the Board of Directors of the Congressional Hispanic Caucus Institute. In 1989, Mr. Romero was named National Hispanic Businessman of the Year by the U.S. Hispanic Chamber of Commerce. Mr. Romero is actively engaged in a variety of civic and charitable activities. He has received numerous awards and acknowledgments from such organizations as the National Kidney Foundation, the New Mexico Anti-Defamation League, the National Hispanic Scholarship Foundation and the Multiple Sclerosis Society.

Mr. Romero studied from 1955 to 1958, in California at Los Angeles State College and Citrus College.

LOCAL GOVERNMENT

	Phone	Fax
HBLE. COMÚ D'ANDORRA LA VELLA **Plaça P. Benlloch, 1** **ANDORRA LA VELLA**	**873 100**	**861 499**
HBLE. COMÚ DE CANILLO **Cra. General** **Casa Comú**	**851 036**	**851 477**
HBLE. COMÚ D'ENCAMP **Plaça Arinsols** **Ed. Comú** **ENCAMP**	**873 200**	**832 532**
HBLE. COMÚ D'ESCALDES - ENGORDANY **Parc de la Mola, 5** **ESCALDES - ENGORDANY**	**890 890**	**890 886**
HBLE. COMÚ DE LA MASSANA **Casa Comunal** **LA MASSANA**	**835 093**	**835 834**
HBLE. COMÚ D'ORDINO **Plaça** **ORDINO**	**835 119**	**837 918**
HBLE. COMÚ DE SANT JULIÀ DE LÒRIA **Av. Verge de Canòlich, 46** **SANT JULIÀ DE LÒRIA**	**841 123**	**842 814**

TOURIST INFORMATION

	Phone	Fax
SINDICAT D'INICIATIVA Oficina de turisme - C/ Dr. Vilanova ANDORRA LA VELLA **Timetable:** 10 a.m to 1 p.m / 3 p.m to 7 p.m	**820214**	**825823**
UNIÓ PROTURISME DE CANILLO Av. Sant Joan de Caselles, s/n **Timetable:** de dimarts a dissabte: de 10 am to 1 p.m / 3 pm to 7 pm diumenges: de 10h a 13h	**851002**	**851002**

Timetable(july, august): 10 am to 1 pm / 3 pm to 8 pm		
UNIÓ PROTURISME D'ENCAMP Plaça del Consell, 1 **Timetable** 9 am to 1 pm / 3.30 pm to 7 pm	**831405**	
UNIÓ PROTURISME D'ORDINO Caseta de turisme - Nova cruïlla, s/n **Timetable** Monday to Saturday 9 am to 1 pm / 3 pm to 7 pm Sunday 9 am to 12 pm	**836963**	**836963**
UNIÓ PROTURISME DE LA MASSANA **Timetable** Monday to Saturday 9 am to 1 pm / 3 pm to 7 pm Sunday 9 am to 12 pm / 3 pm to 6 pm	**835693**	
CASETA D'INFORMACIÓ I TURISME D'ANDORRA LA VELLA Plaça de la Rotonda	**827117**	
UNIÓ PROTURISME LAUREDIÀ Plaça de la Germandat	**841352**	**844345**
UNIÓ PROTURISME D'ESCALDES-ENGORDANY Av. de ls Escoles, 26 - Ed. Tossal, 1er. 3a. **Timetable** 9.30 am to 1 pm / 4 pm to 8 pm	**828721**	**866697**
CASETA PROTURISME D'ESCALDES Plaça Coprinceps **Timetable** 9.30 am to 1 pm / 3.30 pm to 8 pm	**820963**	
CASETA CRUÏLLA D'ENGOLASTERS Cruïlla d'Engolasters **Timetable** 9.30 am to 1 pm / 3.30 pm to 8 pm	**860464**	

Prat de la Creu, 8 -Edifici Le mans
Despatx 204-205
Andorra la Vella
Tel. +376 86 32 32
Fax. +376 86 32 33
E-mail ccis@andorra.ad

BANKS

ASSOCIATION DES BANQUES ANDORRANES – ABA (http://www.aba.ad)
C/ Ciutat de Consuegra 16
Escala A - 2cn 4a.
Andorra la Vella
Tel. : (00 376) 866 845 or (00 376) 824 955
Fax : (00 376) 866 847

Winter Office Hours : Monday to Friday from 9:00 to 13:00 and from 15:00 to 19:00;
Summer Office Hours: Monday to Friday from 8:00 to 15:00

Banc Agricol i comercial d'Andorra
http://www.banc-agricol.ad
Av. fiter i Rossell, 4 bis
Escaldes Engordany
Tel: 00 376 873 345 Fax: 00 376 873 350 E-mail: internacional@banc-agricol.ad

Banc Internacional i Banca Mora - (http://www.bibm.ad)
Av. Meritxell, 96 (Andorra la Vella)
Tel: 00 376 884 488 Fax: 00 376 884 499 E-mail: bibm@bibm.ad

Banca Privada d'Andorra - (http://www.bpa.ad)
Av. Carlemany, 119 (Escaldes-engordany)
Tel: 00 376 873500 Fax: 00 376 873 517 E-mail: bpa@bpa.ad

Banca Reig
Av. Meritxell, 79 (Andorra la Vella)
Tel: 00 376 872 872 Fax: 00 376 872 875

Banc Sabadell d'Andorra - (http://www.bsa.ad)
Av. del Fener, 7 (Andorra la Vella)
Tel: 00 376 735 600 Fax: 00 376 735 601 E-mail: info@bsa.ad

Caixabank - (http://www. caixabank.ad)
Plaça Rebés, 3 (Andorra la Vella)
Tel: 00 376 874 874 Fax: 00 376 862 762 E-mail: info@caixabank.ad

Crèdit Andorrà - (http://www.creditandorra.ad)
Av. Meritxell, 80 (Andorra la Vella)
Tel: 00 376 888 035 Fax: 00 376 888 881
http://www.andorraonline.ad/pages/bancs/bancs.

LIBRARIES

NATIONAL ARCHIVES (http://www.andorra.ad/arxius/index.html)
Edifici Prada Casadet, baixos
Andorra la Vella
Tél : (00 376) 861 889
Fax : (00 376) 829541

E-Mail : sacultura.gov@andorra.ad
Winter opening hours : Monday to Friday : 8:30 to 17:30
Saturday : 9:00 to 13:00

NATIONAL LIBRARY (http://www.andorra.ad/bibnac/index.html)
Casa Bauró Placeta Sant Esteve s/n
Andorra la Vella
Tél : (00 376) 826445
Fax : (00 376) 829445
E-Mail : bncultura.gov@andorra.ad
Winter opening hours : Monday to Friday : 10:00 to 13:00 and 16:00 to 19:00
Saturday : 9:00 to 13:00
Summer opening hours : Monday to Friday : 10:00 to 13:00 and 16:00 to 19:00
Saturday: closed

CANILLO MUNICIPAL LIBRARY
Edifici Cal Metge
Canillo
Tél : (00 376) 851 888
Winter and summer opening hours : Monday to Friday from 17:00 to 20:00

ENCAMP MUNICIPAL LIBRARY
Centre Esportiu i sociocultural
Encamp
Tél : (00 376) 832 830
Winter and summer opening hours : Monday to Friday from 9:00 to 21:00
Saturday from 9:00 to 13:00 and from 15:00 to 19:00

PAS DE LA CASA MUNICIPAL LIBRARY
Centre Esportiu
Avinguda Consell General
Pas de la Casa
Tél : (00 376) 856 830
Fax : (00 376) 855677
Winter opening hours : Monday to Sunday from 10:00 to 23:30
Summer opening hours : Monday to Sunday from 10:00 to 23:30

ORDINO MUNICIPAL LIBRARY
(http://www.andorra.ad/comuns/ordino)
Edifici la Font, 3r
Ordino
Tél : (00 376) 837 811
Fax : (00 376) 873 353
E-mail : ito@andorra.ad
Winter opening hours : Monday to Friday from 16:00 to 20:00
Saturday: from 10:00 to 14:00
Summer opening hours : Monday to Friday from 16:00 to 20:00
Saturday: from 10:00 to 14:00

LA MASSANA MUNICIPAL LIBRARY
Cap del Carrer, s/n

La Massana
Tél : (00 376) 836 920
Winter opening hours : Monday to Friday from 15:00 to 20:00
Closed on Saturday
Summer opening hours : Monday to Friday from 15:00 to 19:00
Closed on Saturday

SANT JULIÀ DE LÒRIA MUNICIPAL LIBRARY
Centre Cultural i de Congressos Lauredià
Sant Julià de Lória
Tél : (00 376) 844044
Fax : (00 376) 844000
E-mail : biblioteca.lauredia@andorra.ad
Winter opening hours : Monday to Friday from 10:00 to 13:30 and from 15:30 to 20:30
Saturday from 10:00 to 13:30

ESCALDES-ENGORDANY MUNICIPAL LIBRARY
Edifici comú d'Escaldes-Engordany, 5è
Escaldes-Engordany
Tél : (00 376) 890 890
Fax : (00 376) 890 886
Winter and summer opening hours: Monday to Friday from 10:00 to 13:00 and from 16:00 to 21:00.
Saturday from 9:00 to 13:00

GOVERNMENT PUBLIC LIBRARY
Edifici Prada Casadet,Baixos
Andorra la Vella
Tél: (00 376) 828750
Fax: (00 376) 829541
E-mail: bibliopublica@andorra.ad
Winter opening hours : Monday to Friday : 10:00 to 20:30
Saturday : 10:00 to 13:00
Summer opening hours : Monday to Friday : 8:30 to 19:00
Saturday : closed

EDUCATION

UNIVERSITY OF ANDORRA http://www.ev.ad
Centre Cultural i de Congressos Lauredià
Planta 1era
Plaça de la Germandat
Sant Julià de Lória
Tél: (00 376) 841 806
Fax: (00 376) 843 538
E-mail: candorra@campus.uoc.es

NURSING COLLEGE
Dr. Vilanova Edifici Davi,1er
Andorra la Vella

Tél : (00 376) 861564
Fax : (00 376) 861536

INFORMATION TECHNOLOGY COLLEGE OF ANDORRA
Plaça de la germandat
Centre Cultural Lauredià,1r
Sant Julià de Lória
Tél : (00 376) 841 806
Fax : (00 376) 861536

BTS : PME/PMI
Prada Motxilla
Andorra la Vella
Tél : (00 376) 872 500
Fax : (00 376) 852 517

SPORTS AND MOUNTAINEERING TRAINING CENTRE
Av. de les Escoles, 10
Santa Coloma
Tél : (00 376) 829 240

ADULT EDUCATION CENTRE
Prada Casadet, Baixos
Andorra la Vella
Tél : (00 376) 822 075

APPRENTICE TRAINING CENTRE
Prada Casadet, Baixos
Andorra la Vella
Tél : (00 376) 822 075

CATALAN SELF-STUDY CENTRE
Av. del Travès, s/n 1er
La Massana

PROFESSIONAL COLLEGES

Andorra is not only an amusement centre, somewhere to practice sports and enjoy unforgettable landscapes, it is also a resource centre where many organizations and companies work and draw up projects, hold congresses and organize conferences which may well turn out to be of great interest to you. The following are the most qualified professional organizations in Andorra.

	Dean:
COLLEGE OF ARCHITECTS	Fèlix Vicente **Secretary:**
	Víctor Blasi

Address: Ciutat de Valls, 6. 1r 2a. Andorra la Vella
Phone.: 861202
Fax: 861111
Office hours: from 9 a.m. to 1 p.m. and from 3 p.m. to 7 p.m.
e-Mail: coaa@andorra.net
web: http://www.coea.net

President:

Alfred Huarachi
Secretary:

Jaume Forné

ANDORRAN COLLEGE OF HIGHER ENGINEERS

Address: Carretera Ribeaygua, 11.

5è 1a. Apartat de Correus 1051. Andorra la Vella
Phone: 828219
Fax: 828219
Office hours: from 9 a.m. to 7 p.m.

Dean:

Manuel M. Pujadas
Secretary:

Daniel Arqués

COL.LEGI D'ADVOCATS

Address: Dr. Nequi, 7. 2n pb. Andorra la Vella
Phone: 869996
Fax: 869669
Office hours: from 9 a.m. to 1 p.m. and from 3 p.m. to 7 p.m.

ANDORRAN COLLEGE OF DISPENSING CHEMISTS

President:

Josep Anton Montané
Secretary:

Montserrat Sebastià

Address: Joan Maragall, 2
Andorra la Vella
Phone: 829914
Fax: 829914
Office hours: Tuesday and Thursday from 4 p.m. to 8 p.m.

ANDORRAN COLLEGE OF PSYCHOLOGISTS

Presidenta:

Meritxell Camp
Secretary:

Montse Gil

Address: Isabel Sandy, 6, 1r. 6a.
Escaldes-Engordany
Phone: 866919
Fax: 860067
Office hours: Dimarts i dijous, de 9 a 13 h.

COLLEGE OF NURSES, MIDWIVES AND NURSING

SPECIALISTS

President:

Lourdes Font
Secretary:

Ramon Badia

Address: C/ del Pui, 16
Andorra la Vella

ANDORRAN COLLEGE OF PHYSICIANS

President:

Dr. Vicenç Martinez-Vecina
Secretary:

Dr. Jordi Ripoll Dorma

Address: Verge del Pilar, 5
Edifici Plaza, 4t. Despat 11
Andorra la Vella
Phone: 823525
Fax: 860793
Office hours: From 9 a.m. to 2 p.m.
e-Mail: junta@col-legide metges.ad

and secretaria@col-legide metges.ad

web: http://www.col-legidemetges.ad

President:

Josep Burgués
Secretary:

Lluís Burgués

COLLEGE OF ECONOMISTS

Address: Cra. Armengol, 15. 6è.
Andorra la Vella
Phone: 824136
Fax: 862174
Office hours: From 3 p.m. to 6 p.m
e-Mail: aedes@andorra.ad

TOWN HALLS

COMÚ DE CANILLO

Comú de Canillo, Av. Sant Joan de Caselles s/n
Canillo
Tél : (00 376) 851 036
Fax : (00 376) 851 477
Winter office hours : Monday to Friday from 8:00 to 17:00
Summer office hours : Monday to Friday from 8:00 to 15:00

COMÚ D'ENCAMP (http://www.encamp.ad)

Plaça dels Arinsols
Encamp
Tél : (00 376) 873 200
Fax : (00 376) 832 918
E-Mail : comu.encamp@andorra.ad
Winter office hours: Monday to Friday from 8:00 to 17:30
Summer office hours : Monday to Friday from 8:00 to 17:30

COMÚ D'ORDINO (http://www.andorra.ad/comuns/ordino)

Casa comuna
Ordino
Tél : (00 376) 835119
Fax : (00 376) 837918
Winter office hours : Monday to Friday from 8:00 to 13:00 and from 14:00 to 1 7:00
Summer office hours : Monday to Friday from 8:00 to 13:00 and from 14:00 to 17:00

COMÚ DE LA MASSANA

Av. del Travès, s/n
La Massana
Tél : (00 376) 835093
Fax : (00 376) 835834
Winter office hours : Monday to Friday from 8:30 to 17:30
Summer office hours : Monday to Friday from 8:00 to 15:00

COMÚ D'ANDORRA LA VELLA

Plaça Princep Benlloch,1
Andorra la Vella
Tél : (00 376) 873103
Fax : (00 376) 861 499
E-Mail : comu.andorra@correu.andorra.ad
Winter office hours : Monday to Friday from 8:30 to 17:30
Summer office hours : Monday to Friday from 8:00 to 15:00

COMÚ DE SANT JULIÀ DE LÒRIA

Av. Verge de Canòlich, s/n
Sant Julià de Lória
Tél : (00 376) 841 123
Fax : (00 376) 842 814
E-Mail : turisme.lauredia@andorra.ad
Winter office hours : Monday to Friday from 8:30 to 17:30
Summer office hours : Monday to Friday from 8:00 to 15:00

COMÚ D'ESCALDES ENGORDANY

Parc de la Mola, 9
Escaldes-Engordany
Tél : (00 376) 890 890/ 890 888
Fax : (00 376) 828 959
E-Mail : escaldesengordany@andorra.ad
Winter office hours : Monday to Friday from 8:00 to 17:00
Summer office hours : Monday to Friday from 8:00 to 17:00

HOSPITALS

HOSPITAL NOSTRA SENYORA DE MERITXELL
Av. fiter i Rossell, 1-13, 4rt
Tél : (00 376) 871 000
Fax : (00 376) 868 100

CLÍNICA GERIÀTRICA ST VICENC D'ENCLAR
C/ de les Escoles, 25
Santa Coloma
Andorra la Vella
Tél : (00 376) 868 368

PRESS

DAILY NEWSPAPERS :

Diari d'Andorra (http://www.diariandorra.ad)
C/ Bonaventura Riberaygua 39, 4rt
Andorra la Vella
Tél : (00 376) 863700
Fax : (00 376) 863800
E-Mail : diaridigital@diariandorra.ad

El Periòdic d'Andorra
Andorrana de publicació
C/ Sant Salvador, 10
Andorra la Vella
Tél : (00 376) 800 555
Fax : (00 376) 826 777
E-Mail : elperiodic@andorra.ad

WEEKLY MAGAZINES :

7 Dies (http://www.diariandorra.ad)
C/Bonaventura Riberaygua, 39, 4rt

Andorra la Vella
Tél : (00 376) 863 700
Fax : (00 376) 863 800
E-Mail : diaridigital@andorra.ad

Informacions
C/ de la Unió, 2 3er
Andorra la Vella
Tél : (00 376) 821 134
Fax :(00 376) 860 839

MONTHLY MAGAZINES

Actual
Av. Princep Benlloch, 68
Andorra la Vella
Tél : (00 376) 865 776
Fax : (00 376) 867 771

Andorra Magazine
C/ Verge del Pilar,5,3r,Despatx 12
Andorra la Vella
Tél : (00 376) 867 888
Fax : (00 376) 867 887

GUILDS, ASSOCIATIONS AND PROFESSIONAL GROUPS:

ANDORRAN ASSOCIATION OF VEHICLE IMPORTERS (AIVA)

Address: Garatge Sport-Av. Verge del Pilar, 10-12
Andorra la Vella

Phone: 822353
Fax: 820383
Office hours: from 9 a.m. to 1 p.m. and from 3 p.m. to 7 p.m.

ANDORRAN GROUP OF DOCUMENT HANDLERS AND REAL ESTATE AGENTS (AGIA)

Address: Sant Salvador, 7
Despatx, 45
Andorra la Vella

Phone: 826142
Fax: 826142
Office hours: from 9 a.m. to 1 p.m. and from

3.30 p.m. to 7 p.m.
e-mail: agia@andorra.ad

ASSOCIATION OF PUBLIC WORKS CONTRACTORS

Address: Baixada del Molí, 48-3r.
Andorra la Vella

Phone: 862772
Fax: 861696

ASSOCIATION OF IMPORTERS AND EXPORTERS OF INDUSTRIAL GOODS (ANIM)

Address: Dr. Vilanova, 9. 4t D. Despatx 45
Andorra la Vella

Phone: 869686
Fax: 869686

PROFESSIONAL ASSOCIATION OF COOKS AND PASTRY COOKS (APCR)

Address: Antic Carrer Major, 18 (UHA)
Andorra la Vella

Phone: 820625
820602
Fax: 861539

ANDORRAN ASSOCIATION OF FLORISTS AND GARDENERS (AFIJA)

Address: Av. Francesc Cairat, 24
Sant Julià de Lòira

Phone: 841725
Office hours: from 8 a.m. to 1 p.m. and from 4 p.m. to 8 p.m.

ASSOCIATION OF BAKERS

Address: Centre Cultural Parc de la Mola.

	Escaldes-Engordany
ASSOCIATION FOR THE DEVELOPMENT OF QUALITY (ADEQUA)	**Address:** Placeta Monjó, 2. Andorra la Vella
ASSOCIATION OF PEASANTS AND LIVESTOCK BREEDERS OF THE PRINCIPALITY OF ANDORRA	**Address:** Av. Dr. VIlanova. Edifici Thais, 4t. Andorra la Vella
ASSOCIATION OF IMPORTERS AND DISTRIBUTORS OF ALCOHOLIC BEVERAGES	**Address:** Avda. Fiter i Rosell, 72. Escaldes-Engordany
ASSOCIATION OF IMPORTERS AND DISTRIBUTORS OF ELECTRONIC GOODS	**Address:** Avda. Fiter i Rosell, 72. Escaldes-Engordany
GROUP OF BUILDERS OF THE VALLEYS OF ANDORRA	**Address:** Urbanització Ciutat Jardí Valira, Bloc, 4 Botiga Andorra la Vella **Phone:** 824991
GROUP OF CAKE MAKERS IN THE PRINCIPALITY OF ANDORRA	**Address:** AMA-Miquel Mateu, s/n. Escaldes-Engordany **Phone:** 829107 **Fax:** 860888
HISPANO-ANDORRAN BUSINESS ASSOCIATION	**Address:** Avda. Tarragona, 75

	Edifici Tarragona. Andorra la Vella
ANDORRAN ASSOCIATION OF ENGINEERING FIRMS	**Address:** Avda. Meritxell, 30-baixos. Andorra la Vella **Phone:** 826543 **Phone:** 860688
ASSOCIATION OF CARPENTERS, CABINET MAKERS AND VARNISHERS	**Address:** Decor Andorra-Avda. Fiter i Rossell, 72 Escaldes-Engordany
ASSOCIATION OF ACCREDITED REPRESENTATIVES IN THE PRINCIPALITY OF ANDORRA	**Address:** C/ Bra Armengol, 5-5 A Andorra la Vella **Phone:** 867666-822081 **Fax:** 867556-860978 **e-Mail: cpa-auge@andorra.ad**
ASAAR	**Address:** Avda. Meritxell, 88 Andorra la Vella
ANDORRAN ASSOCIATION OF GOODS AND FUEL	**Address:** Carretera de la Cornella, 29 Andorra la Vella
ANDORRAN ASSOCIATION OF PUBLIC PASSENGER TRANSPORT	**Address:** Avda. Tarragona, 42, Planta Baixa. Andorra la Vella

ASSOCIATION OF IMPORTERS AND EXPORTERS OF INDUSTRIAL GOODS	**Address:** Avda. Doctor Vilanova, 9. 4 D. Andorra la Vella
ASSOCIATION OF MECHANICAL WORKSHOPS	**Address:** Garatge Martí. Carretera de Nagol, s/n. Andorra la Vella
ANDORRAN TRAVEL AGENTS' ASSOCIATION (AAVA)	**Address:** C/ Maria Pla, 19-21. Hotel Pla. Andorra la Vella
ASSOCIATION OF ANDORRAN INSURANCE COMPANIES	**Address:** La Patrimoine. Pl. Guillemó, 6. Andorra la Vella
ANDORRAN UNION OF MORTICIANS	**Address:** L'Aigüeta, 14. Despatx, 12. Andorra la Vella
ASSOCIATION OF FUEL IMPORTERS AND DISTRIBUTORS	**Address:** Rosaleda Carburants. Encamp
SHOPKEEPERS OF THE UPPER PART OF ESCALDES (CALIDAE)	**Address:** Av. Fiter i Rossell, 72 Andorra la Vella **Tél:** 820829
	Address: Av. Sant Antoni. Casa

APAV	Montané- Post box 53. La Massana
FIABCI-ANDORRA	**Address:** Sant Salvador, 7-Despatx 4 Andorra la Vella **Office hours:** from 9 a.m. to 1 p.m. and from 3.30 p.m. to 7 p.m. **e-mail:** **fiabci-andorra@andorra.ad**
ANDORRAN GUILD OF JEWELERS AND WATCHMAKERS	**Address:** Joieria Flor de Lis. Av. Verge de Canolich, 56 Sant Julià de Lòira
ANDORRAN HAIRDRESSERS' GUILD	**Address:** Casa Hort del Pont, 1r. La Massana
EMPLOYERS' ASSOCIATION OF THE PRINCIPALITY (PDP)	**Address:** Avda. Príncep Benlloch, 75. Andorra la Vella **Phone:** 822711 **Fax:** 828208 **Office hours:** from 9 a.m. to 1 p.m. and from 3 p.m. to 8 p.m.
UNION OF ANDORRAN TAXI DRIVERS	**Address:** Avda. Tarragona, 93. Andorra la Vella **Phone:** 863000 861005 867330

HOTEL UNION OF THE VALLEYS OF ANDORRA	**Address:** Antic Carrer Major,18. Andorra la Vella
ASSOCIATION OF NEIGHBOURS AND SHOPKEEPERS OF RIBERAYGUA AND PRADA RAMON I PRADA RAMON	**Address:** Tintoreria Sant Jordi. C/ Bra Armengol. Andorra la Vella
GUILD OF PHILATELIC TRADERS	**Address:** C/ Engordany, 16 Escaldes-Engordany
ANDORRAN ASSOCIATION OF TAXI OWNERS AND **WORKERS**	**Address:** Carretera d'Engolasters. Escaldes-Engordany
ANDORRA COMPUTER ASSOCIATION	**Address:** C/ Anna Ma. Pla- Hotel Pla. Andorra la Vella
AMI	**Address:** C/ Bonavista, 33. 2n. 3a. Andorra la Vella
ANDORRAN TAXI DRIVERS' ASSOCIATION (ATA)	**Address:** Avda. Santa Coloma, 89 3r.2a. Andorra la Vella
ASSOCIATION OF TAXI DRIVERS IN THE PRINCIPALITY	**Address:** Avda. Dr. Mitjavila, 15 - 6 B. Andorra la Vella
ANDORRAN VEHICLE IMPORTERS	**Address:** Garatge Internacional. Avda. Tarragona.

Andorra la Vella

GROUP OF ANDORRAN BANKS

Address: C/ Ciutat de Consuegra16. Escala A. 2n 4a. Andorra la Vella

Phone: 866845
824955
Fax: 866847

IMPORT BY COUNTRY

2005			2006	2007	2008	2014
KG	Kyrgyzstan	54.81	6.21	0.21	-	-
KH	Cambodia	156.21	24.38	16.83	16.87	49.59
KP	North Korea	47.97	-	0.02	5.64	15.98
KR	South Korea	9,808.35	9,131.53	4,227.70	3,394.84	883.24
KW	Kuwait	-	-	5.83	-	-
KZ	Kazakstan	0.27	13.31	4.30	44.95	35.10
LA	Laos	19.14	31.52	34.77	13.34	4.20
LB	Lebanon	0.08	-	4.84	4.00	0.07
LC	Saint Lucia	-	-	-	-	0.64
LI	Liechtenstein	0.01	-	0.03	-	-
LK	Sri Lanka	214.71	115.74	94.59	106.67	198.27
LS	Lesotho	-	-	-	0.40	-
LT	Lithuania	23.09	58.66	6.19	150.43	42.31
LU	Luxembourg	838.95	493.70	403.89	426.46	475.99
LV	Latvia	4.47	22.06	8.27	45.88	1.79
LY	Libya	-	-	-	3.22	2.25
MA	Morocco	841.55	738.99	830.26	754.47	842.63
MD	Moldavia	5.31	78.45	44.13	38.59	105.82
MG	Madagascar	26.98	9.06	9.14	23.63	16.28
MK	Macedonia	4.09	22.04	6.00	17.24	8.66
ML	Mali	-	0.39	-	-	5.14
MM	Myanmar (formerly Burma)	-	-	8.60	10.74	7.21
MN	Mongolia	-	-	0.17	-	-
MO	Macau	66.55	78.44	61.72	180.54	86.46
MR	Mauritania	4.40	24.83	58.83	76.61	15.14

MS	Montserrat	0.18	-	-	-	-
MT	Malta	7.11	20.49	9.63	1.67	0.86
MU	Mauritius	11.53	32.01	149.65	134.78	164.28
MV	Maldives	-	-	7.22	-	-
MW	Malawi	-	-	1.03	-	0.29
MX	Mexico	319.20	354.75	374.01	398.25	469.22
MY	Malaysia	1,593.38	2,065.68	1,282.68	890.34	570.39
NA	Namibia	-	2.31	-	0.53	0.21
NC	New Caledonia	-	6.60	1.29	-	-
NE	Niger	22.52	27.47	0.22	1.96	6.48
NG	Nigeria	-	-	-	3.19	9.73
NI	Nicaragua	11.51	5.06	-	2.60	15.47
NL	Netherlands	15,187.04	13,363.34	11,813.58	11,394.11	11,725.11
NO	Norway	601.86	33.04	345.02	32.69	23.98
NP	Nepal	2.70	0.42	13.92	0.25	3.24
NR	Nauru	-	-	-	0.03	-
NZ	New Zealand	362.22	45.66	37.62	17.39	142.10
PA	Panama	0.61	-	12.97	5.21	0.52
PE	Peru	28.13	11.16	41.55	67.37	166.43
PF	French Polynesia	146.38	-	7.17	-	-
PH	Philippines	1,094.56	331.66	449.16	512.73	347.95
PK	Pakistan	264.28	205.65	343.84	276.81	232.46
PL	Poland	2,480.99	2,319.27	1,289.31	3,729.35	4,325.07
PT	Portugal	5,242.11	4,652.99	6,296.66	11,097.34	9,298.02
PY	Paraguay	0.01	-	-	-	-
QA	Qatar	0.61	-	-	-	-
RO	Romania	857.11	885.30	1,040.07	1,008.42	1,230.46
RU	Russian Federation	40.00	37.78	429.98	26.48	8.95
SA	Saudi Arabia	-	-	-	-	179.90
SC	Seychelles	0.59	-	0.05	-	-
SE	Sweden	2,773.41	1,970.91	2,048.40	2,553.00	1,370.99
SG	Singapore	194.42	246.19	125.23	526.50	161.79
SI	Slovenia	385.63	633.07	340.83	342.71	349.24
SK	Slovakia	313.76	398.79	286.77	823.02	559.58
SL	Sierra Leone	0.57	0.16	-	6.31	0.87
SM	San Marino	115.28	77.94	0.25	10.25	17.74
SN	Senegal	1.55	3.29	7.42	0.11	-
SR	Surinam	1.61	-	-	-	0.59
ST	São Tomé and Príncipe	0.70	-	-	-	-
SV	El Salvador	1.00	-	12.74	3.31	29.48

SY	Syria	0.07	1.13	1.03	2.52	-
TG	Togo	0.48	6.05	-	-	-
TH	Thailand	2,133.88	1,869.66	2,074.89	1,129.21	1,468.96
TJ	Tajikistan	-	-	2.66	0.72	-
TK	Tokelau	-	-	-	0.95	4.22
TM	Turkmenistan	-	-	-	-	0.76
TN	Tunisia	273.27	396.72	553.60	556.34	1,031.46
TO	Tonga	0.62	-	-	-	-
TR	Turkey	2,708.28	2,172.65	3,106.52	3,253.19	2,405.82
TT	Trinidad and Tobago	0.39	-	-	-	-
TW	Taiwan	4,870.45	3,928.59	2,866.08	2,019.31	1,378.82
TZ	Tanzania	0.03	-	0.08	-	-
UA	Ukraine	24.81	32.13	20.03	55.54	41.78
UG	Uganda	37.67	90.37	25.34	71.26	19.58
US	United States of America	16,546.19	9,012.46	12,086.84	9,069.56	7,477.76
UY	Uruguay	263.52	324.03	176.15	45.26	12.62
UZ	Uzbekistan	-	-	-	1.98	0.09
VA	Vatican City	0.03	0.19	-	-	-
VE	Venezuela	125.33	106.57	164.26	228.40	76.40
VI	Virgin Islands (USA)	-	0.38	0.74	4.54	-
VN	Vietnam	1,734.12	1,267.99	2,114.12	2,437.53	3,342.79
WS	Samoa	-	1.48	1.34	0.54	0.09
XC	Ceuta	-	0.23	-	-	-
XL	Melilla	-	1.95	-	-	-
XM	Montenegro	-	-	1.81	-	5.72
XS	Serbia	-	-	1.67	1.46	-
YE	Yemen	0.72	0.36	-	-	-
YU	Yugoslavia Federal Republic	24.98	8.77	-	-	-
ZA	South Africa	5.15	17.75	14.71	64.58	215.69
ZW	Zimbabwe	-	-	16.53	-	-
Total		1,441,579.93	1,415,681.45	1,395,349.11	1,312,680.15	1,137,351.51
Note: After 2007 the figures are provisional.						

Source: Andorran Customs

EXPORT BY COUNTRY

2005			2006	2007	2008	2014
DZ	Algeria	167.18	-	-	31.77	41.84
EE	Estonia	-	-	-	0.11	-
EG	Egypt	-	-	-	1.00	6.80
ES	Spain	67,390.95	83,462.67	56,179.62	45,382.88	31,978.97
FI	Finland	28.26	0.18	25.21	1.60	7.51
FR	France	19,427.76	18,152.81	14,929.38	10,140.88	9,145.89
GA	Gabon	-	-	-	4.70	-
GB	United Kingdom	5,664.21	1,977.26	50.76	191.07	86.23
GI	Gibraltar	-	-	-	-	6.08
GM	The Gambia	-	-	-	2.00	-
GN	Guinea	-	-	37.24	10.49	1.05
GQ	Equatorial Guinea	-	-	7.70	-	-
GR	Greece	54.54	-	2.22	0.16	0.98
GT	Guatemala	4.92	-	-	-	-
GY	Guyana	5.78	-	-	-	51.27
HK	Hong Kong	-	8.00	6.80	13.05	21.18
HR	Croatia	-	-	0.02	-	-
HU	Hungary	-	-	1.62	-	-
ID	Indonesia	-	-	0.09	-	-
IE	Ireland	0.11	0.27	0.45	1.21	2.67
IL	Israel	-	1.78	2.57	0.10	119.60
IN	India	5.79	-	34.40	1,700.00	28.00
IR	Iran	0.73	-	1.56	0.39	6.10
IT	Italy	634.33	489.90	2,034.93	1,167.45	951.27
JO	Jordan	-	-	-	-	5.80
JP	Japan	108.35	181.54	17.55	70.20	20.23
KR	South Korea	-	-	24.11	-	-
LI	Liechtenstein	-	1,886.89	-	-	-
LK	Sri Lanka	-	-	-	0.03	-
LT	Lithuania	11.20	-	-	-	0.65
LU	Luxembourg	-	9.10	3.50	1.87	0.70
MA	Morocco	613.80	1,879.11	3.17	14.74	6.73
MG	Madagascar	-	-	-	-	3.29
ML	Mali	0.60	-	-	-	-
MR	Mauritania	-	15.00	3.00	-	0.36
MT	Malta	-	-	-	0.11	90.11

MX	Mexico	6.90	-	22.17	4.60	-
MY	Malaysia	7.98	-	-	-	0.05
NC	New Caledonia	-	-	-	-	0.20
NE	Niger	-	-	-	-	0.33
NI	Nicaragua	-	-	-	-	23.21
NL	Netherlands	361.00	497.80	645.82	547.19	482.25
NO	Norway	15.38	-	2.27	0.20	0.74
NZ	New Zealand	-	-	1.45	-	-
PA	Panama	-	-	-	-	0.13
PE	Peru	-	-	-	184.68	-
PF	French Polynesia	-	15.00	-	0.25	-
PH	Philippines	0.30	-	-	-	-
PL	Poland	7.79	3.94	23.26	25.19	1.22
PT	Portugal	4,474.39	1,415.98	373.40	320.86	406.01
RO	Romania	3.32	-	-	5.23	1.50
RU	Russian Federation	41.23	34.03	171.36	361.85	0.91
SA	Saudi Arabia	-	-	-	5.76	1.15
SD	Sudan	-	-	-	3.53	1.25
SE	Sweden	3.36	0.10	3.75	5.50	2.80
SG	Singapore	8.51	4.50	-	18.00	-
SI	Slovenia	-	7.43	6.56	0.46	0.08
SK	Slovakia	-	-	17.55	48.69	41.24
SM	San Marino	7.84	-	31.32	-	-
SN	Senegal	-	13.00	-	-	-
SY	Syria	-	2.50	-	4.00	-
TG	Togo	-	-	2.00	1.00	-
TH	Thailand	-	-	5.31	-	-
TR	Turkey	-	-	-	-	0.10
TW	Taiwan	0.10	2.09	0.20	-	-

EXPORT BY COUNTRY

		2005	2006	2007	2008	2014
UA	Ukraine	3.33	13.00	-	84.43	4.56
US	United States of America	108.88	64.65	61.83	3.32	184.92
UY	Uruguay	-	-	2.39	-	11.10
VE	Venezuela	54.15	-	-	-	-
VN	Vietnam	0.85	-	-	0.05	0.00
WF	Wallis and Futuna	-	-	-	-	1.06
XL	Melilla	2.34	0.10	0.60	-	-

XM	Montenegro	-	-	4.39	-	-
XS	Serbia	-	-	-	0.37	-
YU	Yugoslavia Federal Republic	27.25	-	-	-	-
ZA	South Africa	4.01	-	-	-	4.00
Total		114,117.96	119,994.33	91,299.22	65,255.24	45,583.52
Note: After 2007 the figures are provisional.						
					Source: Andorran Customs	

IMPORTANT LAWS AND REGULATIONS AFFECTING BUSINESS AND INVESTMENTS

COUTRY	LAW TITLE
Andorra	Law 5/2004, of April 14, Code of Customs (BOPA 29, year 16)
Andorra	Act to amend the Act of indirect goods tax 2000
Andorra	Act 31/2008, of 18 December, on measures of economic revival
Andorra	Foreign Investment Law
Andorra	Law 35/2008, of December 18, Code of relations
Andorra	Law 1/2014, of January 23, amending the General Health Law
Andorra	General Health Law of 20 March 1989
Andorra	Law 14/2006, amending Law on indirect tax on commercial activities, 27 October 2006 (BOPA 86, year 18)
Andorra	Qualified Law of modification of the Penal Code. 27-11-1997
Andorra	Excise Act 27/2008 of 20 November 2008 (BOPA 94, year 20)
Andorra	Act Qualified Police Force
Andorra	Law control of sensitive goods, 4 March 1999
Andorra	Law indirect goods tax (IMI), 26 June 1991
Andorra	Law on indirect taxation service delivery
Andorra	Amending the tax law of indirect goods, May 25th
Andorra	Law amending the Law on indirect goods tax
Andorra	Law amending the Law on indirect goods tax
Andorra	Law 19/2004, on Indirect Taxation on commercial activities
Andorra	of the Administrative Code (03/29/1989) - 6/1989 BOPA
Andorra	Constitution of the Principality of Andorra (04/28/1993)
Andorra	Law on the Court of Accounts
Andorra	Law Audit
Andorra	Law 5/2005, of February 21 on qualified campaign finance
Andorra	Law amending the Law of qualified electoral system and the referendum dated 15 December 2000.
Andorra	Qualified campaign finance law.
Andorra	Qualified law to amend the Articles 6.1 and 7.1 of the Act and described the electoral system referendum of 26 November 1999.
Andorra	Law 2/2008, of April 8, foreign investment in Andorra
Andorra	Official Bulletin
Andorra	Law 3/2007, of 22 March, the Corps Penitentiary.
Andorra	Law 17/2008, October 3, Social Security
Andorra	Act ordering the Andorran educational system
Andorra	Nationality Act
Andorra	Act 16/2008 on Code of Criminal Procedure, 10 December 1998
Andorra	Qualified Penal Code Law 9/2005 of 21 February 2005 (BOPA 25, year 17)

COUTRY	LAW TITLE
Andorra	Law 9 / 2005 Qualified Criminal Code
Andorra	Act Police
Andorra	Qualified law and the electoral system referendum dated 3 September 1993.
Andorra	Patent Law of 10/06/1999
Andorra	Tax Law on consumption, 30 December 1985
Andorra	Law 15/2008 on the Penal Code
Andorra	Law 6/2014, of 29 December, The Electronic Signature.
Andorra	Regulations for the Implementation of the Taxation Law Office of Trademarks
Andorra	Trademark Law
Andorra	Law on trading names, names and fellow shop Signs
Andorra	Law on the use of State emblems and Signs
Andorra	Law on Public Broadcasting and Television and the incorporation of the Public Company Radio and Television of Andorra SA
Andorra	General Law of Public Finance (19/12/1996) - 5/1997 BOPA
Andorra	Rules of application of the indirect tax on commercial activities
Andorra	Basic law of the tax system (19/12/1996) - 5/1997 BOPA
Andorra	Excise Rules, 21 January 2014 (BOPA 4, year 21)
Andorra	Draft law where copyright and Neighboring Rights
Andorra	Regulation implementing the Law on Control of sensitive goods,
Andorra	Law 29/2008, of 11 December, The Cadaster

BASIC TITLES ON ANDORRA

IMPORTANT!
All publications are updated annually!
Please contact IBP, Inc. at ibpusa3@gmail.com for the latest ISBNs and additional information

Title
Andorra A "Spy" Guide - Strategic Information and Developments
Andorra A Spy" Guide"
Andorra Business and Investment Opportunities Yearbook
Andorra Business and Investment Opportunities Yearbook
Andorra Business and Investment Opportunities Yearbook Volume 1 Strategic Information and Opportunities
Andorra Business Intelligence Report - Practical Information, Opportunities, Contacts
Andorra Business Intelligence Report - Practical Information, Opportunities, Contacts
Andorra Business Law Handbook - Strategic Information and Basic Laws
Andorra Business Law Handbook - Strategic Information and Basic Laws
Andorra Business Law Handbook - Strategic Information and Basic Laws
Andorra Business Law Handbook - Strategic Information and Basic Laws
Andorra Company Laws and Regulations Handbook

Title
Andorra Constitution and Citizenship Laws Handbook - Strategic Information and Basic Laws
Andorra Country Study Guide - Strategic Information and Developments
Andorra Country Study Guide - Strategic Information and Developments
Andorra Country Study Guide - Strategic Information and Developments Volume 1 Strategic Information and Developments
Andorra Ecology & Nature Protection Handbook
Andorra Ecology & Nature Protection Handbook
Andorra Ecology & Nature Protection Laws and Regulation Handbook
Andorra Energy Policy, Laws and Regulation Handbook
Andorra Export-Import Trade and Business Directory
Andorra Export-Import Trade and Business Directory
Andorra Foreign Policy and Government Guide
Andorra Foreign Policy and Government Guide
Andorra Industrial and Business Directory
Andorra Industrial and Business Directory
Andorra Investment & Business Guide
Andorra Investment & Business Guide
Andorra Investment and Business Guide - Strategic and Practical Information
Andorra Investment and Business Guide - Strategic and Practical Information
Andorra Investment and Trade Laws and Regulations Handbook
Andorra Land Ownership and Agriculture Laws Handbook
Andorra Offshore Investment and Business Guide - Strategic and Practical Information
Andorra Offshore Investment and Business Guide - Strategic and Practical Information
Andorra Offshore Tax Guide
Andorra Offshore Tax Guide
Andorra Recent Economic and Political Developments Yearbook
Andorra Recent Economic and Political Developments Yearbook
Andorra Recent Economic and Political Developments Yearbook
Andorra Starting Business (Incorporating) in....Guide
Andorra Taxation Laws and Regulations Handbook
Andorra Telecommunication Industry Business Opportunities Handbook
Andorra: How to Invest, Start and Run Profitable Business in Andorra Guide - Practical Information, Opportunities, Contacts

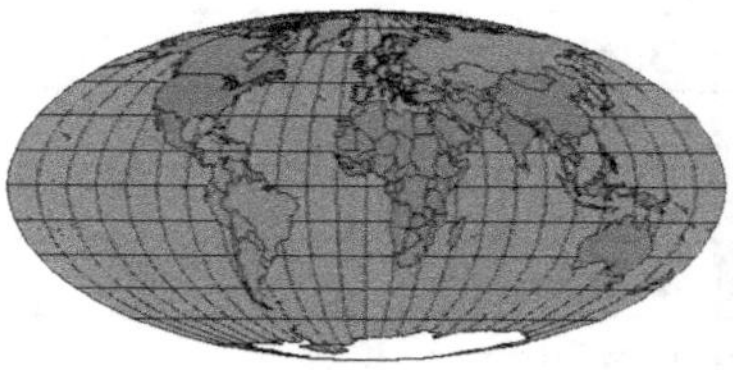

WORLD INDUSTRIAL AND BUSINESS DIRECTORIES LIBRARY

Price: $149.95 Each

1. Albania Industrial and Business Directory
2. Algeria Industrial and Business Directory
3. Andorra Industrial and Business Directory
4. Angola Industrial and Business Directory
5. Antigua & Barbuda Industrial and Business Directory
6. Antilles (Netherlands) Industrial and Business Directory
7. Argentina Industrial and Business Directory
8. Armenia Industrial and Business Directory
9. Australia Industrial and Business Directory
10. Austria Industrial and Business Directory
11. Azerbaijan Industrial and Business Directory
12. Bahamas Industrial and Business Directory
13. Bangladesh Industrial and Business Directory
14. Barbados Industrial and Business Directory
15. Belarus Industrial and Business Directory
16. Belgium Industrial and Business Directory
17. Belize Industrial and Business Directory
18. Bermuda Industrial and Business Directory
19. Bolivia Industrial and Business Directory
20. Bosnia and Herzegovina Industrial and Business Directory
21. Botswana Industrial and Business Directory
22. Brazil Industrial and Business Directory
23. Brunei Industrial and Business Directory
24. Bulgaria Industrial and Business Directory
25. Cambodia Industrial and Business Directory
26. Cameroon Industrial and Business Directory
27. Canada Industrial and Business Directory
28. Cayman Islands Industrial and Business Directory
29. Chile Industrial and Business Directory
30. China Industrial and Business Directory
31. Colombia Industrial and Business Directory

For additional analytical, business and investment opportunities information, please contact Global Investment & Business Center, USA at (202) 546-2103. Fax: (202) 546-3275. E-mail: rusric@erols.com

32. Comoros Industrial and Business Directory
33. Cook Islands Industrial and Business Directory
34. Costa Rica Industrial and Business Directory
35. Croatia Industrial and Business Directory
36. Cuba Industrial and Business Directory
37. Cyprus Industrial and Business Directory
38. Czech Republic Industrial and Business Directory
39. Denmark Industrial and Business Directory
40. Dominica Industrial and Business Directory
41. Dominican Republic Industrial and Business Directory
42. Dubai Industrial and Business Directory
43. Ecuador Industrial and Business Directory
44. Egypt Industrial and Business Directory
45. El Salvador Industrial and Business Directory
46. Equatorial Guinea Industrial and Business Directory
47. Estonia Industrial and Business Directory
48. Falkland Islands Industrial and Business Directory
49. Fiji Industrial and Business Directory
50. Finland Industrial and Business Directory
51. France Industrial and Business Directory
52. Georgia Industrial and Business Directory
53. Germany Industrial and Business Directory
54. Gibraltar Industrial and Business Directory
55. Greece Industrial and Business Directory
56. Grenada Industrial and Business Directory
57. Guam Investment & Business Guide
58. Guatemala Industrial and Business Directory
59. Guernsey Industrial and Business Directory
60. Guyana Industrial and Business Directory
61. Haiti Industrial and Business Directory
62. Honduras Industrial and Business Directory
63. Hungary Industrial and Business Directory
64. Iceland Industrial and Business Directory
65. India Industrial and Business Directory
66. Indonesia Industrial and Business Directory
67. Iran Industrial and Business Directory
68. Iraq Industrial and Business Directory
69. Ireland Industrial and Business Directory
70. Israel Industrial and Business Directory
71. Italy Industrial and Business Directory
72. Jamaica Industrial and Business Directory

For additional analytical, business and investment opportunities information, please contact Global Investment & Business Center, USA at (202) 546-2103. Fax: (202) 546-3275. E-mail: rusric@erols.com

73. Japan Industrial and Business Directory
74. Jersey Industrial and Business Directory
75. Jordan Industrial and Business Directory
76. Kazakhstan Industrial and Business Directory
77. Kenya Industrial and Business Directory
78. Kiribati Industrial and Business Directory
79. Korea, North Industrial and Business Directory
80. Korea, South Industrial and Business Directory
81. Kuwait Industrial and Business Directory
82. Kyrgyzstan Industrial and Business Directory
83. Laos Industrial and Business Directory
84. Latvia Industrial and Business Directory
85. Lebanon Industrial and Business Directory
86. Libya Industrial and Business Directory
87. Liechtenstein Industrial and Business Directory
88. Lithuania Industrial and Business Directory
89. Luxemburg Industrial and Business Directory
90. Macao Industrial and Business Directory
91. Macedonia, Republic Industrial and Business Directory
92. Madagascar Industrial and Business Directory
93. Malaysia Industrial and Business Directory
94. Malta Industrial and Business Directory
95. Man Industrial and Business Directory
96. Mauritius Industrial and Business Directory
97. Mauritius Industrial and Business Directory
98. Mexico Industrial and Business Directory
99. Micronesia Industrial and Business Directory
100. Moldova Industrial and Business Directory
101. Monaco Industrial and Business Directory
102. Mongolia Industrial and Business Directory
103. Morocco Industrial and Business Directory
104. Myanmar Industrial and Business Directory
105. Namibia Industrial and Business Directory
106. Netherlands Industrial and Business Directory
107. New Caledonia Industrial and Business Directory
108. New Zealand Industrial and Business Directory
109. Nicaragua Industrial and Business Directory
110. Nigeria Industrial and Business Directory
111. Northern Mariana Islands Industrial and Business Directory
112. Norway Industrial and Business Directory
113. Pakistan Industrial and Business Directory

114. Panama Industrial and Business Directory
115. Peru Industrial and Business Directory
116. Philippines Industrial and Business Directory
117. Poland Industrial and Business Directory
118. Portugal Industrial and Business Directory
119. Romania Industrial and Business Directory
120. Russia Industrial and Business Directory
121. Samoa (American) Investment & Business Guide
122. Samoa (Western) Industrial and Business Directory
123. Saudi Arabia Industrial and Business Directory
124. Scotland Industrial and Business Directory
125. Singapore Industrial and Business Directory
126. Slovakia Industrial and Business Directory
127. Slovenia Industrial and Business Directory
128. South Africa Industrial and Business Directory
129. Spain Industrial and Business Directory
130. Sri Lanka Industrial and Business Directory
131. St. Helena Industrial and Business Directory
132. Sudan Industrial and Business Directory
133. Suriname Industrial and Business Directory
134. Sweden Industrial and Business Directory
135. Switzerland Industrial and Business Directory
136. Syria Export Import & Business Directory
137. Taiwan Industrial and Business Directory
138. Tajikistan Industrial and Business Directory
139. Thailand Industrial and Business Directory
140. Tunisia Industrial and Business Directory
141. Turkey Industrial and Business Directory
142. Turkmenistan Industrial and Business Directory
143. Uganda Industrial and Business Directory
144. Ukraine Industrial and Business Directory
145. United Arab Emirates Industrial and Business Directory
146. United Kingdom Industrial and Business Directory
147. United States Industrial and Business Directory
148. Uruguay Industrial and Business Directory
149. US Industrial and Business Directory
150. Uzbekistan Industrial and Business Directory
151. Venezuela Industrial and Business Directory
152. Vietnam Industrial and Business Directory
153. Yugoslavia Industrial and Business Directory

www.ingramcontent.com/pod-product-compliance
Lightning Source LLC
LaVergne TN
LVHW080038210926
848481LV00011B/3221